PLATO'S TIMAEUS

The Focus Philosophical Library

PLATO'S TIMAEUS

Translation, Glossary, Appendices, and Introductory Essay

Peter Kalkavage
<small>St. John's College, Annapolis</small>

Focus Publishing
R. Pullins Co.
Newburyport, MA

Cover: Greek red-figure amphore ca. 490 BC, attributed to the Berlin
Painter; Metropolitan Museum of Art, Fletcher Fund.

To my parents

CONTENTS

PREFACE

The aim of this edition is to provide the English-speaking reader with a reliable translation of Plato's *Timaeus*. It is intended mainly for the adventuresome beginner. A veritable museum of Greek mathematics and physical science, the *Timaeus* is Plato's most forbidding dialogue. To offer the reader what I hope is the right amount of help, I have provided footnotes, a glossary, and appendices on music, astronomy and geometry. The appendices are intended as a primer for reading the *Timaeus*. Readers who want more detailed information are encouraged to consult *Plato's Cosmology* by F. M. Cornford, the commentary by A. E. Taylor, or Albert Rivaud's lucid introduction to his French translation in the Budé series. The Introductory Essay is intended more to provoke further questioning than to settle issues.

The *Timaeus* has a remarkable history. It is the dialogue most referred to (and criticized) by Aristotle. Thanks to the Latin translation by Chalcidius,* it was the only Platonic dialogue known to the medieval western world. Over the centuries the dialogue has inspired and instructed such diverse thinkers as Proclus, Plotinus, Dante, Montaigne, Kepler, Leibniz, Vico, Schelling, Goethe, Whitehead and Heisenberg. In the last century there has been a search for "Plato's cosmology," to use the phrase of Cornford's title. The search has unearthed valuable information but has been almost entirely historical and philological in nature. Little has been done to show why the *Timaeus* might be of enduring philosophic value. The dialogue has been treated as though it were an antique.

---

* Calcidius, *Timaeus a Calcidio Translatus Commentarioque Instructus*, ed. J. H. Waszink, Leiden: Brill, 1962. Chalcidius translated only about *half* the dialogue into Latin (up to the end of 53B). For a brief account of Chalcidius on the *Timaeus* and Christian doctrine, see C. S. Lewis, *The Discarded Image*, Cambridge: Cambridge University Press, 1978, pp. 49-60. "Chalcidius determined what the name of Plato should chiefly stand for throughout the middle ages" (ibid., p. 52).

Now, antiquarianism is one of the central themes of the *Timaeus*. The Egyptian priests of Critias' tale record all the goings-on of the cosmos. They reduce the life of the whole to an infinite set of meaningless facts that are recorded—or rather, mummified—in the Egyptian archives. In this, his most antiquarian dialogue, Plato indirectly warns the reader not to become an Egyptian priest. The reader must resist the very spell of antiquarianism that the dialogue playfully casts. My hope for this edition is that it will help bring the *Timaeus* out of its Egyptian bondage to merely historical curiosity and the deciphering of this or that technical detail. I hope that readers will be encouraged to find in the *Timaeus* not merely a repository of Greek science but an occasion for their own thinking about the power of myth, the nature of the soul, history and politics, wholeness and the love of beauty, the human fascination with origins, the will to order, and the prospects of physical science for giving an adequate account of the world and man's place in the world.

The would-be translator of the *Timaeus* is keenly aware of his debts. In the course of completing this edition, I have relied extensively on the efforts of previous translators and commentators. The appendices and notes owe much to Cornford in particular. My colleagues and fellow translators, Eva Brann and Eric Salem, offered their continued encouragement and insightful responses to early drafts. Without our collaborative effort in translating the *Sophist* and *Phaedo* for Focus Press, this edition of the *Timaeus* would not have been possible. Another colleague and friend, Adam Schulman, was enormously helpful in the physical preparation of the text. Keith Whitaker, the editor for Focus Press, worked long and hard on my drafts and made incisive suggestions and corrections. Professor Alejandro Vallega of California State University offered valuable suggestions for the overall shape of the edition as well as for the translation. I am also indebted to St. John's College, whose wide-ranging liberal arts curriculum has allowed me to gain first-hand experience in teaching the disciplines central to the dialogue.

Above all, I wish to thank my wife, Christine, with whom I have had countless talks about the *Timaeus* over the last twenty-five years. My debt to her is beyond measure. Her patience, long hours of proof-reading and mastery of Greek were responsible for catching many errors and for helping to make the translation more consistent, accurate and interesting than it would otherwise have been.

PETER KALKAVAGE
ANNAPOLIS
DECEMBER 2000

INTRODUCTORY ESSAY

"But," said I, "perhaps in heaven a model is laid up for one who wants to see—and by seeing, found—a city within himself. It makes no difference at all whether it is or will be somewhere; for he would do the things of this city alone, and of no other."

"At least that's likely," he said.

Republic 9. 592B

The *Timaeus* is the strangest of Plato's dialogues. It is so strange that one wonders whether anything in it can be taken seriously. Here the conversation and joint inquiry that are habitual with Socrates are suspended. Instead, Plato presents us with long speeches. Socrates for the most part is silent. In exchange for his speech yesterday about the best political order, he is feasted on stories that go back in time to things old and original. We too are feasted. We hear about Solon among the Egyptians, the lost continent of Atlantis, an ancient Athens that once defended the free world, about a noble craftsman-god who constructed the world out of mathematical elements. We are also treated to stories about ourselves. These are the most bizarre tales the dialogue has to offer—tall tales, it would seem, about our souls and bodies, about how we came to have a sphere-shaped head, a neck and torso, eyes and ears, liver and spleen, bone and flesh; about the manifold diseases that afflict body and soul; about where sex came from, and how birds evolved from feather-brained astronomers.

The *Timaeus* is strange not only to us but also in itself. It bears the mark of a deliberate, artfully crafted strangeness that invites deep reflection about the familiar, visible world and our place within that world. Why is this dialogue about the world so strange, and what can we learn from this strangeness?

1

The following introductory essay is divided into four parts. The first three parts follow the largest divisions of the drama; the fourth offers some final reflections on the dialogue as a whole:

I.   The Feasting of Socrates

II. Solon in Egypt

III. The World According to Timaeus:

    i.   The First Founding: the Story of Intellect

    ii. The Second Founding: the Story of Necessity

    iii. Completing the Whole: the Story of Man

IV. Concluding Remarks: the Perils of Order

The Feasting of Socrates

The Platonic dialogues are not treatises but philosophic dramas. In reading them, we must attend to what is done as well as to what is said. Only when we combine speech and deed—*logos* and *ergon*—are we really reading a Platonic drama.[1] Here in the *Timaeus* speech expressly imitates deed. The story Timaeus tells is a playful imitation of the greatest deed the world has ever known: the generation of the world itself. To understand what Timaeus is saying about the cosmos, and what Plato might be showing us through what Timaeus is saying, we must get into the spirit of this playful imitation, even as we pose our serious questions and exert our technical intelligence.

The greatest obstacle in reading the dialogue is that it does not appear to be a dialogue at all. Far more than other Platonic dramas, it has the appearance of being a treatise, a poetic presentation of Plato's teaching. Over the centuries, that is precisely how the dialogue has been read. The modern debate over how to read the *Timaeus* is defined by the disagreement between the dialogue's most famous modern commentators in English: A. E. Taylor and F. M. Cornford.[2] According to Taylor, we must distinguish between Plato and Timaeus: we must not confuse the cosmology presented in the dialogue with Plato's own views on the cosmos. Against this view, Cornford argued that to put Plato at a distance from his character Timaeus was to rob the dialogue of its philosophic worth and seriousness. With this polemic in mind he entitled his book *Plato's Cosmology*.

---

[1] For an account of what it means to take the drama of a Platonic dialogue seriously, see Jacob Klein, *A Commentary on Plato's* Meno, Chicago: University of Chicago Press, 1989, pp. 3-31. See also Stanley Rosen's introduction, "Some Questions of Method," in *Plato's Symposium*, New Haven: Yale University Press, 1969, pp. xi-xxxviii.

[2] A. E. Taylor, *A Commentary on Plato's Timaeus*, Oxford: Oxford University Press, 1928; F. M. Cornford, *Plato's Cosmology*, New York: Library of Liberal Arts, 1957 (first edition, London, 1937).

The view put forth in this essay is that Taylor was, in a sense, right after all. He was right to insist that Plato must not be confused with any of his characters. The dialogues are about all sorts of topics: virtue, happiness, friendship, the best regime, Being, knowledge, love, discourse, and the cosmos. But the central, underlying concern for Plato is always the human soul. By soul I mean not just soul in general and as a metaphysical topic, but soul as displayed in the colorful array of human types that we find portrayed in the dialogues, types that Plato encountered in his day and we still encounter in ours. The dialogues may have been written with just this intention: positively, to preserve the growth of philosophy from the soil of everyday life and discourse and, negatively, to prevent the aspiring philosopher from simply identifying philosophy with the systematic study of general philosophic topics, thus forgetting both himself and the human beings around him.

Here in the *Timaeus* Plato's fascination with individual human souls continues. The dialogue invites us to ask, What is the cosmos? But it also prompts the question, Who is Timaeus? What sort of human being tells a story like the likely story? By inviting us to examine the souls of others, the Platonic dialogues help us gain access to our own souls. They hold up a mirror. What we see in that mirror depends ultimately on what we are open to seeing. In reading a dialogue, we do well to recall the warning of Heraclitus: "If you do not expect the unexpected, you will not discover it."

It is in fact no easy matter to say what the *Timaeus* is really about. It does not begin with cosmology. Socrates does not meet Timaeus by chance in the marketplace or the gymnasium and ask him, What is the cosmos? At the very beginning of the dialogue, after counting his hosts and thereby discovering a missing fourth,[3] Socrates addresses Timaeus as though he were the group's spokesman and gives what seems to be a summary of the *Republic*. Then he expresses a desire to see the best city showing off its well-educated nature in the words and deeds of war. Critias has just the story for Socrates—an amazing tale he heard a long time ago from his grandfather, who heard it from *his* father, who heard it from the great Solon. The story tells how, once upon a time, Athens defeated the insolent kings of Atlantis. Critias then gives Timaeus his role in the day's proceedings: he is to pave the way for Critias' praise of Athens by generating the cosmos in speech all the way down to the birth of human nature (27A). Thereafter Critias will take this newborn nature and give it its political stamp—its *Athenian* citizenship. The role of the other character, Hermocrates, is left mysteriously unspecified. Timaeus then embarks on his magnificent story about the birth and construction of the cosmos. Finally, in the dialogue that bears his name, Critias describes Atlantis and gives the reason for

---

[3] As John Sallis remarks, "The first three words of the *Timaeus* bespeak the dialogue as a whole. These three words, the words *one, two, three*, enact an operation that will be repeated at several decisive junctures and in several basic articulations in and of the dialogue" (*Chorology: On Beginning in Plato's Timaeus*, [Bloomington: Indiana University Press, 1999], p. 7).

its decline and eventual disappearance. His speech breaks off suddenly and unaccountably, just before the war epic that presumably would have gratified Socrates' desire. This is the drama of the *Timaeus-Critias*.[4]

The drama suggests that the *Timaeus* is about beautiful order brought to life—brought to life, that is, through the playful and elusive medium of speech, which in this dialogue appropriately imitates the very process by which the visible order came to be. Through the sequence of projected speeches—the first about man as the child of nature, the second about man as the child of convention—Plato invites the reader to wonder what the connection might be between cosmic order and political order. A cursory reading of the *Timaeus* suggests an obvious connection. Just as Socrates on the previous day had constructed the best city in speech, so today Timaeus will construct the best cosmos in speech. Unlike Anaxagoras, whom the disenchanted young Socrates rejects in the *Phaedo*, Timaeus portrays Becoming as a true cosmos—a genuine whole ruled not by chance and necessity but by divine care and intelligent purpose. To use Leibniz' famous phrase, he builds "the best of possible worlds."[5]

But this neat analogy between the best political order and the best cosmic order only renews our wonder. Why should politics and cosmology be connected in the first place? *Why is the greatest philosophic work on the cosmos framed by politics?*

The dramatic action of the dialogue consists in the feasting of Socrates. Yesterday Socrates had feasted his hosts on a speech about the best regime. Today *justice* as the paying of one's debts compels them to feast him in return (17B). Feasting combines the satisfaction of private, bodily desire with a public show of tribute and a celebration of community. Festivals for the Greeks always involve the gods. They also combine the seriousness and playfulness that are so characteristic of this dialogue. The *Timaeus* takes place during the Panathenaea, the feast in honor of Athens' divine patron and namesake. Critias' tale in particular, which will unearth the buried past of Athena's great city, will be especially relevant to the praise of the goddess, as Socrates points out (26E). The festival in honor of Athena raises important questions: What is the divine? How is the divine related to human

---

[4] For a recent translation of the *Critias*, see Diskin Clay and Andrea Purvis, *Four Island Utopias*, Newburyport MA: Focus Publishing/R. Pullins Company 1999.

[5] The most straightforward statement of Leibniz' "optimism" may be found in *On the Ultimate Origination of Things* (1697), G. W. Leibniz, *Philosophical Essays*, tr. Ariew and Garber, Indianapolis: Hackett Publishing Co., 1989, pp. 149-155. In his *Discourse on Metaphysics* Leibniz patterns his attempt to revive final causes in physics after Socrates' "turn" in the *Phaedo* (19-22). He even inserts his translation of the appropriate passage from the dialogue into his text. The implication is clear: Leibniz is to Descartes as Socrates is to Anaxagoras. For an interesting reflection on Leibniz and Plato, see Paul Schrecker, "Leibniz and the *Timaeus*," *The Review of Metaphysics*, Vol. IV, no. 4, June 1951, pp. 495-505.

beings? How should human beings speak of the divine, celebrate their bond with the divine? What constitutes an appropriate and intelligent tribute to the gods? What sort of theology—if any—is consonant with the philosophic life? These questions are at the very heart of Timaeus' likely story, which is just as much about the gods as it is about the cosmos.

Socrates' hosts are no ordinary, run-of-the-mill fellows but well-known men of political experience and consequence. Two of them are foreigners. They are here in Athens no doubt in part because of the current festival, which surely outdid the festivals in other cities and justly attracted the attention of non-Athenians. Its sheer magnificence transcended political boundaries. These hosts are Timaeus of Italian Locri, Hermocrates of Syracuse, and Critias of Athens. Unlike his two partners, whose historical existence is certain, Timaeus seems to be a creature wholly of Plato's devising—a noble construct. In light of the tension revealed in the *Republic* between the claims of the best and the claims of Becoming—between the "ideal" and the "real"—Timaeus seems to be the consummation devoutly to be wished, the harmonious union of theory and practice. He comes from a city famous for its strict and long-standing enforcement of law; he is rich, wellborn, prestigious and politically powerful (20A). His very name resounds with *timê* or honor and thus proclaims his worldly accomplishment and recognition. Furthermore, Socrates praises him for having reached "the very peak of all philosophy" (20A).

It is far from clear what philosophy is for Timaeus, or what we are to make of Socrates' praise. Indeed, it is not clear what the word "philosophy" (the love of wisdom) means in its various appearances in the dialogue. Like his modern counterpart Leibniz, Timaeus is a harmonizer.[6] His very life and character embody the sort of harmony of disparate things that comes up often in the likely story. To all appearances, he has done what Socrates could not: he has harmonized the pursuit of philosophy with public life. But how has he managed to do this? What understanding of philosophy and conventional politics makes them capable of being harmonized? The gods of Timaeus' speech make all sorts of compromises in order to bring about the harmonies that make the best of possible worlds. What sort of compromise, we wonder, has Timaeus made to be the glorious harmony he appears to be?

Socrates praises Timaeus not for being philosophical but for having been *successful* in philosophy. The praise has the sound of a left-handed compliment.

---

[6] Leibniz' greatest feat of philosophic harmonization is the reconciliation of final and efficient causes (that is, the reconciliation of Aristotle and Descartes). For a description of his famous "pre-established harmony" as a cosmic principle, see *Theodicy* (1710), tr. E. M. Huggard, La Salle, Illinois: Open Court, 1985, pp. 64 ff. For an application of this harmony to the soul, see *A New System of the Nature and Communication of Substances; and of the Union of the Soul and Body* (1695) in G. W. Leibniz, *Philosophical Essays*, tr. Ariew and Garber, Indianapolis: Hackett Publishing Co., pp. 138-145.

"All philosophy," which in Greek can also mean "every philosophy," suggests not the knowledge of one's own ignorance and the erotic striving for wisdom that we hear about in other dialogues but the mastery of a complete set of intellectual specialties.[7] Timaeus comes before us not as a lover of wisdom but as an accomplished knower. He clearly merits our admiration, and Socrates seems genuinely fond of him. He is the only character here whom Socrates refers to as *philos*, which means "dear" or "friend" (17A, 19A). But as a professional philosopher, whose expertise puts him on a par with the sophists, he also arouses our suspicion. Is Timaeus himself a true whole, a true cosmos? Or is he merely a sum of beautiful parts that never conflict because they never come into contact with one another? In any case, it seems that Timaeus has enjoyed a successful political career in part because philosophy for him never calls the city's customs and opinions into question. Unlike the gadfly Socrates, Timaeus does not sting the city into knowledge of its own ignorance (*Apology* 30E ff.).

The identity of Critias has been disputed. Socrates simply relates that everybody in Athens knows that he is no mere private man (20A). Is he or is he not the notorious Critias, who was one of the Thirty Tyrants? If the dialogue takes place in 421, as Lampert and Planeaux argue in their recent article, then the Critias we have here must be the *grandfather* of the famous tyrant.[8] Still, it is impossible to see so notorious a name and not to think of the grandson who helped overthrow the democracy. The name suggests that behind the civil and ceremonious drama of the *Timaeus-Critias* there lurks the civil war and tyranny that infected Athens when ambitious aristocrats tried to impose the rule of the best, when a presumed ideal was tyrannically forced upon the humanly real. Perhaps the seeds of that future tyranny were somehow sown with the Critias we have here in the dialogue, with his political idealism and his nostalgia for "the good old days" of Athenian oligarchy.

Hermocrates too is a character through whom Plato connects the speeches of the *Timaeus* with the actual deeds and sufferings of Athens. Hermocrates is the great Syracusan statesman and rhetorician we meet in the account of Thucydides, who praises him for his intelligence, courage and experience.[9] It was largely through his successful effort to unify the warring factions of Sicily that Athens met her defeat in

---

[7] Timaeus himself uses the phrase "all philosophy" at 88C.

[8] L. Lampert and C. Planeaux, "Who's Who in Plato's *Timaeus-Critias* and Why," *Review of Metaphysics*, September 1998, pp. 88-125. See also Appendix A, "Which Critias?", in Warman Welliver's *Character, Plot and Thought in Plato's Timaeus-Critias*, (Leiden: E.J. Brill, 1977), pp. 50-57. Lampert and Planeaux argue that the missing fourth is Alcibiades. Leo Strauss suggests that Socrates, in his desire for the city in motion, "seems to call for the assistance of a man like Thucydides who could supplement political philosophy or complete it" (*The City and Man*, Chicago: Rand McNally and Co., 1964, p. 140).

[9] *History of the Peloponnesian War* 6. 72.

the Sicilian expedition. The historical Hermocrates thus represents the power of the word to beget deeds. This is the role Plato gives him in the *Timaeus* and *Critias*. His two brief speeches, one in each dialogue, both have the same, practical purpose: to goad Critias into telling his story, to draw him out onto the field of speech (*Timaeus* 20C, *Critias* 108B). The presence of Hermocrates in the *Timaeus-Critias* brings the themes of these dialogues into close connection with Athenian imperialism. Indeed, if the action of the *Timaeus* takes place not long before the Sicilian expedition, then the story of Critias, in which Athens appears as the champion of political freedom, seems to offer an ironic prophecy of Athens' own insolence and defeat. The story in praise of ancient Athens thus seems to point ahead to contemporary Athens as a new Atlantis.

These are the men, each from a different city, who form an alliance to gratify Socrates. A nameless fourth had agreed to join them, but for some reason he is absent. In his very first likely story in the dialogue, Timaeus puts the best construction on this absence and presents the construction as a cause.[10] Foreshadowing his role as an expert on causality, he explains that the fourth failed to show up because he came down with something, thereby absolving the fourth from any accusation of injustice.[11] Are we supposed to believe this explanation and just move on? Or does Plato mean to draw our attention to the political world that Thucydides knows so well, the world in which excuses and pretexts often masquerade as causes? Hermocrates alludes to this world when he says that he and the others have no *pretext* (*prophasis*) for not doing what Socrates orders them to do, as if we are to imagine that if they could come up with a pretext, they might be tempted to use it to avoid paying their debt to Socrates (20C). Timaeus' first likely story offers a perfect example of how human beings appeal to the mitigating circumstances of physical necessity to ward off possible accusations. By conjuring the thought of what people often do when on the spot, Plato invites us to entertain the possibility that the fourth failed to show

---

[10]   Timaeus seems confident in his explanation. He does not say that the fourth *must have* come down with something but that he *did* (the verb he uses, *synepesen*, is past indicative).

[11]   By counting rather than naming his hosts, Socrates suppresses their human identity: for the purposes of a count, the hosts are just so many monads ("Number is a multitude composed of monads or units," Euclid, *Elements* 7, def. 2). Timaeus' first likely story is another dehumanization of the human: he explains the absence of the missing fourth on the basis of what he will later call necessity or the wandering cause. Taylor is one of the few commentators bothered (and rightly so) by Timaeus' tendency, in his later account of the source of moral evil, to cosmologize the individual's moral responsibility out of existence (see Taylor's extended discussion of 86B-87B, ibid., pp. 610-614). Taylor concludes: "We are free, then, to hold that Plato's attitude towards his Pythagorean cosmologist is here, as elsewhere, marked by a certain detachment and by a kindly irony. When we find Timaeus falling into inconsistency we may suspect that his creator is intentionally making him 'give himself away' "(ibid., p. 614).

up precisely because he decided not to.[12] He puts us on guard against explanations which, though plausible, might also turn out to be deceptive.

But what about the desire that sets the speeches of today in motion and thus itself acts as a cause? Why is the drama of the *Timaeus* taking place? To approach this crucial and difficult question, we must go back briefly to the beginning of the dialogue.

The *Timaeus* begins with what is apparently a summary of the account of the best city in the *Republic*. The summary is incomplete. Socrates omits everything that involves an ascent beyond the strictly political: the concern for justice in the individual soul and the analogy between soul and city, the transition from pre-philosophic "best" cities to the city ruled by philosopher-kings, the conversion and ascent of the soul from Becoming to Being and the mathematical education that leads to dialectic, the attack on poets and poetry, and the inevitable degeneration of the best city if such a city ever came into being. In short, the speech Socrates agreed to give yesterday seems not to be the *Republic* but a pale image of the *Republic*—pale because philosophic virtue in its precise sense was missing, because man was present *only* as a political animal.

Whatever Plato's reasons may be for presenting this pale image, this much is clear: Socrates' summary paves the way for treating the best city in speech as though it were a political blueprint, an ideology or theory just waiting to be put into practice. Socrates seems to have tailored the account of the best city (and perhaps had tailored it yesterday) to fit the practical-political temperament of his hosts. He seems to know right from the start that Critias in particular, whom he surely knows best of the three, will be dissatisfied with a merely theoretical (and non-Athenian) city and will seek some way to return political discourse to the realm of doing and making—to real cities as Critias understands them.

Toward the end of his summary, Socrates seems to tempt Timaeus into an admission that something has been left out. He asks him, "Are we yearning for something further in what was said, my dear Timaeus, something that's being left out?" Socrates poses his question in terms of desire. He does not ask "Is this summary complete?" but "Does it really gratify us, my dear Timaeus, or does it perhaps leave us feeling unfulfilled?" What is at stake here is not the city primarily but the soul of "my dear Timaeus," his capacity for desiring more than what the ultra-political summary embodies. That Timaeus responds in the way he does ("Not at all.") seems to reveal the limits of both his philosophic desire and his friendship with Socrates: if thinking succeeds in revealing how a good political order has been achieved, then

---

[12]   This is in fact the view taken by Lampert and Planeaux, who identify the missing fourth with Alcibiades. Alcibiades, they argue, is absent because he refused to submit to the demands of "an orderly and moral cosmos" and is " 'sick' with intractability" (ibid., p. 121).

that is where thinking stops. By giving us a philosophically deficient summary of the *Republic* here at the beginning of the *Timaeus*, and by following this up with Timaeus' willingness to be satisfied with such an account, Plato indirectly signals the importance of philosophic *erôs* for the dialogue.[13] He is perhaps alerting us to the fact that philosophy—which is defined by its *erôs* or love of wisdom—is here being restrained by a practical-political interest in law and order. The abbreviated summary of the *Republic* signals the abbreviation of philosophy itself.

But if Timaeus feels no lack, Socrates certainly does—or at least he claims to. In his longest speech in the dialogue, the speech that presumably explains why the drama is taking place, Socrates announces his desire for a speech about the best city at war. He lays emphasis on the irrational ground of this desire. He calls it a feeling or affection, in Greek, a *pathos*—a word that appears with great frequency in Timaeus' speech—and attributes its arising in him to chance. He does not say that the logical next topic after the city at peace would be the city at war. On the contrary, he confesses to a passion that he says just happened to come over him as he regarded the city in speech (19B). He compares himself to a man who beheld beautiful animals "somewhere" (*pou*) and conceived the desire to watch them contending with one another. It doesn't seem to matter to Socrates whether these animals are works of art or works of nature; the important thing is that they be represented as *moving*.[14] What on earth has gotten into Socrates? Why is he playing the passive victim of a chance feeling, someone who just *feels like* seeing the city stirred up and sent off to war, the way we might just happen to want to see a war movie?

Socrates' professed desire seems not to be directed at truth. As Socrates himself emphasizes, what he wants is not a clearer or deeper insight into the nature of the best city, an insight that could only come from seeing the city in motion, but an encomium or song of praise. This is the task he imposes on his hosts. The goal here is beautification rather than truth-telling or truth-seeking, even if it is also the case that a city in motion reveals more of itself, more of its education and nature, than a city at rest. Unlike the Socrates we see in the *Symposium*, who scorns the company's indulging in the extended praise of Love (198B ff.), Socrates here wants to be treated to a grand piece of rhetoric. This rhetoric is also expected to be an epic poem that shows the best city in all its martial glory. As if in visual confirmation of this desire to hear the city flattered, Socrates has uncharacteristically dressed up for the occasion. He is *kekosmêmenos*—arrayed, that is, made orderly in appearance, just like the beautifully constructed *kosmos* of Timaeus' up-coming speech (20C1).

---

13 On the disjunction in Plato between *erôs* and mathematics (which rules the world in Timaeus' likely story), see Stanley Rosen, "The Role of Eros in Plato's *Republic*," *The Review of Metaphysics* 18, March, 1965, pp. 452-475.

14 Sallis rightly asks: "Why does setting the city in motion require sending it off to war?" See his discussion of this crucial point in *Chorology*, pp. 27-30.

It is hard to believe that Socrates' desire is sincerely meant, that what he says he wants is what he really wants. What then is the true object of Socrates' desire, and how is that object related to what he actually requests (or rather, demands)?

In other dialogues, Socrates gets his interlocutors to show themselves in the act of joint inquiry and to reveal their ignorance by experiencing the self-contradictions inherent in their opinions. Here in the *Timaeus* there is repeated emphasis on the *pronouncement* of opinion, but there is no joint inquiry or direct *testing* of opinion.[15] But Socrates may nevertheless be the same old Sphynx-like examiner of souls. By ironically imitating the spirited desire for action and political motion—the desire in the souls of his political hosts—Socrates may be hoping to draw out the motions and opinions of their souls, to induce (indeed, compel) his hosts to reveal their natures in the act of making long speeches. He assumes the attitude of one of the cave dwellers in the *Republic*, one who is enthralled by the image-opinions cast by cunning projection-ists.[16] Having set up the whole test with his speech of yesterday, Socrates can now just sit back, enjoy, and learn from the spectacle of ambition and self-disclosure that he has evoked from his hosts. Through the cunning desire of Socrates—if this reading is correct—Plato shows us what happens when men of a worldly or practical character get their hands on at least one version of the city of the *Republic*. The uncharacteristic silence and receptivity of Socrates would then have a double function: to signal the appropriate withdrawal of philosophic inquiry from proceedings devoted to glorifi-cation or flattery, and to make a receptive space for the designs of men who think of truth in terms of doing and making.

Central to Socrates' speech is what he has to say about poets and sophists, neither of whom, he claims, are up to the task of gratifying his desire (19D-E). The reason he gives has to do with the human tendency to be either excessively attached or not attached enough to a political *place*. Much later, at the most critical moment in his speech, Timaeus will unveil the extremely hard-to-pin-down nature of space or place (*chôra*).[17] Here in what he says about poets and sophists, Socrates seems to

---

[15]   Socrates lays emphasis on his *opinion* of poets and sophists (19D) and his *opinion* of Timaeus (20A). Opinion and high repute are central themes of Critias' long speech. Timaeus too stresses his connection with opinion. Just before he makes his fundamental distinction between Being and Becoming, for example, he declares that *in his opinion* one must begin with this distinction (27D).

[16]   *Republic* 7. 514A ff. In his description of the cave, Socrates uses the word *pathos* to designate our condition (and affliction) of lacking education (514A). It is the same word he uses here in the *Timaeus* to describe his desire for the city in motion (19B).

[17]   The word *chôra* first appears in the dialogue in Socrates' summary of the best city (19A). The results of sexual generation are ultimately incalculable: worthy souls will sometimes spring up among the unworthy, and vice versa. The guardians must reshuffle misplaced souls in a way that resembles the receptacle's reshuffling of the four kinds (52E-53A).

divine the central role that space and place will have for the speeches to come. (He also seemed prophetic in this regard when he asked Timaeus *where* the missing fourth was, and when he compared himself to a man who beheld beautiful animals *somewhere*.) Poets are too attached to their cities. According to Socrates, they are steeped in convention and therefore cannot be expected to know how to depict a city whose goodness is according to nature. Sophists, by contrast, have no attachments to a particular city at all. They wander from city to city and are thus politically rootless. The right sort of man to gratify Socrates' desire must steer between these two extremes and embody the right relation to political place. He must be the mean between provincialism and political promiscuity. Socrates draws the conclusion that such a man must be a combination of statesman and philosopher—the very class to which his three hosts, so he says, happen to belong.

It is impossible to overestimate the complexity of Socrates' long speech, with its simile of the man who beholds beautiful animals either natural or artificial, the remarks about poets and sophists, and the ambiguous praise of the three hosts for their apparent synthesis of theory and practice. By invoking poets and sophists, Socrates seems indirectly to be saying that the right sort of speaker would have to be both: a poet in order to depict beautiful motion in beautiful words, a sophist in order to capture the sometimes deceptive speeches and subterfuges that cities employ in time of war. Again the question of harmony arises: Do the three hosts really overcome the tension between philosophy and conventional cities? Or do they simply incorporate the extremes of poets and sophists—the too-political and the non-political—and thus merely seem to have overcome that tension?

The desire of Socrates in the *Timaeus* signals the descent from the quest for eternal truth in the *Republic* to the preoccupation with Becoming. Plato is always attentive to how metaphysical depth is hinted at by the casual surface of everyday life. Here in the *Timaeus* he plays on the various ways in which human beings display a bond with *genesis*, which in Greek means both Becoming and birth.

The clearest indication of this bond is the central role that genealogy plays in the dialogue. Critias reveals the potent spell that our memories cast over us. He enacts our bond with the past and with time generally. His nostalgia reminds us with great vividness and detail that human beings for the most part locate the meaning of their lives in the temporal flow of their lives: they find their being in their becoming. Critias also displays the vanity that attends our interest in our own families and genealogies. He is clearly proud of the fact that the story he has for Socrates is a family heirloom passed down from generation to generation and that the great Solon is a distant relative. His aggrandizement of ancient Athens, in other words, is also a personal self-aggrandizement. Genealogies are accounts (*logoi*) that are also stories (*mythoi*): they show how later generations derive from earlier ones in temporal succession. To be able to give our genealogy is to know our temporal origins and roots, to know who we are as children of Becoming. And the farther back we can go in time, the better we think we know our origins and ourselves. All this is mixed together with our love of flattery. We engage in genealogies in the belief that we will be ennobled, that somewhere down the line we will turn out to be related to someone great and famous.[18] This rootedness in the love of our own—in our own families and family histories—is one of the reasons why it would be so difficult to actualize the city according to nature, a city that paradoxically goes against nature in trying to suppress our natural attachment to our own possessions and families. Critias is the very paradigm of this all-too-human rootedness in time, Becoming, and self-love.[19] Through him, wisdom in the dialogue comes to be identified not with the *recollection* (to use Socrates' term from the *Meno*) of eternally unchanging Being but with the detailed *memory* of our own past.

Solon in Egypt

Like the long speech of Socrates, the preview of coming-attractions that Critias presents is extremely complex. It is also mysterious. Why has so amazing a story in praise of Athens been kept secret? Was it because of its political incorrectness, because it would have been praise of an aristocratic Athens in democratic times? Does Critias feel safe in revealing it now because he is in some sort of alliance with two foreign aristocrats (who are his house guests, 20C-D) and has recently heard Socrates, a fellow Athenian, reveal his own apparent preference for the rule of the best?[20]

Whatever the reason is for its having been kept secret for so long, the story immerses us in life as process. Its themes are youth and old age, forgetfulness and memory, destruction and rebirth, science and myth, and political and cosmic order. A very old Egyptian priest tells Solon about an Athens of which the celebrated Athenian lawgiver and poet never dreamed—a glorious, aristocratic Athens that once defended the entire free world from the encroachments of an insolent kingdom called Atlantis. Furthermore, this ancient Athens possessed just the political order that Socrates had

---

[18]   Socrates states his opinion of genealogies in the *Hippias Major*. Hippias reports that the Spartans are fond of hearing him recount the generations of gods and humans, the founding of cities in ancient times, and antiquities in general (*archaiologias*). Socrates remarks that the Spartans use Hippias as children use old ladies—to tell stories pleasantly (285E-286A).

[19]   See *Laws* 5. 731 ff. The Athenian stranger declares that the *aition* or cause of all transgression is excessive love of self. The vanity of Critias comes out with great force at the opening of the dialogue that bears his name. Calling attention to his *philotimia* or love of honor, he tries to minimize the impressiveness of Timaeus' speech in order to make his own speech seem more impressive (*Critias* 106B-108A).

[20]   The nature and extent of the alliance among Timaeus, Hermocrates and Critias is unclear. In addition to being in Athens for the current festival, Timaeus and Hermocrates may also be conspiring with the oligarchically inclined Critias to bring oligarchy to Athens—not just in speech but also in deed.

presented the day before and which the *nomos* or district of Egyptian Sais possesses even now. Who says the best political regime cannot be made actual? Why, it not only *can* be made actual—it *is* actual in Sais and once upon a time *was* actual in Athens' own history! Critias admits that his story about Athens is strange (*atopon*, literally, *placeless*). But he nevertheless insists that it is "altogether true" (20D), that it is history rather than poetry. He calls it a *logos* or account and never refers to it as a *mythos* or story. The word *mythos* in Critias' long speech always has a negative, condescending tone. At one point, this condescension is directed at Socrates himself, who, according to Critias, spoke of the best regime yesterday "as though in a story." Critias makes a bold claim: he will transfer the merely mythical city of Socrates into "the truth" (26D).

What *is* truth in the long speech of Critias and in the account Solon heard in Egypt? This is a question well worth asking in light of the cosmology of Timaeus, who limits the aspirations of physical inquiry to mere trust and likelihood (29C-D). At the very beginning of the dialogue, Plato gave us food for thought—a little drama of scientific account-giving in Timaeus' explanation of why a fourth was missing. The drama put us on our guard against possibly deceptive explanations. The themes of trust and suspicion regarding speeches that purport to be scientifically true are given elaborate treatment here in Plato's drama of Solon in Egypt. Socrates seems to express a certain sarcasm when, echoing Critias' claim, he says that it is of the utmost importance that the feast of speech he is being offered is "no fabricated story but a truthful account" (26E).[21]

Truth for Critias and for the Egyptians (and apparently for Solon as well) is the record of things that have happened in the cosmos and continue to happen. Truth is fact—fact without rhyme or reason. Solon tries to impress the old priests with genealogical accounts of things long past. He puts forth these accounts as though they were historically accurate, whereas in truth they appear to be no more than stories passed down through tradition or public hearsay. Indeed, it is very difficult to see how human beings can go back in time to the very oldest things without having recourse to myth, which seems to go where history as factual chronicle cannot. The strange thing here is that such mythical accounts are put forth as though they were factually, literally true, as though they were historical report rather than poetry. But like all the Greeks, Solon is a parvenu when it comes to going back in time. The Egyptians are the real experts in things old: for them, wisdom is paleontology. Furthermore, truth in Egypt can be written down. That's how concrete it is. And it is here in the concreteness of the sacred writings that Solon is allowed to read the flattering but forgotten "truth" of his city's past.

---

[21] The word for truthful that Socrates uses—*alêthinon*—can also mean honest. The word for "fabricated" is from *plattein*, which can mean "produce a forgery." What is at stake here is not just whether or not the story is factually true but whether Critias is or is not being willfully deceptive.

What truth means in Egypt is nicely captured in what the old priest has to say about the myth of Phaethon (22C-D). Phaethon, son of Helios, tried to drive his father's sun-chariot in order to prove that, having descended from a god, he too was a god. The result was fiery destruction for him and for a large portion of the earth. The myth is a warning to ambitious political idealists (like the tyrant Critias) who try to steer the ship of state in order to prove their wisdom and excellence. The Egyptian priests totally reject this power of myth as myth to shed light on the human realm. Myths for them are no more than popular renditions of cosmological events, the real truth of which is known only to the scientific intelligentsia. Myths are for the many, scientific explanations for the few. The truth of the Phaethon story, the priest tells Solon, "is a shifting of the bodies that move around the earth and along the heavens, and the destruction that comes about on the earth by a great deal of fire at long stretches of time" (22D).

The priests in their scientific "wisdom" thus appear to lack imagination.[22] As professional debunkers of myth (a strange priesthood indeed), they are blind to the power of myth to reveal the human soul in its relation to the cosmos—blind, that is, to what might be argued is the whole purpose of myth. Their scientism is what Socrates in the *Phaedrus* calls "a rude sort of wisdom," which tries to explain away the creatures of myth according to what is probable or likely (*kata to eikos*, 229E). For the Egyptian priests, the visible world is not a true cosmos—a beautifully ordered whole—but a material non-cosmos of mindless repetition, mere cycles of destruction and rebirth. Circles are important here, as they are in the speech of Timaeus, but they have no meaning, no connection with anything intrinsically intelligent. The science of the Egyptians seems, furthermore, totally lifeless. It makes us yearn for a more poetically conceived cosmos in which human nature has a real place and grounding, and the world of the imagination is allowed to flourish. It also makes us wonder whether physical science can ever explain the world without making man and man's power of account-giving aliens in that world, whether physical science and an understanding of the human soul can ever be united. Such a union of science and human values, as we shall see, is precisely the goal of Timaeus' likely story.

The superficiality of Egyptian science is reflected in the Egyptian regime, which Critias identifies with Socrates' best city according to nature. Socrates' sum-

---

[22]   The absence or presence of different kinds of imagining is crucial in the *Timaeus*. In the divided line, we hear about the sort of imagination—*eikasia* or likeness-recognition—that is basic to the soul's capacity for a philosophic ascent to the forms (*Republic* 6. 509C-511E). This is the soul's power of recognizing a likeness as a likeness (and, by extension, a hypothesis as a hypothesis and an opinion as an opinion). For the definitive account of *eikasia* and its extension from sensed images to hypotheses, see Jacob Klein, ibid., pp. 112-125. The likely story of Timaeus, for all its reliance on imagination, seems not to involve this sort of imagining, the imagining that allows the soul to move beyond the image to that of which the image is an image.

mary had presented the best city in such a way as to highlight its schematic character and to exclude or at least downplay all the deep complexities to which serious political discourse leads. He presented the city as a *solution* and treated problems, especially the problems having to do with marriage and children, as if they could be overcome by sufficiently ingenious social engineering. Here in Egyptian Sais, order takes the form of a rigidly observed caste-system in which a scientifically enlightened priesthood plays a hierarchical role that mimics that of the philosopher-kings in the *Republic*. Everything in Sais seems weirdly ossified and dead. Solon resembles an Odysseus visiting shades in some enlightened region of Hades. Even the fact that knowledge in Egypt is *written down* suggests general stagnation and the absence of soul—a mummification of the truth.[23] The spirit of Egypt is represented by old men who speak condescendingly of youth. In the *Republic* the control of *erôs* seems to be the central problem of a political founding.[24] Indeed, the best city, if it ever came into being, eventually degenerates because mathematical calculations cannot prevent the rulers from engaging in sexual generation at cosmically inappropriate times (8. 546A ff.). Plato presents Egyptian Sais (comically) as though it solved the political problem at one fell swoop by simply not having any *erôs* in it at all![25] We meet very old men (that is, human males on the brink of death) but no young males and no women or children. And in his proud show of the Egyptian regime to Solon, the priest shuns any reference whatsoever to women, unlike Socrates, whose summary included the unconventional view that women and men had all occupations in common, including that of ruling the city (18C-D).

By crafting an amazing tale about Solon in Egypt, Plato invites us to think about a political order that distorts the city of the *Republic* even as it claims to transcend it by making it concretely real. It is only human to be taken in by false images and to be more impressed than we should by accounts that claim to be either historically accurate or scientifically true, especially when historical-seeming accounts from the mouths of reputed experts are genealogies that cater to our self-love. In the *Timaeus* no less than in other dialogues, Plato thus reminds us, this

---

[23] In the *Phaedrus* Socrates tells of the Egyptian god, Theuth, who was the inventor of numbers, calculation, geometry, astronomy, and *writing* (274C ff.). Theuth presents these gifts to King Thamus (also a god) and claims that writing is "an elixir or drug of both memory and wisdom" (274E). Thamus observes that this drug will in fact produce not wisdom but only the appearance of wisdom (275A-B).

[24] Speaking of the *comedy* of the city in the *Republic*, Sallis observes: "What the comedy of the city brings to light is the failure, the incapacity, of the fabricated capital city to incorporate *erôs* and all that is linked to the erotic: procreation, mating, birth, sexual difference, corporeity itself in its singularity" (ibid., p. 26).

[25] In the *Republic* old Cephalus exemplifies the disdain for erotic love. In agreement with the opinion of Sophocles, he is glad in his old age to be finally rid of this "frenzied and savage master" (1. 329C). Cephalus would have been at home in Egyptian Sais.

time on a grand cosmic scale, of our extreme vulnerability and subjection to *doxa*, which in Greek means both opinion or seeming and—glory.

How does Timaeus fit into the picture? How is his cosmology different from that of the Egyptian priests, and how is it similar? What is the place and function of human nature in the world as Timaeus depicts it? These are just a few of the questions we must keep in mind as we now turn to the likely story.

The World According to Timaeus

The First Founding: the Story of Intellect

Before launching into his speech proper, Timaeus delivers an apology or defense before the fact. He wants to make sure that his judges, as he calls them (29D), and Socrates in particular, do not expect more from him than he can deliver—more than is fitting for the discursive power of human beings in the face of such risky topics as gods and Becoming. In this prefatory speech, Timaeus introduces four important things: the distinction between Being and Becoming, the fact that everything that comes to be does so by some cause or *aition*, the famous craftsman or demiurge, and the most famous phrase of the dialogue—"the likely story" (*ton eikota mython*).

The distinction between Being and Becoming strikes us as familiar—so familiar, in fact, that we may not stop to think about it. It is one of those things we grow accustomed to finding in a Platonic dialogue. Timaeus sharply distinguishes Being and Becoming. It is the first of many distinctions that Timaeus wants us to *get straight*. The sharpness makes it difficult to see how Being and Becoming could ever have anything to do with one another and consequently how a Being-based cosmos could ever come into existence. The distinction seems to be precisely what must be overcome in some way so that Becoming can be what Timaeus insists it is—an image or likeness of an eternally changeless model or paradigm.

After introducing the distinction between what always *is* and what always comes to be—Being and process—Timaeus introduces his famous craftsman or demiurge. This mythical figure, the divine hero of the likely story, hovers between the realms of Being and Becoming. He seems to be the mythical means by which the two distinct realms are connected. The word *dêmiourgos* means "one who works for the people or *dêmos*." It is a humble, everyday word and refers to anyone who crafts anything whatsoever.[26] We all delight in a thing well made—a well-made chair, building or piece

---

[26]   Socrates refers to a "craftsman of heaven" at one point in the *Republic*. As part of his strategy to get Glaucon to turn from the visible to the intellected, Socrates acknowledges that the works of this craftsman might indeed be as beautiful as they can be, but that it would be strange (*atopon*) for someone to look for any constancy or truth in such objects (7. 530A-C). For the sake of a truly philosophic astronomy, Socrates paradoxically concludes, "we shall let the things in the heaven go" (530B).

of music. We love the way everything fits together beautifully and how a thing well made is a thing that lasts. In the likely story, Timaeus counts on and seeks to gratify this human delight in technical perfection. Through the agency of his mythical craftsman, he makes the world of nature into a well-made and long-lasting artifact. He thus inspires admiration for the beauty of the world that both contains and determines us. By invoking a being that consciously deliberates over the world he would make, Timaeus makes the existent world-order an intended order. The world is the way it is because it was *meant* to be that way.

The divine craftsman is simply postulated. There is no proof for his existence. The question is not whether there really is such a being but what he was looking at when he made the world. Was it a changeable, or an unchangeable model? At one point, Timaeus expresses skepticism regarding our ability to discover what he calls the true "poet and father" of the world (28C). He leads us to suspect that the demiurge is a practical postulate that fills the gap of our theological ignorance, that he is not necessarily the true god but the god who ought to be believed in if we are to affirm the best of possible worlds. Later we hear that this divine craftsman, unlike the gods as Herodotus depicts them, lacked envy, bore no grudge (29E). He did not jealously guard his divine prerogative, the Promethean fire of artful intelligence, but wished that all things should possess it to the extent that their natures allowed. In this way, the world comes to be an image or likeness in a double sense: it is the likeness of a purely intelligible and eternal original *and* the likeness of its divine maker. Artful intelligence for Timaeus is always in the mode of generosity and public-spiritedness. It seeks to bestow itself on the world as a divine gift. It does not keep itself huddled up within itself but rejoices in seeing itself multiplied, reflected and embodied for all to see. The world according to Timaeus comes about not through chance and necessity, nor through the sex and violence depicted in Hesiod's *Theogony*, but through the sober professionalism of *technê* or art. By thus presenting god as a generous craftsman, a divine being who does all things for the common good, Timaeus saves us from making god in the image of a tyrant.

Timaeus expresses his preference for a changeless model through an appeal to piety. He does not argue for the existence of this model any more than he argues for the existence of his demiurge. Rather he says that it would be "not right" (*ou themis*), that is, blasphemous, to say otherwise (29A). Herein lies one reason why the likely story is likely. Likely, *eikôs*, means, has the character of a likeness. It also means probable, reasonable, and equitable or fair. Speech for Timaeus is mimetic: it imitates the condition of its objects. Accounts of what is abiding and intelligible, he says, "are themselves abiding and unchanging" (29B), while accounts of the non-abiding and changing, accounts of mere likenesses, are characterized by likelihood. In an echo of Socrates' divided line in the *Republic*, Timaeus says: "just as Being is to Becoming, so is truth to trust" (29C). Likely stories, we must conclude, are not really put forth for the sake of knowledge and insight. They are a kind of rhetoric. We must be persuaded by them, trust them, and put up with their necessary flaws.

The infirmity of speech about divine origins points to a more deeply rooted infirmity—our own human nature. Timaeus tells Socrates that he must not wonder if many of the things said about the gods and the birth of the all are self-contradictory and imprecise (29C). Adopting the formal tone of a man warding off a possible accusation, Timaeus says: "But if we provide likelihoods inferior to none, one should be well-pleased with them, remembering that I who speak as well as you my judges have a human nature, so that it is fitting for us to receive the likely story about these things and not to search further for anything beyond it" (29C-D).

This sentence points to the connection that physical account-giving has for Timaeus to both piety and prudence. Timaeus draws a line beyond which prudent human beings should not go in speaking of things divine. But the drawing of this line is not just an admission of infirmity. It also demarcates the sphere within which human beings, precisely because they are aware of their limitations and the contingencies of life, are all the more able to exert their powers of productive intelligence. This self-confident aspect of the likely story is conveyed by Timaeus when he says, after Socrates reminds him to invoke the conventional gods, that we must also invoke *to hêmeteron*, "what has to do with ourselves" (27D).[27] By reminding Socrates of the infirmity of the speech to come, Timaeus guards what he later calls the *power* (*dynamis*) of likely accounts (48D).

Timaeus' defense of the inevitable shortcomings of his speech is a not-so-veiled warning against the immoderateness or hybris of philosophy as Socrates practices it. This hybris stems from the philosopher's erotic longing to be beyond all human constructs and opinions—to get out of the cave. Timaeus cautions Socrates against being Socrates. He warns him against striving to go beyond the boundaries of plausibly established grounds. Socrates must be receptive to, and rest content with, the likely story about divine origins. If he wants to enjoy his feast, he must mind his manners and act like a gentleman. In hearing about the divine, he must control the philosophic striving to *be* divine and remember that as Timaeus' potentially harshest judge he too is, after all, only human.

Socrates is more than happy to accept the terms on which his guest-gift is offered. In the most telling moment of the dialogue, he calls the likely story not a *logos* or a *mythos*, not an account or a story, but a *nomos* (29D). *Nomos* is both law and song, as well as custom and convention. Timaeus is our singer for the day. He

---

27   In response to Socrates' curious reminder that Timaeus invoke the gods "according to custom," Timaeus invokes "both gods and goddesses" (27C). Why he does so is not clear. In one sense, he may be signaling the importance of the sexual distinction for the likely story, which, like the city-story of the *Republic*, is composed of a "male drama" and a "female drama" (see Sallis, ibid., pp. 25-27): the story of a cosmic father (the divine craftsman) and the story of a cosmic mother (the receptacle). But he may also be alluding to the sexual madness of the conventional gods—a madness that is soon to be corrected by the likely story and its praise of art, mathematics and sobriety in general. In the *Symposium*, Alcibiades also calls on gods and goddesses (219C). For a discussion of this point, see Rosen, *Plato's Symposium*, p. 308.

will entertain us. But he will also lay down the law. His *logos* is a form of music. It sings of nature as both a divine artifact and a divinely established convention. It celebrates the prudent founding of the cosmic regime and invites us to join in by following all the mathematical constructions—all signs of a god's handiwork. Before Critias gives man his Athenian citizenship, Timaeus will attempt to make us dutiful citizens of the world at large—good cosmopolitans.

In the *Republic*, Socrates and Glaucon rise above politics in their discussion of philosophic education. They talk about what it would be like to get out of the cave of opinion and convention and to reach the sunlight of intelligibility, to undergo a conversion from Becoming to Being (7. 518C-D). Whereas the *Republic* in its central discussion takes us up, the *Timaeus* brings us back down. It is in this respect an *undoing* of the *Republic*, although the *Republic* in another sense already contains an undoing: the tragic degeneration of soul and regime that Socrates outlines in pointed detail in Books 8 and 9. The descent we see in the *Timaeus* takes us down in two senses: back down into the realm of opinion and convention, and back down from Being to Becoming.

This descent is evident in the different roles that mathematics plays in the two dialogues. In the *Republic* mathematics is invoked as the conversionary art by means of which the soul is "turned around" from Becoming and utility to Being and contemplation (7. 518C ff.). In the *Timaeus* mathematics is used to give order to the world and to the soul, and to turn the soul's attention and care to Becoming and prudent story-telling about Becoming. Timaeus is exhorting us not to transcend the cave of body, change and opinion but rather to beautify it with mathematical adornments, to make the cave more enlightened in its opinions and more livable.[28] Mathematics here is not valued for its theoretical or contemplative power but as a form of productive practice or moral demiurgy. It is the means by which world and soul are made law-abiding and well-behaved.

The likely story is the chronicle of a gradual descent or fall from the divine. It depicts making, *poiêsis*, as an activity that starts with the highest things and proceeds to the lower. The divine craftsman begins with changeless Being. He looks to this Being as he makes his images. He does so not because he is a lover of gazing, a lover of wisdom, but because a changeless model guarantees the stability and fine formation of a likeness. For the purposes of beautiful image-making, Being is *useful*. First he makes the cosmic soul and body. Then he makes time and the star-gods. Next he orders the star-gods, in imitation of their father, to make the animal just below them—man. Timaeus refers to the divine original, provocatively but obscurely, as "the intelligible Animal." This animal-archetype prescribes the four living kinds that

---

[28]   To return to the earlier theme of *eikasia* (note 22), Timaeus employs a productive imagination (to use Kant's phrase) that establishes likenesses but which does not enable the soul to reach the forms on the basis of those likenesses. The self-containment of likely stories thus resembles the self-containment of poetry, which has the power of making us believe that its imitations are the truth.

are to populate and fill the world (39E-40A). Man *per se* is not one of the kinds but is instead the ingenious device by which these kinds gain birth. He is a mix of kinds, an unstable blend of god and beast, who, in his unraveling and moral devolution, falls into the various subhuman animals that suit his particular forms of fallenness. In this way, the divine craftsman takes the purely organizational blueprint of the intelligible Animal and transforms it, upon actualization, into a moral order writ large—a moral-cosmic order. As man falls and his originally divine and healthy nature comes to be mixed more and more with mortality, the cosmos paradoxically gets more and more perfect. It becomes better for having become worse. The penultimate moment of the likely story spells out our fall in comic detail. The original "males" go from women (the first degeneration) to birds,[29] to four-footed animals, to more-footed animals, to no-footed animals, and finally to shellfish, who dwell literally in the lowest region of the world—the abyss (91D-92C).

Timaeus takes us through a series of ingenious constructions. He continually calls upon us to imagine that the shape of the world emerged only gradually, as a series of steps that succeeded one another in time. Everything is by analogy with ordinary human craftsmanship. At each point, we are called upon to decipher these steps, to see what mysterious meaning the temporally presented order reveals. The listener-reader's participation in cosmic work is an initiation into the cosmic order. By following the constructions, the listener acquires experience in the ways and means of the world to which the listener himself belongs. He shares in the divine work by which the realm of body is made respectable or decent, in Greek, *kosmion*, thereby activating his own decency of mind. Socrates had dubbed the likely story a *nomos*, a law or song. As a *logos*, the physics of Timaeus indeed seeks in some fashion to explain the world to us. But its primary function seems to be more musical than theoretical: it is an intellectual hymn in honor of our god and cosmic fatherland. This is Timaeus' contribution—and corrective—to the Panathenaea.

Early in his account Timaeus asserts that the world must be intelligent if it is to be most beautiful, and alive if it is to be intelligent (30A-C). The god therefore puts intellect in the soul and soul in the body. He first constructs the cosmic body. He does so by taking the four elements—earth, air, fire and water—and fitting them together in

---

[29]   The story of the birds is one of the wittiest in the dialogue. Birds come from human souls that were not evil but simply naïve. They are the souls of empirical astronomers who betrayed their intellectual vocation by placing the truth of the heavens in sensuous appearance rather than in the workings of intellect (91D-E). The comic attack on empirical astronomers in the *Timaeus* recalls Socrates' critique of empirical musicologists in the *Republic*. There Socrates and Glaucon reject this empiricism as a suitable part of philosophic education on the grounds that in busying itself with the minutiae of observation it makes itself ridiculous (7. 528E-531D). Socrates and Timaeus are united in their attack on empiricism. But unlike Socrates, the Pythagorean Timaeus is devoted to *embodied* intelligibility. On cosmology as the central concern of the Pythagoreans, see Jacob Klein, *Greek Mathematical Thought and the Origin of Algebra*, tr. Eva Brann, New York: Dover Publications, Inc., 1992, "The Science of the Pythagoreans," pp. 63-69.

a geometric proportion (31C-32B). Nothing is said yet about how the elements actually interact with one another and in doing so constantly *change into* one another. That comes later with the account of necessity. Here Timaeus uses mathematical reasoning about three-dimensional objects and mean proportionality to make the four elements of body logically necessary to the very existence of body. He rationalizes body, makes body thinkable, although we must remember that the sort of thinking Timaeus has in mind is not the dialectical quest for insight into the nature of nature but the construction of ingenious models. His goal is to make, *poiein*, rather than to search, *zêtein*. In other words, mathematical physics for Timaeus is a form of *poiêsis* or poetry. This fact raises important questions for the dialogue: What is actually revealed about the cosmos in the act of building models of the cosmos? How and to what extent do these mathematical poems embody insights into the world as it really is?

After thus ordering the elements, the god makes the cosmic body into a sphere. The cosmos is the totality of all things. Timaeus describes this totality as though it itself were one of the beings we find within the totality—the super-animal of all minor animals.[30] What is most interesting about this part of the story is how human nature by its very absence indirectly governs the account of the all. The super-animal needs no hands for grabbing or warding off, no feet for walking, no lungs for breathing, and no mouth for eating or speaking. A strange sort of animal to be sure, which Timaeus does not shrink from describing with scatological boldness as a being that feeds on its own waste-matter (33C-D)! The animal also has no need for organs of sexual genera-tion, although Timaeus demurs to say so. It is nevertheless clear from what he does say that the cosmos in its self-sufficiency experiences neither erotic love nor ambition. This self-sufficiency leads Timaeus to call the cosmos "a happy god" (34B).

The lengthy description of the cosmic body is a darkly humorous reminder of the extreme neediness of our human nature. In the spherical cosmos we encounter what we would like to be but are not—self-sufficient and therefore happy gods. All the things we must have if we are to live, all the appendages and organs that we have and the cosmos does not have, are only signs of our lack. For Timaeus as well as for Aristophanes in the *Symposium*, human unhappiness derives ultimately from the fact that we are not spheres (189C ff.).[31] But is this cosmic happiness really happiness? Timaeus purges the god Cosmos of all desire and makes it its own best friend (34B). Presumably this god lacks philosophic desire. In the self-sufficient, non-erotic nature of the cosmic god we seem to get Timaeus' disagreement with Socrates regarding the need for philosophic inquiry for a truly happy life.

---

[30]   Sallis, drawing on Nietzsche, offers an extremely interesting critical reflection on the positing of cosmos as animal (ibid., p. 58, note 13).

[31]   The circle-people in Aristophanes' myth are, however, very different from Timaeus' spherical cosmos. They have sexual organs (although they use them to procreate not on one another but "on the earth, like cicadas") (191B). And, although they lack erotic longing, they are high-minded and ambitious—so much so that they try to take Olympus by storm (190B-C).

Timaeus constructs the cosmic soul *after* he first constructs body, thus implying, mistakenly, that body is older and therefore higher than soul. He apologizes for this mistake (34B-C). The problem of before and after is chronic for the likely story. The account suffers, one might say, the infirmity of being a creature of Becoming that sometimes gets its priorities mixed up. Timaeus periodically draws our attention to this problem, as if the occasional breakdown of order was part and parcel of the intended teaching about order. His cosmology is the temporal unfolding of hierarchy conceived as seniority—hierarchy as patriarchy. But the problems of before and after—the temporal image of higher and lower, ruler and ruled—show that hierarchy in Becoming is not always easy to establish. The reversed order of body and soul is the first manifest sign that the likely story is indeed at times incoherent, as Socrates had been warned. Here too, as in the earlier warning, the cause of the breakdown is our vulnerable, not entirely rational humanity. We do not always do and say what we intend to do and say. We are only human—subject to what Timaeus calls "the wandering cause" (48A). We are reminded here that the likely story is not a purely theoretical or detached activity. Unlike the dialectical striving for divine insight, it does not transcend the human condition in explaining the world. On the contrary, it imitates, arises out of, and also ministers to that condition.[32]

The god's construction of the cosmic soul is an amazing accomplishment—a true work of art. The central teaching about the soul seems to be that the soul is made out of music—four octaves and a major sixth in Pythagorean tuning, to be precise (see Appendix A). The resultant *harmonia* or scale is the paradigm of order for Timaeus, and the ingenious work of tuning the scale with mathematical ratios is the paradigm of what it means to make a cosmos or beautiful whole. This musical arrangement is then used for the construction of the celestial orbits. The implication seems to be that music has the power to bring mathematics and astronomy to a greater pitch of perfection. Music in a sense reveals the true beauty and significance of these sciences. It incorporates grace, flexibility and vitality—features of soul—into the domain of an otherwise lifeless, *Egyptian* mathematical order. Thanks to the power of music, the world does not simply have mathematical order but is inspired and animated by order.[33] In this way, the teaching of Timaeus serves as the inspiration for a very similar project undertaken by Kepler in his *Harmonies of the World*.[34]

---

[32] The likely story is, among other things, a form of psychic medicine or therapy. This is clear not only from Timaeus' long discussion of diseases and their treatments (81E-90D) but also from the opening of the *Critias*, where Timaeus calls knowledge, *epistêmê*, the "most perfect and best of medicines" (*pharmakôn*, 106B).

[33] In the Appendix to his *Plato's Phaedo: An Interpretation*, Kenneth Dorter offers an interesting discussion of philosophy and music in the Platonic dialogues (Toronto: University of Toronto Press, 1982, pp. 193-203).

[34] Book Five of the *Harmonies of the World* (1619) may be found in *Great Books of the Western World* 16, Chicago: Encyclopaedia Britannica, Inc., 1975, pp. 1005-1085.

Music is clearly central to the likely story. Pre-cosmic genesis—the original chaos that was there "before" god intervened—is described as unmusical or out of tune (30A). The celestial bodies "dance" to the music of time (40C). And ordinary music—the music that has sound and rhythm—was given to us as a gift from the gods to restore us to psychic health, which for Timaeus is the deepest form of musicality (47C-E). Even the geometric solids that are constructed later in the speech are said to be *harmonized* or fitted together out of their elemental triangles and numbers (53E), by analogy with how ratios are fitted together to make a musical scale.[35] As we know from the *Republic*, music is powerful (and dangerous) in a way that the visual arts are not. It takes possession of us, insinuates itself into our very souls, and forms our likes and dislikes (3. 401D-402A). As something essentially fluid, it overcomes the distance between inner soul and outer world, between the private and the public. For all these reasons, music is the lawgiver's greatest ally in his effort to bring order and balance to the human soul.

Critias had alluded to the political importance of music when he mentioned the Apaturia, the feast at which Athenian boys chanted songs and were initiated into their tribe (21B). Singing binds us to our political place (think of the rousing effect of "The Star-Spangled Banner" or the "Marseillaise"). It appeals to our *thymos* or spiritedness, which is the seat (among other things) of patriotic loyalty. In Critias' example, sing-ing—in fact, the singing of songs composed by the lawgiver Solon—is the act by which the souls of budding citizens are rooted in their communities. Here in this musico-political context, *nomos* as song combines beautifully with *nomos* as law or custom. The scientific song of Timaeus does something similar. It roots us in the laws and customs of our cosmic fatherland. The music of the likely story invites us to be young again and to take part in our cosmic Apaturia.

But musicality comes in only after the god has used force or violence to mix the forms of Same and Other (along with Being) in order to get the soul-stuff that is subsequently made into the Pythagorean scale (35A ff.).[36] This is the second manifest incoherence in the account. Timaeus stresses the fact that the kind Other was "loath to mix" with the kind Same. The divine craftsman here does what any self-respecting craftsman does: if the parts of his intended whole do not fit, he makes them fit. Were it not for this craftsmanlike use of force, the most fundamental union

---

[35]   Music as a metaphor for good condition is still with us. We speak of a *tune-up* for automobile engines and of *toning* our bodies.

[36]   The three forms or *eidē* of Being, Same and Other remind us of the "greatest kinds" from the *Sophist*: Being, Same, Other, Motion and Rest (254B ff.). But whereas the Eleatic stranger is interested in the dialectical interweaving of these kinds, Timaeus seems interested in no such intelligible connection. For the purposes of cosmic founding, the forms Being, Same and Other are kneaded together rather than dialectically interrelated. The result is not, in other words, purely eidetic but is a strange hybrid of the intelligible and the corporeal—a material-like stuff that is nevertheless amenable to intellectual "molding."

of Same and Other would not have come about and there would be no cosmos: no original force, no subsequent world-music. The likely story is thus both justification and praise of the use of force in a noble cause.

The story of soul begins with a tangled, convoluted sentence that seems to mimic the very mélange of Same and Other that it describes (35A).[37] The construction takes place in three separate stages. First the god mixes Same, Other and Being with force. Then he gives this soul-stuff a Pythagorean tuning. Finally he bends this musical order into circles to form the orbits of the stars, Sun, Moon and the other planets. We are called upon to *imagine* all this and to trust that something like it happened, without having a clear idea of what any of it really means.

Timaeus uses the music of myth to overcome the distance between inner and outer, soul and world. The apparently outer orbits of the heavenly bodies are imagined as the inner revolutions of sound judgement (36E-37C). They are the divine paths from which human judgement tends to stray. The "external world," as we call it, is really embraced by and in some sense *within* the soul's all-embracing circles of thought. As we gaze into the heavens at night, we are really gazing into our innermost and highest selves. Astronomy, the study of the musically tuned heavens, tunes us as we lead our minds down orderly and regular paths of thinking. By causing us to imitate the orderly objects of our study, it restores our capacity for clear-headed and unwandering judgement. The stars, we learn, are our true home and origin, and astronomy takes us back to what Timaeus calls the "form" (*eidos*) of our "first and best condition" (42D). It leads man, the "heavenly plant" (90A), back to his roots. Philosophic education for Timaeus (if we may call it that) thus aims not at transcendence of, but at assimilation to, the intelligent order of the visible heaven.[38]

After finishing the cosmic body and soul, the god joins them "center to center" (36E). He rejoices in his noble offspring just as an artist rejoices in his handiwork or a father in seeing a living likeness of himself. But the divine artist-father, as if recoiling from the thought of his offspring's mortality, resolves to make his likeness even more like its eternally unchanging model: he makes *time*. Time is said to be "a moving likeness of eternity" (37D). It is constructed neither before nor after but together with the construction of heaven (37D, 38B).

Normally we think of place as something stable and time as something fleeting

---

[37]   Taylor calls this passage "the most perplexing and difficult passage of the whole dialogue" (ibid., p. 106). Cornford, following Proclus, gives a fairly clear description of how the mixing of Same, Other and Being involves two stages; in other words, it is a mix of mixes (ibid., pp. 59-66). For difficulties in this construal, see Sallis, ibid., pp. 65 ff.

[38]   The alternative to cosmic assimilation is given inspired utterance in the great myth of the *Phaedrus*, where Socrates sings of "the region *above* the heaven" (*ton hyperouranion topon*, 247C ff.).

and unstable—as the image, in a sense, of mortality.[39] Timaeus reverses this perspective. He associates time with stability and order, and place (as we shall see) with instability and process. Time imitates eternity by making motion regular and periodic. It is the self-sameness within the perpetual self-otherness of motion. Time makes the heavens into a cosmic *clock*, by which all other motions are measured.[40] The Sun, Moon and planets come into being only after the birth of time. They are like the hands of the cosmic clock, which mark off and "guard" the numbers of time (38C). Ominously, Timaeus ends his account of time, which gives the world a vicarious eternity, with the thought of death. Time, he says, came into being with the heaven "in order that, having been begotten together, they might be dissolved together—should some dissolution of them ever arise" (38B). Does Timaeus mean to suggest that such dissolution *will* arise? Is he hinting at the fact that *everything* that has a coming to be, as Socrates says in the *Republic*, necessarily has a passing away (8. 546A)? What is supposed to happen when the Perfect Year, as Timaeus calls it (39D), reaches its end? Does the world literally *run out of time*? Is there perhaps a never-ending cycle of successive worlds that mimics the cycle of civilizations in the priest's tale?

After making time, the craftsman does something unique in the likely story—he speaks. The craftsman-father (as he ambiguously calls himself) refers to the apparent inevitability of death mentioned above. He reassures his star-god sons that although they too are generated and therefore subject to dissolution, they have a vicarious immortality through the goodness of his will (41B). Addressing his star-god sons (the gods of Homer and Hesiod are summoned, it seems, only to be disregarded), he entrusts them with the completion of his work. They, not he, are to be the makers of man. Again Timaeus reminds us that making is inevitably a descent from perfection—a fall. Man must be mortal. But that can come about, says the god, only if beings lower than him do the making. Man's mortality has several meanings here. It means first of all that we literally die. But it also means that our nature is not purely immortal and divine. Our divine, intellectual nature is mixed with mortality—with the mortality of our bodies, which are perpetually subject to flux, disease, and old age as well as death; the mortality of sensation, which is a perpetual being struck by the impressions of an external and unpredictable world; and the mortality of our passions, which make us inconstant, unstable and generally unintelligent. We begin to die in manifold ways at the moment we are born. Education is the antidote to this condition of having been born mortal. It is the means by which we return to our originally healthy selves.

---

[39]   The instability of time is given eloquent and succinct expression by Hegel: "[Time] is that being which, inasmuch as it *is*, is *not*, and inasmuch as it is *not*, *is*; it is Becoming directly intuited" (Hegel's *Philosophy of Nature*, Part Two of the *Encyclopaedia of the Philosophical Sciences*, tr. A V. Miller, [Oxford: Clarendon Press, 1970], p. 34).

[40]   For a highly suggestive parallel between Timaeus and Einstein on time as a clock, see Eva Brann, *What, Then, Is Time?*, New York: Rowman and Littlefield Publishers, Inc., 1999, pp. 4-12.

The making of man for Timaeus is a pious desecration. This fact is signaled by his later juxtaposition of the words *sebomenoi*, being reverent, and *miainein*, to defile (69D), in describing the paradoxical situation in which the makers of man find themselves. In pious obedience to their intelligent begetter, they must complete the cosmos by defiling the very principle of intelligence that the begetter embodies. They must immerse the sacred substance of intellect in the troubled sea of Becoming. They must, in a sense, beget chaos. Much of their construction of man is in response to this paradox of piety and defilement. They start with the head, which is the most divine part of our body. It is the part that contains the divine circuits of Same and Other—the paths of sound judgement. They then proceed to make the rest of the body the head's vehicle or chariot (44D-E). Again, on the principle that making proceeds from the best and works its way down, the gods first make the sublime nature of our eyes. These are given to us primarily so that we might see the heavens, learn to count (by observing periods or complete cycles) and take up the study of astronomy, thus rectifying our warped condition (47A-C). It is here in the context of vision, more specifically in Timaeus' Empedoclean account of how mirrors can be used to produce distorted images (46A-C), that the likely story approaches its central crisis.[41]

The Second Founding: The Story Of Necessity

In the *Phaedo*, Socrates tells Simmias and Cebes about his youthful fascination with cause and Becoming, with the "inquiry into nature" (96A ff.). He sought a cause for why things were the way they were and came to be the way they came to be. The book of Anaxagoras, in which *nous*, intellect, was the cause of all things, seemed at first to be just what Socrates was looking for. Surely *nous* "would order all things and position each thing in just the way which was best" (97C).[42] Socrates' youthful hopes are dashed once he discovers that Anaxagoras is just one more materialist who abandons the world to chance and necessity.

The *Timaeus* is Plato's most extensive treatment of causality. Like the young Socrates in the *Phaedo*, Timaeus honors above all the cause that has to do with what is best, the causality of the good. In his first attempt to found the best of possible worlds in speech, he had relied almost exclusively on this sort of cause. The divine craftsman was good; his sons were dutiful; and the world, although in a state of flux, was governed by principles of order and thoughtfulness. In the likely story, *nous* really does rule the world. Timaeus, a master of many distinctions, gets straight what Anaxagoras did not: the all-important distinction between a cause and that without which the cause cannot be a cause. At the end of his long excursion into the secondary order of cause, he even presents this distinction as a lesson to live by, thus again affirming the bond between his physics and the virtue of prudence: "one should mark off two forms of

---

[41]   Empedocles is of crucial importance for the likely story as a whole. See M. Wright, *Empedocles: the Extant Fragments*, New Haven: Yale University Press, 1981.

[42]   *Plato's Phaedo*, tr. Brann, Kalkavage, Salem, Newburyport MA: Focus Publishing/R. Pullins Company, 1998, p. 77.

cause—the necessary and the divine—and seek the divine in all things for the sake of gaining a happy life, to the extent that our nature allows, and the necessary for the sake of those divine things" (68A-69B).

The assistant or secondary cause is *anankê*, necessity. It is the source of power as opposed to goodness. Timaeus also calls it "the wandering cause" (48A), thereby revealing necessity as a potential hindrance as well as a help to rational accomplishment in the sphere of Becoming. This is the cause that most physicists are always talking about, the cause to which they reduce everything. Timaeus doesn't simply incorporate this cause into his first founding. Instead, he takes the emergence of necessity in the account as an occasion for "another new beginning," as he calls it (48B).[43] This second account of origins will be more radical than the first, and stranger. It will take us down into the not-to-be-trusted heart of Becoming as such and its passing show. The two beginnings are never combined into a single, coherent whole. Timaeus never tries to derive the content of the first founding from the more radical second founding. The likely story thus remains three separate stories: a story of intellect, a story of necessity, and a final story that refers to the first two without ever explaining their connection. This is the most serious as well as most interesting incoherence of the entire account of the cosmos. By presenting us with so blatant an incoherence, Plato causes us to wonder why the definitive dialogue on the cosmos offers no single and continuous account of the world's beginning.

The problem that gives rise to the need for a new beginning is the perpetual transmutation of the elements and, more generally, the fascinating but deceptive process known as *appearing*. In the first founding, the four elements of body were serenely related by a continuous *analogia* or proportion (31B ff.). Timaeus gave no account of their possible interactions. Here in the second founding, the elements appear, come on the scene, as always turning into each other—a fact that can in no way be explained if the elements were as elemental or atomic as the previous account had made them seem. As the work of the first founding goes on, Timaeus gets closer and closer to Becoming as such, to the very *process* of coming to be and passing away. Here in his second account of cosmic origins, he openly confronts the basic and formidable question: What is Becoming?[44]

---

[43]   For the possible implications of this new beginning, see Sallis, ibid., p. 91 ff.

[44]   Timaeus' descent into Becoming bears a certain dramatic and philosophic likeness to the Eleatic stranger's "descent" into Non-being in the *Sophist* (237A ff.). (For a lively translation of the stranger's adventure of Being and Non-being, see *Plato's Sophist*, tr. Brann, Kalkavage, Salem, Newburyport MA: Focus Publishing/R. Pullins Company, 1996, pp. 40 ff.) There too a lengthy, technical excursus is interrupted for the sake of a direct confrontation with a deep and dangerous topic. In the *Sophist* no less than in the *Timaeus*, Plato raises a question: Are the technically determined "looks" of things what the things themselves actually look like (to the intellect), or are they the *artifacts* of technical speech? Does technical speech belong in the class of "getting" or "making" (*Sophist* 219A-D)?

Timaeus begins his journey by informing us that the cosmos was in fact "begotten from a standing-together [a *systasis*] of necessity and intellect" (48A). Intellect, we are told, *persuaded* necessity to lead things to the best—that the world is in effect held together, constituted, by a kind of cosmic rhetoric.[45] The metaphor of persuasion serves to keep the two orders of causality separate even as it brings them together. The construction of soul had required force. Here, as we approach the construction of body, the gentler, statesmanlike force of persuasion is sufficient. Body is apparently more tractable than soul and more open to the designs of artful intelligence. Perhaps this is because the soul is by nature more heterogeneous than body, made out of elements (the forms of Same and Other) that are more disparate than the more homogeneous *magnitudes* out of which body is composed. There is also perhaps the suggestion that the soul is a more terrible force to reckon with than body, that its potential for recalcitrance and disorder is greater.[46]

The excursion into necessity, as we are reminded several times, is *chalepon*—a word that means both difficult and dangerous (see, for example, 48C and 49A). Timaeus pauses, as though on the brink of an abyss, and prays that Zeus, the savior god, will lead him "out of a strange and unusual narration to the decree based on likelihoods" (48D). The word for decree is *dogma*, which is related to *doxa* or opinion. A dogma is an official opinion or public proclamation. It is also the decision of a court or assembly. We are reminded here that the likely story strives not to transcend opinion in order to reach genuine knowledge but to craft persuasive opinions which, like ordinary human laws, provide stability and guidance in the face of Becoming and all its dangers and deceptiveness. Just before Timaeus had begun to speak, Socrates reminded him to invoke the gods "in accordance with custom" (27B). This time the invocation of a god needs no prompting from Socrates. Well might Timaeus pray for divine help! The new principle he is about to unveil is elusiveness itself—a duplicitous, sophistic form or *eidos*, as Timaeus provocatively calls it (49A), which is itself only when it is being something else.

Timaeus revises his original count of principles or kinds. Before, he needed only two: the likeness and the model. Now he needs a third. This third he calls a

---

[45]   Given the presumably mindless character of necessity, it is difficult to see in what this persuasion consists. According to Klein, it points ahead to the geometric construction of the four primary bodies out of scalene and isosceles triangles (54A-B) (*A Commentary on Plato's Meno*, p. 196). In any case, persuasion would not be an appropriate metaphor if necessity were not somehow predisposed to order and beauty. For an interesting discussion of this point, see Hans-Georg Gadamer, "Idea and Reality in Plato's *Timaeus*" in *Dialogue and Dialectic: Eight Hermeneutical Studies on Plato*, New Haven: Yale University Press, 1980, pp. 156-193.

[46]   In his critique of music in Book 3 of the *Republic*, Socrates admits only two modes into the well-founded city: the Dorian and the Phrygian. (On the Greek modes, see Appendix A.) These correspond, respectively, to force and persuasion (399A-C). The two beginnings in the likely story are thus in accord with the two acceptable modes in the *Republic*: a song of force and a song of persuasion.

receptacle and wet-nurse for all Becoming (51A, 52D). As the formless ground of all imaging or doubling, the receptacle resembles the surface of a mirror. We recall that mirror-reflections had first reminded Timaeus of the necessity for the necessary cause (46C). What had earlier been regarded as the four elements of body—earth, air, fir and water—are not, strictly speaking, elements at all. They are not ultimate, discrete atoms that provide stable building-blocks for the body of the world. Fire, for example, the most robust and interesting of the elements, is not really a "this" (*touto*) but only an "of this sort" (*toiouton*) (49D ff.). In the language of Spinoza, fire is but a passing *mode* in the ever-abiding sea of *substance*.[47]

Timaeus tries to clarify his strange and unheard of principle through an image—something he does often in this section of his speech. Once more using productive art as the model of nature, he asks us to imagine a strange sort of demiurge who works in gold, ceaselessly changing the shapes he impresses there into other shapes (50A). Timaeus gives a little foretaste of things to come when he singles out the *triangle* as one of these possible shapes. The image of the gold-fashioner makes the receptacle seem like a second divine craftsman, whose work, however, is done only to be undone—a perverse sort of craftsman, or rather magician, bent on perpetuating instability and inconstancy of shape. If, while we were watching the amazing spectacle of all these shapes in motion, someone pointed to one of them and asked us, What is it?, then, says Timaeus, the *safest* answer—the answer least likely to be unsettled and destabilized—would be "gold." Strictly speaking, however, although it is a molding-stuff for all generated things, the strange receptacle cannot simply be identified with matter.[48] As Timaeus' image clearly suggests, the motion or instability of the third kind is spontaneous. When the elements turn into one another, this is not the result of some goldsmith's external hand but of change from within. The receptacle is simultaneously stuff and process. It is the unstable medium not of things but of emergencies and things happening.

We noted earlier that Timaeus reshapes our sense of inner and outer. The motions of the heavens were mythically revised as the inner revolutions of thought. In this section of the likely story, we seem to get another such projection of the inner into the outer. In the receptacle we seem to encounter the corporeal image of our own imagination or *phantasia* writ large—the inner ground of our soul's spontaneous production of, and desirous receptivity to, images of all sorts. Timaeus suggests this very analogy when he speaks of the *dreaminess* induced by the third kind (52B-C).[49] When Socrates expressed his desire at the beginning of the dialogue,

---

[47]   *Ethics Demonstrated in the Geometrical Mode*, Part One, Definitions 3 and 5, tr. Samuel Shirley, Indianapolis: Hackett Publishing Co., 1992, p. 31.

[48]   Sallis offers an illuminating account of why the *chôra* should not be identified with *hylê* or matter (ibid., pp. 151-154).

[49]   This sort of *phantasia* must be distinguished from *eikasia* as it appears on the divided line (see note 22). The *phantasia* associated with Space induces dreams and blurs the distinction between the sensed and the intellected. *Eikasia*, by contrast, is

he was implying that this part of his soul, his imagination, would gladly welcome and be receptive to glorious moving pictures. He was in fact confessing that he too, like the four elements, was under the *sway* (52E) of the ever-abiding force that Timaeus calls the receptacle.

After a slow and mysterious build-up, the third kind eventually gets its name. It is *chôra* or Space (52B). There is no good translation of this word as Timaeus uses it. The *chôra* is not empty space because it is filled with the powers and traces of the four elements (53B). It is not simply place because it is in perpetual motion, both swaying and being swayed by these powers and traces (52E). For this same reason it can't be room or mere extension. Nor can we identify it with Aristotle's *hylê* or matter. Perhaps the name in English that best suits it is Field. First of all the name suggests the field theories of modern physics, which Plato seems to have prophesied here as an ingenious combination of Pythagorean mathematical configurations and Empedoclean process or flux. The electromagnetic field in particular bears a certain resemblance to Timaeus' third kind: it is a medium for the play of forces, a locus of tensions and conflicts, and the medium for the transmission of wave or periodic motion.[50] This modern field, like the third kind, is not a room for stable things but a medium for fleeting events and actions. Field also suggests the field of battle, an image that connects the ongoing war of the elements with Socrates' desire for a war movie.[51] Finally, field suggests tilled soil, an image suited to the third kind as the womb of the world.

As we see from the foregoing discussion, necessity for Timaeus is a multifunctional principle. This is one reason why it is so difficult to describe in any reasonably coherent way. Before proceeding, it may be helpful to enumerate these functions. First, necessity is the source of the necessary *causes* that the craftsman needs in order to accomplish his noble ends—causes like "cooling and heating, coalescing and dissolving" (46D). These are the powers (*dynameis*) associated with

---

the faculty by which we are awakened from our dreaminess, come to regard images as images, and thus begin our ascent to Being. To be sure, Timaeus *mentions* "the unsleeping and truly subsisting nature" (52B), but the imagination employed in telling likely stories does not treat its image-objects as hypotheses and steppingstones that point "upward" to that nature. (For the treatment of hypotheses as steppingstones and springboards to the forms, see *Republic* 6. 510B-511C).

50   For an interesting discussion of the connection between soul in Plato and the modern concept of energy, see Dorter, ibid., pp. 179-191. Just as soul for Timaeus seems to be the world's "thought energy," the receptacle seems to be the source of its "body energy."

51   The polemical condition of pre-cosmic genesis in the *Timaeus* has its political counterpart in Hobbes' "state of nature." Both conditions cry out for an *artifice* (for Hobbes, the social contract) that will transform raw nature into a state of unity and peace. But whereas Timaeus relies on the persuasion of necessity, Hobbes resorts to the *fear* of the sovereign power (*Leviathan*, Part I, Chapter 13; Part II, Chapter 17).

the four elements of body. Second, necessity as the *wandering* cause is the reason why there is contingency, chance, free play and unpredictability in the world: things sometimes happen because they happen to happen (like Socrates' desire at 19B). Third, necessity as an all-receptive medium is the mysterious ground of cosmic *imaging*. This is perhaps the single most elusive function of necessity—the reason why necessity keeps slipping through the net of discourse. Fourth, necessity as Space or *chôra* is the reason why everything in the realm of Becoming is defined in terms of *place* and has *room* to be (52B). Fifth, necessity, like the cosmic soul, is a source of perpetual *motion*, indeed, a kind of circular and circulatory motion. As Timaeus reminds us, the wandering cause doesn't dart out in all directions but sweeps things around (48B) and makes the so-called elements pass into each other, as though in a circle (49C). Sixth and finally, necessity, in some mysterious way, antedates and serves as the ground of *body*.[52]

At one point Timaeus does something especially daring and unsettling. He raises the question as to whether there even is any "Fire itself on its own" or any other things that are "themselves by themselves" (51B). He flirts with nominalism and speculates that perhaps what we call an *eidos* or form is really "nothing but a word" (51C). It is not clear why Timaeus raises this huge issue. Is he just being thorough, making sure that we realize that for the purposes of the likely story—whose boundaries and power alike Timaeus is careful to preserve—the positing of a "by itself" that *is* rather than becomes must remain a hypothesis that dwells in the region of trust? In the end, Timaeus *casts his vote* for the forms (51D). This is an emphatic reminder that cosmological discourse for Timaeus is governed by a certain political or statesmanlike attitude toward even the highest objects of contemplation. To think is ultimately to *judge*.

In the first founding, the image of art predominated. The craftsman, to be sure, had been called a father and the world his offspring. But the act of making was always soberly artistic, always the work of intellect. It was somehow paternal without ever having involved sex. One thinks of the birth of Athena, whose feast day it currently is and who sprang asexually from the head of Zeus. Here in the second founding, the craftsman of the first founding is almost entirely absent (god is referred to in passing at 53B). The accent throughout this section of the dialogue is in fact on our powers of geometric construction and likely account-giving, our generation of Athena-like "brain children." Furthermore, the father that corresponds to the receptacle-mother is not the divine craftsman but the *eidos* or form of each element (50D). In what sense is the form itself a father? Apparently only because it plays the role of the purely intelligible original after which the sensed image is fashioned and whose "look" is somehow manifest in its sensuous instances. In any

---

52   "What distinguishes the 'civilized' state of the 'receptacle' from its primordial chaotic state is nothing but the presence of complete, if transient, *bodies*" (Jacob Klein, *A Commentary on Plato's Meno*, ibid., p. 197).

case, life up to this point in the story had really meant the life of intellect. Soul was the principle of thought and circular motion. Here in the second founding the receptacle, although the ground of body, seems to provide a new and necessary kind of soul or animating principle—soul as the ground of organic life and growth. As Timaeus moves, in other words, from his first to his second founding, astronomy as the primary science gives way to biology, the science of *living* body.

But even in the sphere of organic life, artistry for Timaeus always seems to get the upper hand. The praise of the god Cosmos is also the praise of *technê* or art. Having completed his descent into the underworld of Becoming as such, Timaeus resumes his technical display by adorning Space with beautiful intellectual structures. He *makes body* by constructing mathematical models out of the regular Platonic solids: pyramid for fire, cube for earth, octahedron for air, and icosahedron for water (54D ff.). The fifth solid, the twelve-sided dodecahedron, is used to adorn the heavens, apparently by dividing the inner "wall" of the cosmos-cave into pentagonal panels for the god's interior decorating. The language that Timaeus uses to construct the solids embodies his typical (and confusing) melding of the natural and the artificial that we see throughout his speech. He speaks of the birth of the solids out of each other (54D). These three-dimensional constructs seem to grow, like plants, out of their two-dimensional elements. The pyramid is the element and *seed* of fire (56B). But the faces of the solids are also "stuck together" as if by the hand of a child at play (55B).

The regular solids are a technical rather than philosophical solution to the problem of change. They are an object lesson in how the cosmologist can explain the shiftiness of change in terms of the integrity of form. If the elements were really elements or atoms, then their change into one another would be unthinkable. But if everything flows and there are no relatively stable natures at all, then change is again unthinkable, since to think is to think a determinate something. The regular solids thus mediate between motion and rest, instability and stability. Their structures can be decomposed and recomposed. This constant recombination of structural parts provides a mathematical model for change itself. It is the perfect marriage of Pythagoras (number and geometric shape) and Empedocles (process or flux). Thanks to the sobering, Apollonian influence of mathematics, the wild, Dionysian spree of change becomes the orderly transposition of beautiful geometric "animals" in motion. Change thus becomes a delight to contemplate.

Much earlier in the dialogue, when Critias was telling Socrates about his speech to come, he said that the well-educated citizens of Socrates' speech would "in all ways fit" [*pantôs harmosousi*] the citizens of ancient Athens (26D). That is to say, Critias would make them fit; he would build a likeness so true to its original that the listener would swear that likeness and original were the *same*. The whole enterprise of Critias, as he himself understands it, is the fabrication of detailed correspondences—harmonies or metaphors[53]—that beguile one into thinking that the things harmonized, made to fit, are identical. This sort of beguiling yet deceptive harmonization is what Timaeus seems to be engaged in when he constructs the elements of body. He *harmonizes* the solids, as he says (53E), echoing Critias' use of this word, and proceeds to "explain" their properties on the basis of his geometric poems. In his *Crisis of the European Sciences*, Husserl refers to what he calls the *garb of ideas*, which modern mathematical physics uses to dress up nature, cover its naked truth, with the formal attire of mathematical constructs and symbols.[54] Timaeus is doing consciously and deliberately what Husserl says the modern physicists do for the most part unconsciously. He is adorning nature with a gorgeous dress of number, ratio and figure. This is only one of the ways in which the *Timaeus* transcends its antiquity and appears to be Plato's prophecy of modern mathematical science.

The mathematical story of body is intensely playful. It and the whole account that issues from it constitute what might be called a mythematical physics. It is only apparently more scientific, less mythical than what has preceded it. The source of this mythic quality lies in the attempt to persuade us that mathematical structure is sufficient for the explanation of sensed body and all its properties or affections. We are even treated to a bio-geometric explanation of old age and death (81C-E)! Timaeus builds the four solids he needs and only afterwards assigns them to the four elements. He thus makes us aware that explanation here is really the construction of geometric metaphors and happy correspondences. We are not really accounting for fire, for example. We are instead constructing the elegant geometric analogue or model of fire. When Timaeus had first named the third kind as Space, he said that it was grasped by "some bastard reasoning with the aid of insensibility" (52B). The insensibility or non-sensing to which he refers here may well be the imagination, that is, our capacity both to be affected by and to make images. Timaeus' mathematical-physical explanations, which blur the distinction between physical body and geometric body, seem to be examples of this bastard reasoning. In a sense, they are a kind of noble lie[55]—a combination of poetry (making imitations) and sophistry (arguing). What the pyramid gives us is not the true cause or *aition* of fire and its affections

---

53   The verb *metapherein*, from which our word "metaphor" comes and which means carry from one place to another or translate, was in fact used by Critias to describe his actualization of the city in speech (26C-D).

54   "In geometrical and natural-scientific mathematization ... we measure the life-world—the world constantly given to us as actual in our concrete world-life—for a well-fitting *garb of ideas [Ideenkleid]*" (*The Crisis of European Sciences*, [Evanston: Northwestern University Press, 1970], p. 51).

55   Socrates advocates the noble or well-born (*gennaion*) lie at *Republic* 3. 414B ff. The lie concerns becoming or birth. It consists in persuading first the rulers and soldiers, then the rest of the city, that their true education was taking place while they were under the earth, which nursed and trained them as though it were their mother. Socrates goes on to describe golden souls, silver souls, and souls of iron and bronze.

but the official or alleged cause, the *prophasis*, in which it is healthy for decent and intelligent human beings to place their trust.

The subsequent account of how necessity actually operates in the world is long, detailed and at times tedious. Here Timaeus often sounds like any other materialist process-physicist. On several occasions, he quells our wonder like some ancient Descartes, assures us that marvels like mirrors (46A) and the lodestone (80B-C) are in the end perfectly understandable and not really wondrous at all. All we have to do is make the right assumptions and all the problems will just go away. On he goes about how the elements combine, wage war with each other, seek refuge with their kindred; about how the various kinds of bodies in our world were formed and got both their sensed qualities and their names; about how our senses themselves work. Timaeus seems gleefully immersed in the particulars of all this necessary causality, this renovated spectacle of elemental wars and alliances.

Even after he officially stops his descent into the powers of Becoming and returns to man (69B), the relentless display of necessary causes persists as we march through ingenious accounts of our various organs and the many diseases to which our bodies and souls are subject. At one point, Timaeus reminds us explicitly that physics properly understood is a form of play: "And whenever, for the sake of a rest, a man puts down accounts about things that always *are* and peruses accounts about becoming, thereby gaining a pleasure not to be repented of, then he would make within his life a temperate and prudent sort of play [*paidian*]" (59C-D). Timaeus here defends the business of telling likely stories, defends cosmological play, as though to preempt any quibbles by dialecticians who might accuse it of being frivolous—or worse. In passing he also defines such speech as productive rather than theoretic: the play of physics is not something engaged in but something *made*.[56] But just how playful is this cosmological play? And if it is play, then in what sense may likely stories be said to reach any real insight and truth about the world? What is meant by "putting down accounts about things that always *are*"? Putting them down for now, or putting them down for good? Is this refined sort of pleasure—a gentlemanly pleasure that we can enjoy in good conscience—the *goal* of our account-giving?

It is very difficult to come up with clear answers to these questions. One thing is sure: physics comes on the scene as a form of play with even more comedic force once Timaeus turns to the fabrication of human nature. It is to this third and final part of the likely story that we now turn.

Completing the Whole: the Story of Man

What is human nature for Timaeus, and why were we made in the first place? Man comes about because the cosmos must be complete. If the world is to be perfectly filled, it must contain all the animal kinds dictated by the eternal archetype

---

[56]   In his prelude (as Socrates called it), Timaeus had referred to speeches or accounts (*logous*) as produced or *made* (*poieisthai*, 27C).

that Timaeus calls "the intelligible Animal" (39E). The various animals derive from the mystic number Four, which is alluded to in the dialogue's opening. The four animate kinds correspond to the four elements of body (39E ff.). The star-gods are mostly made of fire. Then come animals that crawl on the earth, fly through the air, and swim in the water. Man is not one of the kinds. He is rather the generator of the mortal kinds, the means by which the lower kinds come to be. Timaeus here appropriates the three-part soul we hear about in the *Republic*—the soul that is composed of a reasoning part, a spirited part, and a desirous part (4. 435B ff.). Timaeus takes these parts and lodges them in separate regions of the body. In his head, man lives the life of the gods, the life of circular perfection and prudence. But in his torso are housed all the lower animal possibilities of rage and desire that lurk, now literally, in the lower regions of his being. In the very shape of his body, man thus unites the two cooperating causes of cosmic order. He is the unity-in-opposition of the good and the necessary. The invisible soul thus becomes visible, in a sense, through the body's structure.

The star-gods, we recall, are entrusted with this unenviable task of man-making. Into our souls they pour all manner of "affections terrible and necessary" (69D), which drive us crazy and pull us away from the gods' intelligent guidance. The subsequent construction of our bodies is for the most part bound up with and in response to this necessary maddening of man. The neck, for example, is invented so that the circles of thought in our head will be minimally perturbed by the passions housed in our torso (69D). The *thymos* or spirited part of the soul is placed in the chest so that it can hearken to the head and subdue the anarchy below (70C). The lungs are a sort of cushion and cooler for the heart when it is excited by anger (70C). And the intestines are invented so that we may have a respite from our desire for food and drink and thus have leisure for philosophy (73A). Our flesh was given to us so that we wouldn't be seriously hurt when we fell (74B-C). The gods of Timaeus are always provident, always looking out for our susceptibility to *falls*. They make our hair, for example, as a compromise between a longer but stupid life and a shorter but more intelligent one (75B-76D). They make rudimentary finger-nails, knowing that women "and the rest of the wild animals" issuing from man's fall would need them some day (76D-E). As we watch this weird and unflattering construction of ourselves, again and again we are made to realize, in darkly comedic ways, the paradoxes of being human and the delicate and endangered condition of our lives—a condition or *pathos* that derives from our subjection to necessity or the wandering cause. Through the ingenious play of the likely story, our body becomes the very parable of our nature.

The mouth is one of the most perspicuous construction stories within this parable (75D-E). It shows how we, like everything else in the cosmos, are defined by the alliance or *systasis* of the good and the necessary. The mouth is the organ that most clearly embodies these two great causes. It is for the sake of the necessary stream of nutriment that flows *in*, and the good and beautiful stream of intelligence that flows *out*. Our whole nature is defined by these two streams. But *systasis* means standing together in conflict with one's enemy as well as allying oneself with a friend. The union of the good and the necessary is both an alliance and a tension. As a point of tension, the mouth is the union of two oppositely directed and conflicting streams. This often happens in the stories of our body: the artificiality of the construction, which in the case of the mouth seems like a happy marriage of opposites, reveals an incoherence or even war within human nature, in this case a war concentrated in one and the same bodily organ.

Next to the brain, and possibly the mouth, Timaeus' favorite organ seems to be the liver, for which he mounts a memorable philosophic comedy (71A-72D). For Timaeus, bodily organs are regarded and constructed in light of their relation to intelligence. Recall that in constructing the intestines, for example, Timaeus said nothing about what they might contribute to the assimilation of food. The all-important thing was that they prevent food from passing from the body too quickly, thus leading to an endless condition of desire that would allow no leisure for philosophy. Here in the case of the liver, the intimate relation between bodily organ and intelligence is especially prominent. The liver also gives Timaeus a chance to defend the right and proper relation between the human and the divine.

The liver, more than any other organ, seems to address our nature as a whole. To explain its structure, placement and function, Timaeus appeals to the hierarchical soul we hear about in the *Republic*. The liver is utterly ingenious and offers yet another example of the constructor-gods' providentiality. It serves as the mediator between intellect and emotion, our highest and our lowest parts. Like the cosmic receptacle, whose all-receptive potency reminded us of the surface of a mirror, it is the medium for *imaging*. Through this organ "the power of our thoughts that courses from the intellect" gains control over the unruly passions by projecting movie-like images into its dense and shiny surface (71B). Timaeus follows *nomos* or custom in making the liver the organ of divination. This is the closest he ever comes to acknowledging some form of divine madness. Timaeus in effect rationalizes this publicly accepted, institutional relation of man to the uncanny and supernatural. Although he does not criticize divination as a form of superstition and psychic disturbance, he does make it clear that inspiration without judgement is useless. The diviners may be receptacles of divine communication, but without the sane and sober prophets or "interpreters of things divined" (72B), successful communication is impossible. This rationalizing of divination reminds us that in Egypt too divination played an enlightened role. Together with medicine, it seemed to sum up prudence or practical wisdom (24B-C).

The story of the liver concludes Timaeus' account of the parts of the three-part soul in its relation to the body. True to the cosmic principle of Space (*chôra*) unveiled in his new beginning, the account is primarily topological: it reveals "where and in what company and through what reasons these [three parts] have been housed separately from one another" (72D). In a way, this shows the whole point of the likely story as it relates to human nature. To engage in cosmology is to activate a detailed awareness of the proper place of things within the economy of the whole. If to be wise is above all to know one's place, then cosmology, as Timaeus understands it, is the highest form of wisdom. Dialectic, in Timaeus' world, seems totally superfluous and perhaps even poses a threat to the cosmic regime.[57]

In the course of his long physiology, Timaeus gives a highly complex and purely mechanical account of the interrelated processes of breathing and digestion. He makes us acutely aware in this explanation of how much our mortal lives are determined by the workings of necessity. Occasionally, the physiological account of man becomes so immersed in non-human, merely corporeal causality that what goes on in breathing and swallowing, for example, is said to be no different from what goes on in the case of projectile motion (79E-80A), the flowing of waters (80B), the falling of thunderbolts (80C), and the apparent but ultimately deceptive "attraction" of amber and lodestones (80C). The main point Timaeus seems to want to make is that genuine, non-superstitious causality consists in the fact that there is no void, and that pushes make sense whereas pulls do not.[58] Explaining man's physiology, therefore, is a matter of showing how this non-wondrous causality, the causality of pushes and displacements, is at work within our bodily processes—a further confirmation of the fact that we are just as much creatures of necessity as we are of intellect and soul.

The account of mortal structures eventually leads to the account of the eventual collapse of those structures. As the divine craftsman-father told his handiwork-sons, "all that is bound together can be dissolved" (41A). Here, as we approach the end of the likely story, necessary causation leads us into the domain of decrepitude, death, and disease. The *prophasis* or official explanation of natural death is ingenious. Staying alive ultimately means that our elemental triangles are winning the continual battle with the outside world, defeating the alien triangles that invade us from without. Metabolism is this on-going polemic interaction with the outer world. But the triangles can fight only for so long. In time, the "root" of our triangles eventually gives way and we begin to die a natural death. Timaeus stresses the naturalness of this death by deconstruction. He tells us that when the soul is released from her body and flies out, she does so "with pleasure" (81E). This virtually painless sort of death is neither wondrous nor terrifying. It does not raise

---

[57] Perhaps this is why there is no place for Socrates in the world as Timaeus constructs it.

[58] The most interesting example of a pull is erotic love. The beloved pulls or draws the lover without being pulled or drawn (like Aristotle's "for the sake of which" at *Metaphysics* 12. 7. 1072A26-B4). Toward the end of his speech, Timaeus explains *erôs* (which for him is a love of generating) with no reference to the beloved whatsoever (91A-D). The sexual impulse is not directed toward an Other but aims rather at the affirmation of the ruling power (the male) and the fruitfulness (the female) of the Self. The Other is simply a necessary means to this end.

the problems that arise in the *Phaedo*, where Socrates ministers to the doubts and fears of Simmias and Cebes.[59]

The theme of naturalness continues in Timaeus' surprisingly long discourse on disease. Perhaps the most interesting thing we hear is that diseases are *constructed* (81E). Timaeus speaks of them at times with a certain admiration and respect. At one point he describes the most dangerous bodily diseases (those that affect the marrow) as "greatest and lordliest" (84C). What does it mean to think like this? In one sense diseases are against nature. They are the bodily substances flowing backwards—against the right and established order for life and health (82E, 84B-C). Timaeus has a provocative way of describing this departure from right order. He says that it is "against the laws [or customs] of nature" (83E). But in another sense diseases are like animals in their own right (89B). They are intelligible structures that go through cycles like everything else in the world and, as the account plainly shows, are amenable to thorough systematic study. Pathology is no less a science of nature, no less a study of intelligible structures and causes, than the physiology of health.

The story (and cosmic defense) of bodily disease leads Timaeus to his account of vice and folly, both of which he treats as forms of disease (86B ff.). Timaeus sounds very modern and enlightened here, like an ancient Spinoza or Descartes. He presents soul and body as intimately related. Furthermore, vice is ultimately due to mental derangement, either madness or stupidity, both of which in turn are due to "some corrupt condition of the body and an uneducated upbringing" (86D-E).[60] Vice, strictly speaking, should not be condemned but treated and, if possible, cured. Timaeus appears to express a kinship with Socrates. He asserts that no one is willingly bad (86D ff.). But the therapy for human badness of soul is not, as it is for Socrates, an inquiry into virtue and a dialectical quest for self-knowledge. It is rather a matter of getting enough exercise, practicing moral virtue (which for Timaeus never prompts the Socratic question, What is it?), studying mathematics and astronomy, and presumably holding the right and prudent opinions about the cosmos.[61] The important thing—indeed, the human good for Timaeus—is simply a matter of harmonizing and striking the right balance between the extremes of our nature, since "all the good is beautiful and the beautiful is not without measure"

---

[59] One wonders whether Simmias and Cebes, both of whom are strongly influenced by the teachings of Pythagoras, would have found consolation in Timaeus' Pythagorean account of death. In any case, Socrates in the *Phaedo* addresses a problem that Timaeus does not: the danger of *misology*, that is, the hatred and distrust of accounts and arguments (89D ff.).

[60] See note 11.

[61] An essential ally in the maintenance of health and bodily integrity is none other than the *receptacle*. Timaeus counsels us to imitate "the nurturer and wet-nurse of the all" by keeping ourselves constantly in motion (88D).

(87C). Here, as elsewhere in his speech, Timaeus exhibits a deceptive likeness to Socrates—a likeness that, on closer inspection, reveals profound differences. The climax of the story of human nature is the gods' invention of sex (90E ff.).[62] Throughout his speech, Timaeus is at odds with *erôs* and its attendant madness. He grounds the world, the paradigm of all that is *kosmion* or decent, in art rather than sex, although along the way we hear metaphors that point to the sort of generating that involves father, mother, offspring and genesis or birth. Sex keeps insinuating itself into the account but is always held back. It comes on the scene in full force only at the end, when the degeneration of man as the means of completing the cosmos, and the role of sexuality in this degeneration, can no longer be postponed. Its dramatic appearance in the likely story is like that of Alcibiades in the *Symposium*, who breaks up the established order of speech-making with his drunkenness and ambition. In fact the outrageously apt description of the male organ as "unpersuadable and autocratic, like an animal that won't listen to reason, and attempts to master all things through its stinging desires" (91B-C) is not a bad likeness of Alcibiades.

Timaeus makes it clear that the reproductive systems of both men and women are grafted onto their natures. They are like independently existing, autonomous creatures who have come to invade our integrity and rob us of *our* autonomy. The male "animal" infects its hosts with the *erôs* for begetting and the tyrannical desire to rule all things; the female "animal" infects its hosts with the irritability and frustration that come from being ready for child-bearing but not yet pregnant. As usual, Timaeus puts great emphasis on the importance of *nous* and *anoia*, intellect and folly. He never tells us the most obvious thing about sex: that without it, the cosmos would not be continually filled with mortal animals, that the whole point of sex is perpetuation. There is no divine "Be fruitful and multiply!" as in the creation story of *Genesis*. Instead, Timaeus weaves sexuality into a myth that makes the cosmic order of animality into the image of a moral order, a best of possible worlds in which fallen, subhuman souls naturally take on the bodies and habitats suited to them. Timaeus says nothing about any possible connection between the sexual impulse and the desire for immortality. He rejects, in other words, one of the erotic teachings of Diotima in the *Symposium* (207A ff.). Just as beauty in the likely story never arouses but always orders, so too erotic desire is never connected with the pursuit of the things that *are* always. The aim of Timaeus' cosmology is to justify the visible world, not to teach us how to transcend it.

---

[62] According to Timaeus, the love of sexual begetting was something *built* (the verb used is from *tektainein*). This appears to be a modification of the origin of *erôs* as Parmenides presents it in the following two fragments: "For she [an unnamed goddess] rules over hateful birth and union of all things, / Sending female to mingle with male, and again conversely / Male with female…" (12), "She devised [*mêtisato*] Love first of all the gods …" (13) (*Parmenides of Elea, Fragments*, tr. David Gallop, [Toronto: University of Toronto Press, 1991], p. 83).

In a bizarre way, what Timaeus says *makes sense*. Human beings do make beasts of themselves in countless ways. What the likely story does is to transform this psychic devolution into an ongoing and perfectly natural feature of the visible, bodily world. He makes the appearance of all the subhuman animals in the world the work of cosmic justice (*dikê*, 92C). On the one hand, this seems to put a curse on the animal kingdom: animals come from the souls of degenerate men. But on the other hand, it raises moral degeneration itself to the level of a cosmic principle: it *dignifies* moral decline. Earlier, Timaeus had stressed the naturalness of disease and even the naturalness of vice and ignorance. Here he shows how vice itself is a kind of demiurge or craftsman. Vice is useful and even plays an important and absolutely necessary role in the completion of the cosmos. The likely story becomes, at the end, a *theodicy*—that is, a justification of the ways of god to man, in which evil not only is allowed to exist but also enhances the beauty of the all and makes it "genuinely all" (41C). Evil is not only necessary: from the cosmic perspective, it seems to be both beautiful and good as well. The very end of the likely story thus indirectly calls into question the whole business of crafting a best of possible worlds—at least as Timaeus understands it.[63]

The last sentence of the dialogue is the closing cadence of Timaeus' song in honor of the god Cosmos, the god playfully generated by the likely story. Timaeus heaps on this god the most glorious superlatives. The god is "greatest and best, most beautiful and most perfect—this one heaven, being alone of its kind" (92C). But the most important word in the sentence is the humble little *houtô*, "thus": "by having acquired animals mortal as well as immortal and having been all filled up, this cosmos has *thus* come to be." The final and finalizing touch is, as we have seen, the devolution of the human soul into its animal forms—a devolution that might be called the demiurgy of evil. From the cosmological perspective, moral degeneration, like bodily disease, doesn't seem bad at all.

One final note before we leave Timaeus' final sentence. The sentence tells us that the cosmos got to be best and greatest by being made full. Perhaps the central problem of a cosmos or ordered whole is this: how to reconcile the demands of hierarchy with the demands of totality or comprehensiveness. This problem is alluded to in the dialogue's famous opening, where Socrates shifts from counting numbers

---

[63]   A similar difficulty comes up in Leibniz' optimism. Leibniz shares Timaeus' aesthetic approach to the cosmos. The world is like "a very beautiful picture" (*On the Ultimate Origination of Things*, ibid., p. 153). We find fault with the world only because we are attending to a part abstracted from the whole. Evil is like darkness in painting or dissonance in music. The distinctly modern optimism that Leibniz adds to Timaeus' beautiful cosmos is the belief in a "constant and unbounded *progress* [my emphasis] in the whole universe" (ibid., p. 154). That is, nature now has a *history*.

[64]   In his recent translation, Donald J. Zeyl mutes the dissonance by rendering the opening, "One, two, three … Where's number four, Timaeus?" (Plato, *Timaeus*, Indianapolis: Hackett Publishing Co., Inc., 2000).

(which express a determinate all) to a ranking number (which expresses where something is in a series or hierarchy): "One, two, three, but where is the fourth?" The shift has the effect of a mathematical dissonance.[64] The praise of Timaeus also contained a reference to hierarchy and totality: Timaeus had attained the *peak* of *all* philosophy. From the hierarchical perspective, the cosmos is an *ouranos* or heaven, something of high and noble rank. From the comprehensive perspective, it is an all. The two perspectives on cosmos reflect the two *archai* or origins of cosmos—intellect and necessity (which, as Space, was "all-receptive").

Has Timaeus succeeded in reconciling the two perspectives? Does he resolve the dissonance of Socrates' opening count? The metaphor of persuasion had kept intellect and necessity *separate* as well as related. But the animal world is generated because intellect as it exists in man pollutes itself and thus declines. Here at the very end of the dialogue the cosmos is finally made whole and therefore perfect through the demiurgy of moral decline, which "fills out" the all. Timaeus sounds enthusiastic and victorious in his completion of a "divine comedy." But his climax, apart from being morally disturbing, is perplexing. What does it mean for the cosmos to be made perfect by all the things in it that represent various degrees of degeneration, to be made better for having been made worse? The end of the *Timaeus* does not really provide a point of closure. It reactivates our questioning and sends us back into the likely story to ask: how is it, again, that a cosmos is both a heaven and an all?

Concluding Remarks: the Perils of Order

For Plato there is no definitive, final myth any more than there is a definitive, final conversation. All the Platonic myths, not just the myth of the *Timaeus*, are about the cosmos. Each is an attempt *from a certain point of view* to depict a divine whole that is responsive to the distinction between good and bad, noble and base. The likely story is not "Plato's cosmology" but a perspective on the cosmos that makes the qualities of decency, prudence and moderation (in addition to ingenuity) essential for the true student of the natural world.

But Timaeus' cosmology does not need to be Plato's cosmology in order to contain some things that Plato thought were true or at least somehow worthy of our trust. It is at least plausible that there is an ordered whole and that, in spite of what modern science tells us, the extraordinary detail and design in the world around us, especially in the realm of organic being, are signs of divine and intelligent *care*; that the physical universe is, as Galileo put it, the book of nature written in mathematical symbols[65]; that the world results from the conflict and cooperation of two great causes, the good and the necessary; that we too should not in our everyday lives

---

[65]   *The Assayer* (1623), *Discoveries and Opinions of Galileo*, tr. Stilman Drake, New York: Doubleday Anchor Books, 1957, pp. 237-238. Plato's dream of a mathematical morphology within *living* nature is amazingly confirmed by D'Arcy Thompson's *On Growth and Form*, New York: the Macmillan Company, 1948.

neglect the necessary things in our aspiration to things divine; that human thinking is the intermittent participation in a divine thinking that goes on continually; that when human beings take up the study of Becoming, they must content themselves with likely or merely probable stories; that in order to be happy, human beings need balance, order and measure; and that a truly comprehensive science of nature should not be indifferent to the human good but should incorporate good sense or prudence in its quest for a genuinely intelligent order to the physical world.

What distinguishes the likely story from other Platonic myths is, first, that it purports to explain in some fashion the visible world to which we sensuously belong—the world of body and Becoming. It purports to be myth that is also scientific explanation. This is one of the main reasons why it is so strange. Second, the likely story is not primarily about the cosmos but about the *making* of a cosmos. This is the great deed that Timaeus imitates. There is a divine craftsman, and everything depends on our grasping that the world is a work of art. Third, although Being is referred to, philosophy as the dialectical quest for Being is absent. The highest science is astronomy, and thinking about the cosmos consists in a strange sort of making or poetry rather than inquiring. Fourth, the highest good for man is not the cultivation of his *erôs* for transcendence and immortality but health, which consists in the enlightened establishment of symmetries and the prudent tempering of psychic and bodily motions.

Here we return to a question raised earlier in this essay: Why is the greatest philosophic work on the cosmos framed by politics? In the *Timaeus*, Plato seems to be reflecting on what happens when the love of wisdom is replaced by what might be called *the will to order*.[66] This will stems from our rootedness in Becoming and consists in the spirited desire to establish a beautiful order within this realm. We love to make images, especially when they reflect our own imagined beauty and nobility. From the perspective of the *Republic* the will to order represents the attempt to glorify the *cave*. Critias and Timaeus both embody the will to order. Critias needs Timaeus as his accomplice. The reason is that before he can carry Socrates' city, as he says, from myth to truth, he must overturn Socrates' understanding of nature as the realm of eternal truth. He must replace the praise of eternal Being and the contemplation that grasps this Being with a praise of Becoming and a physical theory that takes the form of doing and making. Timaeus must renovate Becoming in order to make the world at large receptive to noble designs, including and especially the noble designs of political idealists like Critias and his ambitious grandson. Now, Timaeus himself never derives political communities from cosmic principles, even though his cosmological account is permeated by political metaphors. He presents man as the cosmic rather than the political animal. Nevertheless, his story in its wider context has an important bond with the political designs of Critias. Timaeus' configuration of Becoming "by means

---

66   Borrowing a phrase from Wallace Stevens, we might even call it a "rage to order" (*The Idea of Order at Key West*).

of forms and numbers" (53B) prepares and ennobles Becoming so that it may be receptive to political configuration. The sheer fact that our Critias is the grandfather of the famous tyrant who actually tried to take Athens back to her first and best condition as he saw it, is enough to suggest that Plato wants us to contemplate the extreme danger of this will to order and its potential for political destabilization and chaos. As we saw earlier, the reference to the myth of Phaethon also alludes to this danger. The central insight here seems to be that political idealism always runs the risk of being corrupted by ambition and the love of one's own.

Plato is constantly reminding us of danger—the danger of not knowing our own ignorance about the most important things, the danger of our passions, the danger of intellectualism, even the danger of dialectic itself in its capacity to produce "lawlessness" (*paranomia*) in the souls of its practitioners (*Republic* 7. 537E).[67] In a sense, danger and safety are the most central terms of the Platonic dramas. Down through the ages the great myth of the *Timaeus* has been a port in the storm for many thinkers, a place of doctrinal safety from a world that often seems disorderly and abandoned by the divine. To human despair over the world the myth says, "No, do not despair! The world is the best of possible worlds constructed by a providential god. Believe in the likely story!"[68] The *Timaeus* thus seems to give human nature what Socrates, Simmias, and Cebes were looking for in the *Phaedo*—a raft that would bear us along safely over the waves of uncertainty and fear (85C-D).

But the story as Plato has Timaeus present it is also perilous. The peril consists in the fact that although Timaeus warns us of the deceptive nature of appearances and Becoming, he too practices a deceptive if noble art that connects him with the poetic sophistry of Critias—the ingenious fabrication of intellectual constructs that at times seem to masquerade as true causes. What seems to make this art all the more deceptive is that we, along with Socrates, are being enjoined to suspend inquiry into first principles; we must "receive the likely story about these things" and not "search further for anything beyond it" (29D).

Having sounded the note of blame, I end, as Timaeus does, with praise. The *Timaeus* is one of the greatest feats of the philosophic imagination. In the union of Pythagoras and Empedocles, the likely story presents the paradigm of what it would mean to use mathematical structures to make flux intelligible—at least, as intelligible as possible. The mathematical physics of Timaeus also foreshadows some

---

[67]   The danger of dialectic (its moral neutrality and capacity to generate contradictions) seems to be alluded to in the drama of the *Parmenides*, where the Eleatic's respondent for the logistical treatment of the One is the future tyrant named Aristotle (137B-C). See *Plato's Parmenides*, tr. Albert Keith Whitaker, Newburyport MA: Focus Publishing/R. Pullins Company, 1996.

[68]   The greatest testimony to the consoling power of the likely story is the *Consolation of Philosophy* by Boethius (480-524 AD). Lady Philosophy appears to the imprisoned Boethius and consoles him with the workings of providence, at one point drawing directly on the *Timaeus* (3. 9).

of the features of modern natural science, especially in its presentation of science as theoretical model-building.[69] In its odd mixture of political and cosmological themes, the dialogue also prompts questions about politics and cosmology that we may otherwise never have thought to ask.

The *Timaeus* is indeed strange. But without this strangeness we might fail to realize just how strange our familiar, solid-seeming world of body and motion really is, even when that world is conceived as a mathematically ordered whole. So too, we might fail to realize the strangeness of man, the account-giver, as the most complex and dangerous being in that world.

---

[69] An especially instructive and beautiful example of this model-building is Niels Bohr's essay, *The Theory of Spectra and Atomic Constitution* (1913). Here Bohr develops his famous model for the energy levels of the hydrogen atom by harmonizing the theories of Balmer, Kirchoff, Planck, Lorentz and Rutherford. In language reminiscent of the *Timaeus*, Einstein called this theoretical harmonization "the highest musicality in the sphere of thought" (Autobiographical Notes, *Albert Einstein: Philosopher-Scientist*, ed. P. A. Schillp, [Evanston, Illinois: The Library of Living Philosophers, Inc., 1949], p. 47).

THE *TIMAEUS* IN OUTLINE

Note on the translation

I have tried to stay close to the Greek while conveying the sense that the *Timaeus* is not a treatise but a series of speeches. The technical character of the dialogue makes the latter goal extremely difficult, if not sometimes impossible, to attain. I have also tried to maintain consistency in the translation of the same Greek word wherever possible.

Forms of the verb "to be" are italicized whenever the verb has no predicate and means "has being" (and for emphasis only once, at 38B).

In his long speech, Timaeus sometimes shifts into the present tense (notably at 37D6, just as the god sets out to construct time). These shifts have been preserved in the translation.

The Greek words for "soul" and "city" are feminine. I have followed the old-fashioned practice of respecting their gender. The sexual distinction is central to Timaeus' speech, and the regular occurrence of a "she" in the translation reminds us of that fact. In the case of *psychê* (soul), this practice has the advantage of making certain sentences more readable than they would otherwise have been. Occasionally, another female presence is signaled: Earth, Moon, and necessity.

The dialogue abounds in very long sentences. For the most part, I have kept these sentences intact, breaking them up only when the length seemed to pass far beyond the limits of readability.

The Greek text used was that of Burnet, although frequent reference was made to the texts of Bury, Archer-Hind and Rivaud.

TIMAEUS

Socrates, Timaeus, Hermocrates, Critias

17A **Socrates**: One, two, three ... but now where's our fourth, my dear Timaeus, of yesterday's feasters and hosts of today?

Timaeus: Some illness befell him, Socrates—he wouldn't have been left out of this meeting willingly.

Socrates: Then does the task of filling the missing one's part belong to you and these fellows here?

B **Timaeus**: It certainly does, and we'll do everything in our power, at least, not to fall short in any way. Besides, it wouldn't be at all just for those of us who are left, after being entertained by you yesterday with gifts so befitting to guests, not to host you heartily in return.

Socrates: So then, I take it you remember what I ordered—how many things you were to speak of and about what?

Timaeus: Some of it we remember; and as for what we don't, you're here to remind us—or rather, unless there's some difficulty for you, go through it again briefly from the beginning, just to make it more secure for us.

C **Socrates**: So be it. I suppose the chief part of the speeches recounted by me yesterday was about what sort of regime, as it appeared to me, would come to be best and of what sort of men it would be made.

Timaeus: And to be sure, Socrates, the regime you recounted was very much to the mind of us all.

Socrates: So then, as for the class of those who till the earth, and all the other arts in the regime, didn't we first off distinguish them as separate from the class of those who were to make war on the city's behalf?

Timaeus: Yes.

Socrates: And when, exactly in accordance with nature, we gave to each
D man the one sole occupation that was suited to his very self—one art to each—we said that those who had to make war on behalf of all, and they alone, had to be the guardians of the city, if anyone from the outside
18A or even of those within might set out to do her harm; and that they'd

47

be gentle in dealing out justice to the people ruled by them, since they were by nature friends, but would become harsh in their battles against the enemies they happened to run into.

Timaeus: That's altogether so.

Socrates: For I think we were saying that the soul of the guardians had to be of a certain nature—spirited but at the same time philosophic, in the highest degree—so that they'd be able to become correctly gentle, and harsh, toward the people we mentioned.

Timaeus: Yes.

Socrates: And what about their upbringing? Weren't we saying that they'd been brought up on lessons in both gymnastics and music, in all things, in short, that were appropriate to these men?

Timaeus: Of course.

B   **Socrates**: And I suppose it was said that those brought up this way must never regard either gold or silver or anything else as their own private property. On the contrary, they must regard themselves as auxiliaries who take from those kept safe and sound by them a temperate wage for moderate men; and, in fact, they're to spend it in common and live as companions with each another, continually exercising a care for virtue and staying at leisure from all other occupations.

Timaeus: That too was said, and in just that way.

C   **Socrates**: Furthermore, regarding women, we mentioned that their natures were to be tuned to the men and so made similar to them, and that to all the women all occupations were to be given in common, those pertaining to war as well as to the rest of life's regimen.

Timaeus: That's just the way that too was said.

Socrates: Well, and what about the part that had to do with child-production? Or is that easy to remember because of the unusualness of what was said? We set it down, did we not, that regarding marriages and children

D   all would be in common with all; and we contrived it so that no one might ever recognize his own private progeny, and all will regard all as their very kinsmen—as sisters and brothers if these happened to be within an age that fit their own, but as parents and grandparents if they came before and were upwards in age, and as their own offspring and descendants of their offspring if these were children and lower down in age?

Timaeus: Yes, and that's easy to remember, just as you say.

Socrates: And indeed, in order that they might become, to the best of our power, as good as possible in their natures right from the start, don't we remember how we said that the rulers, male and female, had to contrive some sort of lottery by secret ballots for marital coupling so that the

E separate classes of bad and good men will respectively be mated by lot
with women who were like them; and that no hatred would arise among
them on this score since they'd believe that the cause of the allotment
was chance?

Timaeus: We do remember.

19A **Socrates**: And what's more, do we remember how we said that the offspring
of the good were to be brought up, but the offspring of the bad were to be
handed over in secret to the rest of the city? And as those offspring were
growing up, the rulers always had to keep a sharp lookout for the worthy
ones among them and bring them back again to their former place, and
move the ones among themselves who were unworthy into the place of
those who went back?

Timaeus: That's what we said.

Socrates: Well then, have we by now gone through things exactly as they
were said yesterday so as to go back again over the chief points? Or are we
still yearning for something further in what was said, my dear Timaeus,
something that's being left out?

B **Timaeus**: Not at all. On the contrary, these were the very things that were
said, Socrates.[1]

Socrates: Now then, hear, if you would, what comes next regarding the
regime we went through—how I happen to be affected by it. My affection seems to be something like this: it's as if someone who gazed upon
beautiful animals somewhere, either produced by the art of painting or
C truly living but keeping their peace, were to get a desire to gaze upon them
moving and contending in some struggle that seemed appropriate to their
bodies. I too am affected in the same way toward the city we went through.
For with pleasure would I hear someone giving a full account of her strug-
gling against other cities in those contests in which cities contend—how
she made a fitting entrance into war and rendered appropriate payment
to her education and upbringing in her dealings with each of the cities,
by the way she acted in her deeds and negotiated in her speeches. Now,
D on this point, Critias and Hermocrates, I myself have accused myself of
never becoming capable of praising our men and our city adequately. Of
course there's nothing wondrous in this inability of mine, but I've gotten
hold of the same opinion about the poets, those born long ago as well as

---

[1] Socrates has in fact given a highly incomplete summary of the best city in the
Republic. He leaves out the concern for the proper ordering of the individual
soul; the need for philosopher kings; the mathematical education that paves
the way for dialectic; and the eventual degeneration of the just city. He also
leaves out the whole problem of defining justice and determining whether
the possession of justice makes us happy.

the ones that are around now; not that I dishonor the poetic class, but it's plain to everyone that the imitative tribe will imitate easiest and best what it's been brought up on, and it's difficult for them individually to

E   be good at imitating what arises outside their upbringing—difficult in deeds and still more difficult in speeches. And as for the sophistic class in its turn, I believe them to be highly experienced in many and beautiful speeches on other matters; but I fear that somehow or other, since the members of this class wander from city to city and haven't settled down anywhere in their own private dwellings, the class would stray from the mark in describing how men at once philosophers and statesmen might act and speak when, in war and battles, they acted in deed and engaged each adversary in speech. What's been left is the class in *your* condition,

20A the class that by nature and upbringing partakes of both at once. For Timaeus here—being from Italian Locri, a city with excellent laws,[2] and yielding to no one in those parts in substance and class—has managed the greatest offices and positions of honor in his city and, moreover, has in my opinion reached the very peak of all philosophy; and as for Critias, I suppose all of us in these parts know that he's a layman in none of the things we're talking about. And again, regarding Hermocrates' nature and upbringing, one must trust the many people who testify to their

B   adequacy in all these matters. That's why even yesterday, bearing all this in mind, I gratified you heartily when you obliged me to go through matters of regime, since I knew that none would more adequately than you render the account next in order (that is, if you were willing); for by establishing all things appropriate to the city, you would render her engaged in a fitting war—you alone of those now living—and so, having spoken what was ordered, I ordered you in return to take up what I'm describing even now. Then, after you had looked over it in common among yourselves, you agreed to pay me back today with my guest-gift

C   of speeches; so here I am—arrayed for the occasion and readiest of all men to do my receiving.[3]

---

[2] See *Laws* 638B. According to the *Oxford Classical Dictionary*, Epizepherian or western Locri, a city in the toe of Italy, "possessed Europe's earliest written legal code (attributed to Zaleucus)" (Oxford: Clarendon Press, 2nd Edition, p. 616). The legislation of Zaleucus was known for its severity. Pindar refers to Locri as "the city where dwells Unswerving Strictness [*Atrekeia*]" (*Olympian* 10. 13).

[3] Socrates uses a form of the verb *kosmein* (related to the noun *kosmos*) to convey the fact that he is dressed up. It is the first appearance of a cosmos-word in the dialogue. See Glossary under **cosmos**. The only other dialogue in which Socrates is uncharacteristically dressed up is the *Symposium*—he is wearing shoes (174A).

Hermocrates: To be sure, just as Timaeus here was saying, Socrates, we won't be lacking in heart, nor is there any pretext whatsoever on our part for not doing what you say; so that, even yesterday, from the very moment we left you and arrived back at the guest-room in Critias' house where we're staying—and earlier still as we were on the way—we in our

D   turn were looking into these things. Then this fellow here related to us an account that comes from old hearsay; so now, Critias, tell *him* what you told us, so that he may join us in examining whether it's serviceable or unserviceable for the order we've been given.

Critias: That's what must be done—that is, if it also seems good to our third partner, Timaeus.

Timaeus: Why, of course, it seems good.

Critias: Hear, then, Socrates, an account most strange—and yet altogether true, as Solon, the wisest of the Seven, once claimed. Now Solon was a

E   relative and really close friend of our great-grandfather Dropides—just as he himself often says in his poetry; and Dropides told our grandfather Critias, as the old man in turn related to us from memory, that great and wondrous were the old deeds of this city here, deeds that have disappeared as a result of time and the destruction of mankind; but one was the greatest of them all—a deed that would be fitting for us to remember

21A   now, so as to render our debt of thanks to you and at the same time to praise the goddess on her feast-day by singing, as it were, in a manner both just and true.[4]

Socrates: Well spoken. But now what sort of deed was this that Critias related, a deed not spoken of but genuinely enacted by this city in ancient times, according to the hearsay from Solon?

Critias: I shall proclaim it—having heard an old account from a man not

B   young. For indeed, at the time, Critias, so he claimed, was already fairly close to ninety, while I was somewhere around ten; and it happened to

---

[4] The feast to which Critias refers is probably the Greater Panathenaea, the celebration of Athena's birthday, which took place every four years. The main event was the adorning of the goddess's statue in the Acropolis with a colorful and elaborately woven *peplos* or robe. The robe depicted the Battle of the Gods and Giants and was conveyed to the Acropolis draped on the mast of a ship mounted on wheels. For more on the Panathenaea and Athenian festivals generally, see H. W. Parke, *Festivals of the Athenians*, Ithaca, NY: Cornell University Press, 1977.

be our day of Cureotis during the Apaturia.[5] Now the children's part of the festival that was usually held on that occasion also took place at that time, and our fathers set up contests in the recitation of epic poetry. And so, while many poems by many poets were recited, since those of Solon were new at that time, many of us children chanted them. Then one of the members of our clan said—either because it really seemed so to him at the time or because he was also paying Critias a compliment—that

C   Solon, so it seemed to him, had come to be both the wisest of the Seven in other matters and what's more, in his poetry, the noblest of all poets.[6] At that the old man was very pleased (how well I remember it!) and with a big smile said: "If only, Amynander, he hadn't misused his poetry by treating it as a side-job but pursued it seriously like the others, and if he had finished off the account he brought here from Egypt and wasn't compelled to neglect it because of the factions and all the other evils he discovered when he came back here, then, in my opinion at least, neither Hesiod nor Homer nor any other poet would ever have become more

D   highly reputed than he." "But what account was that, Critias?" said he. "Why," he declared, "it was about the greatest and most justly famous action this city ever enacted, although, through time and the destruction of those who performed it, its account didn't survive down to our day." "Say from the beginning," said he, "what Solon went on to say and how and from whom he heard these things held as true!"

E   "There is, in the Delta of Egypt," said he, "where, at its head, the stream of the Nile splits in two, a certain district called Saïtic,[7] and the greatest city in this district is Sais (where in fact King Amasis also was from),[8] whose originator is a certain goddess—the name in Egyptian is Neith, but in Greek (so their account goes) it is Athena; and these people claim to be great Athens-lovers and in some fashion relatives of the people here.

"Now Solon said that when he had passed through there, he came

22A   to be very much held in honor among them, and that once, furthermore, while putting questions about old things to the priests who were most

---

5   The Apaturia was held in October and came to be associated with the god Dionysus. The Cureotis took place on the third day of the festival, at which time the youths or *kouroi* were initiated into their clan. The word Apaturia derives from *phratria* or brotherhood but also suggests the Greek word for deception, *apatê*. See Parke, ibid. pp. 88-92.

6   "Noblest" here is *eleuteriôtaton*, literally, most free.

7   The word for district is *nomos*, which also means law, custom or song. See Glossary under **law**.

8   Herodotus tells us that "Amasis was a great lover of the Greeks" (*Inquiries* 2.172 ff.).

experienced in them, he discovered that neither he himself nor any other Greek hardly knew anything at all, so to speak, about such things. And once, when he wished to lead them on to give speeches about antiquities, he attempted to speak of the most ancient things of all in the accounts given here—about Phoroneus, said to be the first man, and about Niobe—

B and he proceeded to tell stories about Deucalion and Pyrrha after the flood, and about how they survived it, and to give the genealogy of their descendants; and by recalling how many years it took for the events he was speaking about, he tried to number the periods of time.

"And one of the very oldest of the priests said: 'Solon, Solon! You Greeks are always children, and there's no such thing as an old Greek!' Now when he heard this, Solon said: 'What do you mean by that?' 'You're young,' he declared, 'young in soul, all of you; for in those souls

C you don't have a single old opinion derived from ancient hearsay or any study hoary with time. And the cause of this is the following. Many destructions of mankind in many ways have come to be and will be—the greatest by fire and water, but different and lesser ones by thousands of other means. For what is also told in your parts—that once Phaethon, son of Helios, yoked his father's chariot and, through his not being able to drive it along his father's path, burned up what was on the earth and

D himself perished when he was struck by a thunderbolt—this is told in such a way that it has the figure of a story, but the truth of it is a shifting of the bodies that move around the earth and along the heavens, and the destruction that comes about on the earth by a great deal of fire at long stretches of time. At those times, then, all who dwell on mountains and in high and dry regions suffer a greater destruction than do those who dwell near the rivers and the sea; but for us, the Nile, our savior in other ways as well, at that time too saves us from this impasse by rising up. And when in turn gods purify the earth by flooding it with waters,

E then those who live in the mountains—herdsmen and shepherds—are saved, while those who live in the cities near you are swept into the sea by the rivers. But along this place here, neither then nor at any other time does water stream down on the fields from above: on the contrary, it all tends by nature to come up from below. Hence, and on account of these causes, the things preserved here are said to be the oldest. The truth is that in all the regions where neither excessive cold nor heat is at work, there is always some class of human beings, sometimes more, sometimes less in number. And if anything beautiful or great or that also

23A has something distinctive about it has come to pass somewhere, either near you or here or even in another region that we know by hearsay—all such things have been written down from olden times and preserved here in our temples. But it happens that at any given time your lands

B and those of other people have only just been equipped with writing and all the things that cities need; and after the usual span of years, the heavenly stream comes back again like a plague to sweep your people away, and leaves only the illiterate and uneducated among you, so that all over again from the beginning, you become young, as it were, knowing nothing either of things here or of whatever was in your own land in olden times.

" 'At any rate, Solon, the genealogies you went through just now about the events in your land aren't much different from children's stories. First of all, you all remember only one flooding of the earth, whereas many have come to pass before this; and furthermore, you don't

C know that the most beautiful and best race among men was born in the place where you live, from whose little bit of seed that was left over, there exists both you and the entire city that is now yours; but you've forgotten all this because for many generations the survivors met their end without giving voice to themselves in writing. For indeed, Solon, once, before the time of the greatest destruction by water, what is now the city of the Athenians was the best in war and was outstanding in all respects for her excellent laws. In her the most beautiful works are said to have been born as well as the most beautiful regimes of any of those under heaven that we've inherited through hearsay.'

D "Having heard this, Solon said he was struck with wonder and put all his heart into begging the priests to recount for him, with precision and in order, everything about his fellow-citizens of old. And the priest said: 'No grudge do I bear you, Solon; but on the contrary, for your sake I shall speak and for the sake of your city, and most of all for the sake of the goddess, who took as her lot both your city and this one here and brought them up and educated them—the city in your land first

E by the span of a thousand years, when she took over your seed from Gê and Hephaestus, and the one here at a later point. And the number of years for the arrangement here in our land, as it was written down in the sacred texts, is eight thousand. Now concerning the citizens born nine thousand years ago, I shall make plain to you in brief their laws as well as the most beautiful of deeds enacted by them; but the precise

24A sequence of all this we'll go through at another time at our leisure, once we've gotten hold of the writings themselves.

" 'As for their laws, take a look at the ones here; for you will discover, right here and now, many examples of the things that were once there in your land: first, the class of priests, which is bounded off as separate from the others; and after this, the class of craftsmen, of which each sort does its crafting all by itself without mixing with another; and then the class

B of shepherds, of hunters, and of those who till the earth. And, in particular, regarding the warrior class, you've no doubt perceived that it has been separated off from all the other classes, and its members have been ordered by the law to care for nothing except what has to do with war. Moreover, there's the state of their armament—shields and swords—with which we were the first in Asia to be armed, the goddess having displayed this to us, just as she had first displayed it in those regions around you.

C Again, when it comes to prudence, you no doubt see how much careful attention the law here has paid to the cosmos right from the beginning by having discovered all that accrues to human things from those that are divine, down to divination and medicine, which aims at health, and by having acquired all the other studies that follow them. Now at that time, the goddess, having arrayed you before all others with all this arrangement and order, settled you by singling out the region in which you were born, since she observed in it a good blending of seasons, one that would bear the most prudent men. So inasmuch as she's both a lover of war and a lover of wisdom,[9] the goddess singled out this region as the one likely to bear men who most resembled her, and settled it first. And

D you dwelled in the observance of such laws as these—indeed, laws that were still better—and you surpassed all mankind in every virtue, as was suitable for those who were the offspring and pupils of gods.

 " 'Many and great are the deeds of your city that are written down

E here and that strike people with wonder, yet there is one that rises above them all in magnitude and virtue; for our writings tell of how great a power your city once stopped, which, in its insolence, was advancing against all of Europe together with Asia, having set out from somewhere far out in the Atlantic Ocean. For at that time the ocean there could be crossed, since an island was situated in front of the mouth that you people call, so you claim, the Pillars of Hercules.[10] The island was bigger than Lybia and Asia together, and from it there was access to the other islands for those traveling at that time, and from the islands to the entire

25A opposing continent that surrounds that true sea. For these parts around here, which lie within the mouth we're talking about, are clearly a harbor that has a narrow entrance for sailing into, while that other is genuinely an ocean, and the land surrounding it would in perfect truth be most correctly called a continent. And on this very island of Atlantis there was gathered a great and wondrous power of kings, which mastered the entire island, many other islands, and even parts of the continent; and in addition to these, they further ruled over the lands here within

B Lybia as far as Egypt, and over Europe as far as Tuscany.

---

[9] The word for lover of wisdom here is *philosophos*, philosopher.
[10] The strait of Gibraltar.

" 'Now once all this power had been gathered together into one, it undertook in a single onslaught to enslave the region around you and the one around us, and the entire region within the mouth. It was then, Solon, that the power of your city became illustrious to all mankind for her virtue and might, for she stood before all others in bravery and in all the arts relating to war, at times leading the Greeks, at times standing alone, of necessity, when the others defected; and having taken the most extreme risks and having mastered the invaders, she set up trophies;[11] and she prevented from being enslaved those who were not yet enslaved, while as for the rest of us who dwell within the boundaries of Hercules, she liberated us all ungrudgingly. But at a later time, when monstrous earthquakes and floods came about, and one grievous day and night assaulted them, then the entire assembly of warriors among you sank beneath the earth, and the island of Atlantis likewise sank beneath the sea and disappeared—which is why, even now, the ocean in that spot has become impassable and unexplorable, since it's blocked by the shoal mud the island produced upon settling.' "

You have heard, Socrates—in abridged version, so to speak—the very things uttered by old Critias in accordance with the hearsay from Solon; so when you spoke yesterday about the regime and the men you were describing, I was struck with wonder as I recollected the things I'm telling you now, since I realized that by some divine[12] quirk of chance, your speech wasn't far off the mark from agreeing for the most part with what Solon said. Of course I didn't want to speak up on the spur of the moment: so much time had passed that I didn't remember it adequately. So I thought it would be expedient for me to speak up like this only after I had first recovered it all adequately for myself. That's why I quickly agreed to what you ordered yesterday, since I considered that we'd be moderately well-provided for that which in all such matters is the greatest task: setting down as a foundation some account suited to our plans. Thus it was, just as this fellow here was saying, that the very moment I took off from here yesterday, I brought back the account for these men by recollecting it; and when I left them and went over it during the night, I recovered pretty much everything. Ah, yes, as the saying goes: "How wondrously memorable are the lessons of childhood!" For my part, I don't know if I'd be able to recapture in memory all the things

---

[11] A trophy (*tropaion*) consisted of pieces of armor that were taken from the enemy and hung on trees or displayed on upright posts. See Hermocrates' reference to a trophy at *Critias* 108C.

[12] "Divine" here is *daimoniôs*, demonically. See 40D and note. It is highly interesting that Critias juxtaposes, and apparently identifies, the work of the divine and chance.

I heard yesterday; but as for what I thoroughly heard a long, long time ago, I'd be utterly struck with wonder if any bit of it has escaped me.

C It certainly was all heard then with a great deal of pleasure and boyish delight, and the old man taught it to me heartily, since I kept asking him question after question, so that the account has become fixed in me like the burned-in markings of an indelible painting.[13] What's more, right from the break of dawn I kept telling it to these fellows here so that they, along with me, would be well-provided with speeches.

Now, then, to get to the very purpose for which all this has been said, I'm ready to speak, Socrates, not only on the chief points but also in all the particulars, just as I heard them; and as for the citizens and the city you went through for us yesterday as though in a story, we, having

D now carried them here into the truth, shall set down that city as being this very one I was talking about; and we shall declare that the citizens you had in mind are those true ancestors of ours about whom the priest was speaking. In all ways will they fit one another, and we will not sing out of tune in saying that they are the very ones who existed at that time. All of us in common, each taking his part, will attempt, to the best of our power, to render what's fitting for what you've ordered us to do. So

E then, Socrates, one must consider whether this account is to our mind, or whether one is to search further for another instead of it.

Socrates: And what account, Critias, might we get hold of instead of this one, which is especially fitting to the current sacrifices to the goddess because of its very close connection with her, and is no doubt of the utmost importance in being no fabricated story but a truthful account? How indeed, and from where, shall we discover other accounts if we dismiss these? No, it's not to be, but with Good Fortune to attend you,

27A you must speak; and I, in exchange for my speeches of yesterday, must keep my peace and listen in turn.

Critias: Then consider, Socrates, how we've managed the layout of your guest-gifts. It seemed good to us that Timaeus here—since he's the most astronomical of us and the one who's made it his main job to know about the nature of the all—should speak first, beginning from the birth of the cosmos and ending in the nature of mankind. I am to come after him, as though I had received from him the men born by his speech, and from you certain of them who had been educated in the highest degree.

---

[13] The encaustic or "burned in" markings refer to a popular Greek method of painting that probably originated in Egypt: "it seems that coloured waxes were applied with a kind of palette-knife and fixed by heating with a metal rod. It may have been originally used for securing the colour on marbles meant to stand out of doors" (Martin Robertson, *A Shorter History of Greek Art*, [Cambridge: Cambridge University Press, 1981], p. 173).

B   Then, in accordance with that very word and law of Solon, I am to bring them before us, as before a court of judges, and make them citizens of this city of ours, on the grounds that they are indeed the Athenians of that former time, who, being hidden, were revealed by the oracular voice of the sacred texts, and, in what remains, to make speeches as though about men who are already citizens and Athenians.

Socrates: Perfect and brilliant too, it seems, is the feast of speeches I'm to get in return! So, Timaeus, it seems it would be your task to speak next—that is, after you've called upon gods in accordance with custom.

C   **Timaeus**: Why, Socrates, on that point at least, all men who partake of even a bit of sound-mindedness always call on a god, I suppose, at the onset of any affair be it small or great. And for us who somehow intend to make speeches about the all—telling in what way it was born, or even whether it was without birth—it's a necessity, unless we're utterly deranged, after we've called upon both gods and goddesses, to pray that all we say be to their mind above all and, following that, to our own. And

D   let that be our invocation as it relates to gods; but we must also invoke what has to do with ourselves, so that all of you might most easily learn and I, for my part, most clearly display what I have in mind about the topics that lie before us.

Now then, in my opinion, one must first distinguish the following. What is it that always *is* and has no becoming; and what is it that comes

28A   to be and never *is*?[14] Now the one is grasped by intellection accompanied by a rational account, since it's always in the same condition; but the other in its turn is opined by opinion accompanied by irrational sensation, since it comes to be and perishes and never genuinely *is*. Again, everything that comes to be, of necessity comes to be by some cause; for apart from a cause, it's impossible for anything to have a coming to be.

Now so long as the craftsman[15] keeps looking to what's in a self-same condition, using some such thing as a model, and fashions its look and power, then of necessity everything brought to a finish in this

B   way is beautiful; but if he should look to what has come to be, using a begotten model, the thing isn't beautiful. Now as for all the heaven (or cosmos, or whatever else it might be most receptive to being called, let it

---

[14]   Omitting the second *aei*, "always," that appears in Burnet's text. See John Whittaker, "*Timaeus* 27D 5ff.," *Phoenix* 23, 1969, pp. 181-185.

[15]   This is the first appearance in the dialogue of the famous demiurge or craftsman. He is introduced without fanfare and almost in passing.

be called that by us),[16] the first thing about it one must investigate is the very thing set down at the beginning whenever one has to investigate anything: whether it always was, having no beginning of a coming to be, or whether it has come to be, having begun from some beginning. It
C   has come to be; for it is visible and touchable and has body, and all such things are sensed; and things that are sensed, since they're grasped by opinion accompanied by sensation, came to light as coming to be and begotten. And again, for what comes to be, we claim that it's necessary that it come to be by some cause. Now to discover the poet and father of this all is quite a task, and even if one discovered him, to speak of him to all men is impossible. So one must go back again and investigate the
29A   following about the all: to which of the two models the builder looked when he fashioned it—to the one that's in a self-same condition and consistent, or to the one that has come to be. Now if this cosmos here is beautiful and its craftsman good, then it's plain that he was looking to the one that's everlasting, but if otherwise—which isn't even right for anyone to say—then to the one that has come to be. Now it's clear to everyone that it was to the everlasting; for the cosmos is the most beautiful of things born and its craftsman the best of causes. Since that's how it has come to be, then it has been crafted with reference to that which is grasped by reason and prudence and is in a self-same condition.

     Again, starting from these things, there's every necessity that this
B   cosmos here be the likeness of something. Now what is most important is to begin everything at a beginning that's in accordance with nature. So then, when it comes to a likeness and its model, one must determine how the accounts are also akin to those very things of which the accounts are interpreters. Now accounts of what's abiding and unshakable and manifest with the aid of intellect are themselves abiding and unchanging; and to the extent that it's possible and fitting for accounts
C   to be irrefutable and invincible, they must not fall short of this. But as for accounts of something made as a likeness of something else—since it is a likeness—it is fitting that they, in proportion to their objects, be likenesses: just as Being is to Becoming, so is truth to trust. So then, Socrates, if, in saying many things on many topics concerning gods and the birth of the all, we become incapable of rendering speeches that are
D   always and in all respects in agreement with themselves and drawn with precision, don't wonder. But if we provide likelihoods inferior to none,

---

[16] The problem of choosing the right name for the all also comes up in the *Epinomis* (977B1-5). Both Timaeus and the Athenian stranger seem to be echoing Aeschylus' *Agamemnon* 160-162: "Zeus—whoever he may be—if being invoked by this name is dear to him, let him be so invoked!"

one should be well-pleased with them, remembering that I who speak as well as you my judges have a human nature, so that it is fitting for us to receive the likely story about these things and not to search further for anything beyond it.

Socrates: Excellent, Timaeus! And it must be received entirely as you urge; so now that we've received your prelude so wonderfully, do for us what comes next in order and perform the song itself.[17]

Timaeus: Now let us say through what cause the constructor constructed becoming and this all. Good was he, and in one who is good there never arises about anything whatsoever any grudge; and so, being free of this, he willed that all things should come to resemble himself as much as possible.[18] That this above all is the lordliest principle of becoming and cosmos one must receive, and correctly so, from prudent men. For since he wanted all things to be good and, to the best of his power, nothing to be shoddy, the god thus took over all that was visible, and, since it did not keep its peace but moved unmusically[19] and without order, he brought it into order from disorder, since he regarded the former to be in all ways better than the latter. And it was not right—nor is it right—for him who is best to do anything except that which is most beautiful; so, once he did some calculating, he discovered that of all things visible by nature, nothing unintelligent will ever be a more beautiful work, comparing wholes with wholes, than what has intellect; and again, that it's impossible for intellect apart from soul to become present in anything. Through this calculation, then, by constructing intellect within soul and soul within body, he joined together the all so that he had fashioned a

E

30A

B

---

17   Socrates' word for the upcoming speech of Timaeus is neither *logos* (account) nor *mythos* (story) but *nomos*. In this context, the word can mean either law or song, just as *prooimion* can mean either preamble or prelude. "Perform the song" thus also means "Carry out the law." No doubt both meanings are intended. In the *Republic*, Socrates refers to "the song (*nomos*) that dialectic performs" (7. 532A).

18   The word for grudge here is *phthonos*, which refers to ill will and especially jealousy. The Egyptian priest in Critias' story had used the same expression, "no grudge" (23D); and ancient Athens was said to have liberated the lands besieged by the Atlantians *aphthonôs*, ungrudgingly (25C). In Herodotus the gods are, above all, grudging or jealous. In Book One of the *Inquiries*, Solon tells the tyrant Croesus that "the divine is altogether jealous and troublesome" (32). The sentiment, "The divine is jealous," appears in a letter written by King Amasis (3. 40), to whom Critias had referred at 21E. Aristotle rejects the jealousy of the divine early in the *Metaphysics* (1. 2 983A).

19   *plêmmelôs*, literally, in a way that was out of tune. Timaeus returns to a variant of this word at the end of his speech (92B). See Glossary under **musically**.

work that would be most beautiful and best in accordance with nature. So then, in this way, in keeping with the likely account, it must be said that this cosmos here in truth was born an animal having soul and

C intellect through the forethought of the god.

Again, with this beginning, we must say what comes next in order to these things: in similarity to which of the animals the constructor constructed it. Now we shall not count as worthy any of those that by nature have the form of part—for nothing that's like the incomplete would ever become beautiful—but let us set down the following about the cosmos. Among all animals, it's the one most similar to that of which the others, individually and according to kind, are parts. For that one, having embraced all the intelligible Animals, holds them within itself,

D just as this cosmos holds and embraces us and all the other nurslings constructed as visible.[20] For since the god wanted to make it as similar

31A as possible to the most beautiful of things intellected and in all ways complete, he constructed it as an animal visible and one, holding within itself all those animals that are akin to it according to nature.

So have we spoken correctly in naming the heaven "one," or was it more correct to say that it's many and indefinite in number? One, if indeed it's been crafted in accordance with its model. For that which embraces all the intelligible Animals (however many they are) wouldn't ever be second in company with another one; for again there would have to be another animal surrounding them both, of which both of them would be a part, and then this cosmos would be more correctly spoken of as copied no longer from those two but from that other one which embraced them. So

B then, in order that this cosmos might be similar to the altogether perfect Animal in uniqueness, for this reason the maker did not make two or indefinitely many cosmoses; but rather this heaven here that's come to be, both is and will continue to be one—alone of its kind.

Now what has come to be must be bodily in form and both visible and touchable, but separated from fire nothing would ever become visible, nor would it become touchable without something solid, or solid without earth; hence, in beginning to construct the body of the all, the god proceeded to make it out of fire and earth. But it's not possible for

C two things alone to be beautifully combined apart from some third: some bond must get in the middle and bring them both together. And the most beautiful of these bonds is that which, as much as possible, makes itself and the things bound together one, and proportion is

---

[20] Timaeus does not expressly name *the* intelligible Animal that embraces the other intelligible Animals until 39E1. Is it a living thing or simply the form Animal, which embraces the four kinds of animality?

suited by nature to accomplish this most beautifully.[21] For whenever, of three numbers, the middle term of any two of them, whether cubic or square, is such that as the first is to it so is it to the last—and again, conversely, as the last is to the middle so is this middle to the first—then the middle term becomes first and last, while the last and first in turn both become middle terms, so that of necessity it will turn out that all the terms will be the same; and once they've come to be the same in relation to each other, all will be one.[22] Now if the body of the all had to become a plane having no depth at all, then one mean would have been enough to bind together its fellow terms and itself; but as the case now stands, since it was appropriate that it be solid in form, and since solids are joined together never through one mean but always through two, in this way, then, the god set water and air midway between both fire and earth.[23]

And having fashioned among them the condition of same ratio as far as possible, so that fire was to air as air to water, and air was to water as water to earth, he bound together and constructed a heaven visible and touchable. For these reasons and out of such terms as these, four in number, the body of this cosmos was begotten to agree with itself through proportion, and from them came to have friendship, so that having come together with itself in self-sameness, it was born indissoluble by none other save him who bound it together.

At this point the construction of the cosmos has taken up the whole of each one of the four terms. For the constructor constructed it from all of fire and water and air and earth, having left over no part or power of any of them outside, since he intended the following: first that it be as much as possible an animal whole and perfect, made up of perfect parts; and in addition to this, that it be *one*, inasmuch as there wasn't anything left over, out of which another such animal might come to be; and further that it be free of old age and disease, since he observed that

---

[21] As Timaeus' description makes clear, *analogia* here refers to a *mean* proportion.

[22] The numbers **2**, **4** and **8**, for example, can be used to form the mean proportion **2:4::4:8** (where **4** is a square number and **8** a cubic number). When the two ratios that compose the proportion are inverted, the resulting proportion becomes **4:2::8:4** or **4:8::2:4**. What was formerly the mean term is now at the extremes, and the terms that were formerly extremes are now in the middle. Euclid defines square and cubic numbers in *Elements* 7, Def. 18 and 19.

[23] Empedocles had posited four elements or, as he called them, *roots* of all things (fragment 6). For Timaeus, the elements start out as being rationally interrelated. Water and air are the two mediators between the more fundamental elements of fire and earth.

when hot and cold (and all things that have mighty powers) surround a composite body from the outside and attack it, they dissolve it in an untimely way and make it wither by bringing on disease and old age. Through this very cause and calculation he built it to be this one whole of all wholes taken together, perfect and free of old age and disease.[24] And he gave it a figure that was fitting and akin to it. But for that animal

B that is to embrace within itself all animals, the fitting figure would be the one that has embraced all figures within itself, however many there are; so for this reason too, he worked it in circular fashion, sculpting it into the form of a sphere, the figure that keeps itself in all directions equidistant from its center to its extremities and which, of all figures, is the most perfect and most similar to itself, since he considered that

C *similar* is vastly more beautiful than *dissimilar*. So he made it all smooth on the outside and gave it a rounded finish, and this for many reasons. For of eyes it had no need at all, since nothing to be seen was left over on the outside; nor of hearing, since there was nothing to be heard; nor was there any atmosphere surrounding it that needed breathing; nor again was there need of any organ by which it might take food into itself or send it back out after it was digested. For nothing either went out from

D it nor went toward it from anywhere—since there *was* nothing—for the animal was artfully born so as to provide its own waste as food for itself and to suffer and do everything within itself and by itself, since he who put it together considered that the animal would be much better by being self-sufficient than in need of other things. And as for hands, which would be useless for either taking hold of or again warding off anything, he thought he didn't need to attach these to the animal in

34A vain, nor feet nor anything that on the whole served for standing on. The motion he did assign to it was the one congenial to its body, that motion among the seven kinds which especially attends intellect and prudence; so for this reason, he spun it around uniformly in the same spot and within itself and made it move by revolving in a circle, and he took away from it all the other six motions and fashioned it free from their various wanderings;[25] and since for this revolving motion the animal had no need of feet, he begat it legless and footless.[26]

---

[24] Timaeus just falls short of declaring that the cosmic body is deathless.

[25] The six motions that are taken away are described at 43B. They correspond to the six directions in which a body can move in space. The seventh, privileged motion is rotation. For a very different (and more complex) delineation of motions, see *Laws* 10. 893Bff.

[26] The extended description of what the cosmic sphere lacks is indebted to two fragments by Empedocles (29 and 134). Timaeus suppresses what Empedocles makes explicit in both fragments: that the divine sphere lacks organs of reproduction.

B   All this calculation of a god who always *is* concerning the god who was one day to be—once it had been calculated—made the animal smooth and even and equidistant from its center in every direction, a whole and perfect body made of perfect bodies. And after he put soul at its center, he stretched her throughout the whole, even to the point of covering the body on the outside with her as with a veil;[27] and so, as a circle turning in a circle, he established a heaven that was one, alone, solitary—able by itself, because of its excellence, to be company to itself and to stand in need of no other at all, and sufficient unto itself as acquaintance and friend. For all these very reasons, he begat it a happy god.

C   As for the soul, although at present we are attempting to speak of her as though she came later, the god did not in fact contrive her as younger—for in uniting them, he would never have let an elder be ruled by a younger—but we who somehow partake largely of the accidental and random do so also when we speak.[28] He, however, constructed soul as prior to the body in both birth and excellence and as its elder, since she was to be mistress and ruler of body, and it was to be ruled.[29] And he did so out of the following materials and in the following mode.

35A   Midway between the Being that is non-partitioned and always self-same, and in turn the Being that is partitioned and comes to be in the realm of bodies, he blended out of both a third form of Being; and doing the same thing with the nature of Same and the nature of Other, he constructed in the middle a blend of their non-partitioned form and the partitioned form that applies to bodies; and since they were three, he took hold of them and blended them into one entire look; and since the

B   nature of the Other was loath to mix, he joined it to the Same with force. And once he had mixed them with Being and made one out of three, he again distributed this whole into so many portions as was fitting, each portion mixed from both Same and Other and from Being.[30]

Here's how he began to make the division. First he took away one portion from all of what he had, and after this portion he proceeded to take away its double, and then in turn a third portion half as much again as the second and three times the first, and a fourth double the second,

---

27   Earlier, intellect was in soul, and soul was in body (30B). Now body is somehow in soul.

28   The word translated as "random" is *eikêi*. It is very close in appearance to the word *eikôs*, likely. See Glossary under **random**.

29   The temporal priority of soul to body is also affirmed in the *Laws* (10. 892A-B).

30   According to Cornford, soul here is a blend of the *intermediate* forms of Being, Same and Other—a blend of blends (pp. 59-61).

C

36A

B

C

and a fifth three times the third, and a sixth portion eight times the first, and a seventh twenty-seven times the first.[31] After this he proceeded to fill up the double and triple intervals by cutting off still more portions from the original mixture; and he put them in the intermediate positions between the portions he already had, so as to have two means within each interval—a mean that exceeds one extreme and is exceeded by the other by the same *fractional part*, and another mean that exceeds one extreme by a *number* equal to the amount by which it is exceeded by the other extreme.[32] And since there arose from these bonds new intervals within those he already had (intervals of **3:2**, **4:3** and **9:8**), he went about filling up all the **4:3** intervals with intervals of **9:8**, leaving in each of them a fractional part. And this leftover interval that corresponded to the part had its terms in the numerical ratio of **256** to **243**. And so, that in fact is how the mixture from which he'd been making these cuts at last had all been spent.[33]

Then, once he had split this whole structure in two down its length and attached each strip to the other at their midpoints to make what resembled an X, he bent each of them into a circle, having clasped them together each to itself and to the other at a point directly opposite to where they were first attached. And he took them around in the motion that goes round in the self-same way and in the same spot, and he proceeded to make for himself one of the circles outer and the other inner. Then he designated the outer course to be of the nature of the Same, while the inner course to be of the nature of the Other. Now he led the course of the Same around sideways and to the right, and the course of the Other along the diagonal and to the left,[34] but mastery he gave to

---

[31]   The various portions here result from interspersing the terms of the proportions: **1:2::4:8** and **1:3::9:27**. When expanded, each becomes a geometric proportion with two means: **1:2::2:4::4:8** and **1:3::3:9::9:27**.

[32]   The first mean is the so-called harmonic mean; the second is the arithmetic mean. (See Appendix A.) They are further described in the *Epinomis* (991A-B) in the context of the Athenian stranger's praise of astronomy.

[33]   In the preceding mathematical passage, Timaeus refrains from telling us the meaning of what the god is doing. The educated reader is expected to grasp, without being explicitly told, that the god is constructing the musical scale in Pythagorean tuning for four octaves and a major sixth. (The ratio **256:243** roughly corresponds to our semitone.) See Appendix A.

[34]   The circle of the Same is the celestial equator, and its (daily) motion is from east to west. It is the motion of the "fixed" stars—fixed, that is, with respect to the celestial sphere. The circle of the Other is the ecliptic. This is the great circle that includes the (annual) circuit of the Sun and governs the movement of the other planets. Its motion is from west to east. When both motions are combined, the resulting path for each "wandering" star within the all is a spiral (39B). See Appendix B.

D the orbit of the Same and Similar; for it alone he let be unsplit, whereas the inner orbit he split in six places into seven unequal circles according to each interval of the double and triple—each of which were three. He ordered the circles to go in directions contrary to one another; and of the seven circles into which the inner circle had been split, he ordered that three be of the same speed, while the other four course at speeds dissimilar to one another and to those three, yet in ratio.[35]

E After this, when all the construction of the soul had become agreeable to the mind of her constructor, he proceeded to build within her all that was bodily in form, and he joined them with one another by bringing them together center to center; and once she had been woven in every direction from the center to the outermost heaven and had covered it in a circle from the outside as with a veil, she herself turned within herself and began a divine beginning of a life unceasing and thoughtful and for all time. And while heaven's body was born visible, soul herself was invisible and partook of calculation and attunement[36]—she, the best of 37A begotten things, born by the best of things intelligible and which *are* always.[37] And so, blended as she was from these three portions, from the nature of Same and Other and from Being, and divided into parts and then bound together according to ratio, herself circling back upon herself, whenever she touches on something that has its Being dispersed or, again, something whose Being is non-partitioned, she is moved throughout her whole self and tells what that thing is the same as and what it's other B than, and in what exact relation and where and how and when it turns out that particular things *are* and are affected, both for what comes to be and for what's always in the same condition. The account that arises is similarly true whether it has to do with either the Other or the Same; and this is swept along within the self-moved without sound and noise. And whenever the account becomes concerned with what's sensed, and the circle of the Other, correct in its going, sends its message to all its soul, then opinions and beliefs arise which are firm and true; while in turn, whenever her account concerns what is rational, and the circle of

---

[35] "In ratio" here means "in a ratio of whole numbers." The seven circles form a cosmic seven-stringed lyre for Timaeus' soul music. The three celestial bodies that go at the same speed are the Sun, Venus and Mercury. The four that go at different speeds are the Moon, Mars, Jupiter and Saturn. The divine craftsman makes the paths before he makes the bodies that traverse them.

[36] The word for tuning or attunement is *harmonia*. See Glossary under **tuning**.

[37] Contrast *Phaedrus* 245C-E, where Socrates argues that soul is "of necessity both unborn and deathless."

C   the Same, wheeling smoothly, makes its disclosure, then intellection and knowledge are of necessity brought to perfection. But if anyone should ever say that these two conditions come about in any of the beings other than soul, he'll be speaking anything rather than the truth.

And when the father who begat it noticed that it was moved and living—a sanctuary born for the everlasting gods[38]—he rejoiced in it and, being well-pleased, thought of fashioning it to be still more similar

D   to its model. And just as the model happens to be an everlasting Animal, so too did he attempt as far as possible to bring this all to a similar perfection.

Now to be sure, the nature of the Animal happened to be eternal, and in fact it was just this feature that it wasn't possible to attach perfectly to that which is begotten; so he proceeded to think of making a certain moving likeness of eternity; and just as he's putting heaven in array, he makes of eternity, which abides in unity, an eternal likeness that goes

E   according to number, that very thing we have named *time*.[39] For since there were no days and nights and months and years before heaven was born, he contrives their birth to come about just when heaven was constructed. All these are parts of time, and "was" and "will be" are forms of time that have come to be—exactly those forms which, without noticing it, we incorrectly apply to everlasting Being. For this is just what we say—"it was," and "it is" and "it will be." But "is" alone is suited to it, in

38A   keeping with the true account, whereas "was" and "will be" are fittingly said of becoming, which goes on in time—for both are motions, but it isn't suitable for that which is always in the same unmoving condition

---

[38]   "Sanctuary" here is *agalma*, which can also refer to a statue or an offering to a god. Cornford, following Proclus, takes the word as referring to a shrine for the gods (pp. 99-102). Timaeus is playing on the similarity between *agalma* as a thing of joy (from *agallein*, to glory or delight in) and *agasthai*, to marvel at, admire, take delight in. The word *agalma* occurs only once in the *Timaeus* but several times in the *Critias* (for example, 110B5, 116D7 and 116E4). See *Epinomis* 984A-B, where the Athenian stranger uses *agalmata* and *eikones* (likenesses) interchangeably in reference to the heavenly bodies.

[39]   As Cornford observes, time for Timaeus is "not a pre-existing framework" (not a kind) but a feature of the cosmic order (p. 102). It is not on a par with Space, which exists "before" the birth of the all (52B). Although Timaeus seems to suggest an important distinction between the everlasting or perpetual (*aidios*) and the eternal or timeless (*aiônios*), both terms are used of the intelligible model. In the oft-quoted definition of time, it seems strange to hear that the likeness is eternal (*aiônios*). To avoid this apparent confusion of the sensed likeness with its intellected model, Remi Brague has suggested that the adjective go with "number" rather than with "time" (for a discussion of this point, see John Sallis, *Chorology: On Beginning in Plato's Timaeus* [Bloomington: Indiana University Press, 1999], pp. 81-82).

to be in the process of becoming either older or younger through time, nor suitable that it ever became so, nor that it has become so now, nor that it will be so hereafter, nor on the whole are any of those conditions suitable which becoming has attached to what's swept along in the realm of sense; on the contrary, these were born as forms of time, which imitates eternity and circles around according to number—and there are

B   further expressions besides the ones we mentioned: "what has become *is* become," and "what is becoming *is* becoming," and in addition, "what's about to become *is* about to become," and "what is not *is* not"—none of which we say with precision. But the present would probably not be a fitting occasion for a precise reasoning-out of these matters.

Time, then, has come into being along with heaven, in order that, having been begotten together, they might also be dissolved together— should some dissolution of them ever arise; and it was made in accordance

C   with the model of the eternally enduring nature, in order that it might be as similar as possible to its model. For whereas that model is something that *is* for all eternity, heaven in its turn is something that has become and *is* and *will be*, through the end, for all time. So, on the basis of such reason and such thought on god's part for the birth of time, in order that time be begotten, the Sun and Moon and the five other stars (which have been given the name "wanderers"[40]) have been born for the marking off and guarding of the numbers of time. And once the god had made bodies for each of them, he set them in the orbits in which the circuit of the Other was moving—seven they were, since the stars were seven: the

D   Moon in the first circuit around the earth, the Sun in the second above the earth, the Dawnbearer and the star called "Sacred to Hermes" in those circuits going in a circle at a speed equal to that of the Sun but allotted the power contrary to him;[41] whence the Sun and the Star of Hermes and the Dawnbearer overtake and in the same way are overtaken by one another.[42] As for the others—where and for just what causes he settled them, if someone should go through all this in detail, the account that's a

E   side-job here would provide more work than that for the sake of which it's being given. Maybe later, when there's leisure for it, these matters might happen to meet with an exposition worthy of them.

---

[40]   The wanderers are *planêta* or planets—from the verb *planasthai*, to wander.

[41]   On the much-disputed "contrary power" see Taylor, *A Commentary on Plato's Timaeus*, Oxford: Oxford University Press, 1928, pp. 196-202, and D. R. Dicks, *Early Greek Astronomy to Aristotle*, Ithaca, NY: Cornell University Press, 1970, pp. 123-129.

[42]   The Dawnbearer or Morning Star is Venus; the star that is Sacred to Hermes is Mercury. The overtaking and being overtaken refer to the fact that, unlike the outer planets (Mars, Jupiter and Saturn), Mercury and Venus always appear somewhere within a fixed angular distance on either side of the Sun.

And so, when each body (as many of them as were needed for the fashioning of time) had attained the course that was fitting for itself, and when they had been begotten as animals bound with ensouled bonds and had learned what was ordered them, they went around according to that course of Other, which is slanted and goes through the course of the Same and is mastered by it—this one among them going in a greater circle, that one going in a lesser, those in the lesser circle going around more swiftly, while those in the greater more slowly. Now because of the course of the Same, the ones that go around most swiftly kept appearing to be overtaken by those that go slower, although they really do the overtaking; for the course of the Same (which is the swiftest) twisted all their circles into a spiral (because they proceed in two ways that are contrary and simultaneous), and it made the body most slowly going away from itself appear the nearest to it. And in order that there be some manifest measure of their relative slowness and swiftness, with which[43] they advanced in their eight courses, a light did the god touch off in that circuit second from the Earth—the very light we have now called the Sun—in order that this might shine forth as much as possible to all things everywhere, and that those animals for whom it was appropriate might partake of number by having learned it from the orbit of the Same and Similar. So then, Night and Day have been born in this way and for these reasons, being the circuit of the one and most prudent circling; and Month whenever the Moon, having come around her own circle, overtakes the Sun; and Year, whenever the Sun comes around on his own circle. As for the other stars, humans have not taken note of their circuits (except for a few out of the many), nor do they give them names, nor take exact relative measurements and look at them by means of numbers, so that people scarcely know at all that the "wanderings" of these bodies—baffling in their multitude yet wondrously embroidered—are time. It is nonetheless possible to note that the perfect number of time would fulfil the Perfect Year at that moment when the relative speeds of all the eight circuits, having finished together, come to a head, as measured by the circle of the Same and Similarly-moving. In accordance with these very reasons and for the sake of all this were all those stars begotten that have turnings as they make their way through heaven,[44] in order that this animal might be as similar as possible to the perfect and intelligible Animal in the imitation of its eternally enduring nature.

39A

B

C

D

E

---

[43]   Reading *kath' ha* (literally, according to which) with Archer-Hind.

[44]   The turnings here are not rotations but changes in direction. See Taylor, p. 220 and Appendix B.

Now in other respects it had, up to the birth of time, already been fashioned in similarity with that to which it was likened; but since it had not yet embraced the entire range of animals born within itself, it was still for this reason in a dissimilar condition. Accordingly, this remaining part he proceeded to fashion by imprinting it with the nature of its model. So just as intellect sees looks of whatever sorts and however many that are in the Animal that *is*, those sorts and that many he thought this animal too must have. Now the forms of these looks are four: one the heavenly kind to which gods belong, another the winged and airborne kind, a third the water-dwelling form, and the form that's footed and land-living fourth. So then, most of the look of the divine form he went about fashioning out of fire, so that it would be as brilliant and beautiful to look at as possible; and likening it to the all, he went about making it well-rounded. And he proceeds to set it in the prudence of the most masterful to follow along in its train, having distributed it all around the whole heaven in a circle to be for it a true adornment, cunningly embroidered over the whole.[45] Two motions he attached to each member of this form: one the motion that's self-same and goes around in the same spot, since each in itself always thinks the same thoughts about the same things, the other the motion that goes forward, since it's mastered by the orbit of the Same and Similar. But with respect to the five other motions, each of them is unmoved and standing, in order that they might become as excellent as possible. Now from this cause were born those among the stars that were unwandering—animals that are divine and everlasting and abide always by revolving in a self-same way and in the same spot; and as for those stars that turn and have that sort of wandering, they were born in just the way described at an earlier point. And Earth he contrived to be both our nurturer and, because she's huddled round the pole that's stretched through all, the guardian and craftsman of Night and Day[46]—first and eldest of the gods who have come to be within heaven.

40A

B

C

---

[45] The word for adornment here is *kosmos*, which means both the cosmos and any ornament or beautiful arrangement (see Glossary under **cosmos**).

[46] The question of whether or not the Earth moves according to Timaeus has been debated since antiquity. The controversy revolves around the phrase *heillomenên ... peri ton dia pantos polon tetamenon,* "huddled round the pole that's stretched through all." Burnet (following Aristotle, who cites this phrase in *On the Heavens* 2.13.293b30) reads the participle *illomenên* for *heillomenên. Illomenên* means winding and thus implies that the Earth moves, while *heillomenên* means pressed or crowded together, and implies that it does not. Cornford argues for *illomenên* and a rotating Earth (pp. 120-134). Against Cornford, D. R. Dicks argues that *heillomenên* is the correct reading and that the Earth guards the alternation of Night and Day by

But as for the choric dances of these stars and their juxtapositions with one another, and the return-motions of their circles back upon themselves and their progressions, and which among the gods come to be in conjunction with one another and how many of them in opposition, and how they pass behind and in front of each other and at what times each of these is hidden from our view and, upon reappear-

D   ing, sends terrors and portents of things to come afterwards upon men unable to calculate—to speak of all this without looking at imitations of these very things would be vain labor.[47] But let this and the way we've put it about the nature of gods visible and begotten be sufficient, and let it have an end.

As for the other divinities,[48] to declare and come to know their birth is beyond our power, and one must be persuaded by those who have declared it in earlier times since they were offspring of gods (so they claimed), and presumably they, if anyone, had sure knowledge of their own ancestors. It's impossible, then, to distrust sons of gods, even

E   if they do speak without either likelihoods or necessary demonstrations; but since they profess to be reporting family matters, we must follow custom and trust them. And so, in keeping with what they say, let the birth of these gods so hold and be declared. Of Gê and Ouranos were born the children Okeanos and Tethys; and of these were born Phorkys, Kronos and Rhea, and all those that go with them; and of Kronos and

41A   Rhea were born Zeus, Hera, and all those who, as we know, are called their siblings; and of these again were born still other offspring.

Now when all the gods had their birth—both those who make their rounds in an always apparent way and those who appear to the extent that they're willing—the begetter of this all proceeds to speak to them as follows:

---

resisting the motion of the Same (pp. 132-137 and note 181 on p. 239). See Archer-Hind's note in *The Timaeus of Plato*, New York: Arno Press, 1973, pp. 132-134. A brief summary of the controversy appears in Guthrie's note to his translation of *On the Heavens* in the Loeb edition (pp. 220-223). Forms of the disputed word *heillomenên* occur elsewhere in the dialogue (76C1 and 86E7-A1). For the reasons given by Archer-Hind, Cornford and Dicks, I have omitted the *tên* from the sentence in Burnet's text.

[47] Reading *autôn* for the *aû tôn* in Burnet's text. The *mimêmata* or imitations here are the physical, mechanical models used by ancient astronomers to reproduce, and thereby understand, celestial phenomena.

[48] The divinities are in Greek *daimones*. A *daimôn* can be the good spirit that guides (90A) or an evil spirit—a demon.

"Gods of gods,[49] you works of whom I am both craftsman and father, born through me and indissoluble—unless, that is, I myself were

B   willing to dissolve you! Now, to be sure, all that is bound together can be dissolved, and yet only one who is bad would be willing to dissolve that which is beautifully joined together and in good condition. For these reasons, and since indeed you have been born, you are not immortal nor entirely indissoluble, yet in no way shall you suffer this very dissolution, nor shall you happen to meet with the doom of death, since through my will have you been allotted a bond greater still and more lordly than those bonds with which you, when born, were bound together. So now, learn what I present before you in speech. Three mortal kinds are left unbegotten still; but if these are not born, heaven shall be imperfect, for it shall not have all the kinds of animals within itself—but have them

C   it must, if it is to be sufficiently perfect. And if through me these kinds did come to be and partake of life, they would be made equal to gods. So in order that mortal kinds may *be* and this all be genuinely all, do you turn yourselves, in accordance with nature, to the crafting of animals, imitating my power in giving you birth. And as many of them for whom it is suitable to have the same name, 'immortal,' the part called divine

D   and which has authority within those always willing to follow the just way and yourselves—that part shall I hand down to you after I've sown it and made a beginning. But as for the part that remains, do you, by interweaving mortal with immortal, go about fashioning and begetting animals; and make them grow by giving them nourishment, and, when they've withered away, receive them back unto yourselves!"

Thus he spoke, and once again into the former bowl[50] in which he had blended and mixed the soul of the all he proceeded to pour what was left over from the previous ingredients,[51] mixing it in somewhat the same mode, yet unblended no longer to the same extent but rather in

49 Cornford departs from Burnet's reading of *theoi theôn* ("gods of gods") by interposing a comma, even though there is no dispute over the MS. He does so on the grounds that *theoi theôn* has no discernible meaning (p. 369). But a very simple meaning presents itself if the genitive *theôn* is taken as partitive. Having gathered together both types of gods in one group, the craftsman immediately separates the wheat from the chaff, the legitimate heirs from the usurpers of the title. The gods whom the divine craftsman chooses to address are not the deceptive Olympians but his own well-behaved offspring. These are the true gods among the gods, the *theoi theôn*.

50 The *kratêr* is a bowl in which wine is mixed with water.

51 As Taylor points out, the human soul-mixture is not made out of a residue of the divine soul-mixture but out of the original ingredients of Being, Same and Other. He draws the important conclusion that "our souls are neither 'parts' of the cosmic soul nor 'emanations' from it" (p. 255).

E   second and third degree of purity. And when he had combined all of it, he divided it up into souls equal in number to the stars and assigned each soul to each star; and having mounted them, as it were, in a chariot, he showed them the nature of the all. He told them the laws of destiny: how

42A   the first birth ordered for all would be one, in order that no one might be slighted by him; and how, once he had sown them, each in his own appropriate organ of time, they would have to sprout into the most god-fearing of animals; and how, human nature being twofold, the superior part would be a kind which at a later point would be called Man.[52]

Now when, by necessity, they should be implanted in bodies and made subject to whatever might come into and go out of their body, here's what would necessarily happen. First, there would be sensation, one and the same for all of them and innate, arising from forceful affections; and second, erotic love mixed with pleasure and pain; and in

B   addition to these, terror and anger and whatever goes along with them and all such things that by nature tend to be contrary and set at odds with each other. If they were to master these, they would live in justice, but if they were mastered by them, then in injustice. And he who has lived well throughout his appropriate time would make his way back to the dwelling of his lawful star and would have a life that was happy and

C   habitual to him. But he who had failed to live well would, in his second birth, take on woman's nature.[53] If in that form he still did not refrain from evil, then in whatever mode he might make himself bad, he would always take on some such bestial nature in the similitude of that mode of life that was born in him. And he would keep changing and would not cease from his labors until he had reached the following point: not before he should draw along with the circuit of the Same and Similar that was in himself the vast mob of fire and water and air and earth that

D   had later grown over it and, having mastered by reason that roaring and irrational mob, reach the form of his first and best condition.

After he had laid all these strictures on them, in order that he might be blameless of the future evil from each of them,[54] he went about sowing some in the Earth, some in the Moon, some in all the other organs of time. And after this sowing, he handed down to the young gods the task of molding mortal bodies, and—once they had fashioned

---

[52]   The Greek word here is not *anthrôpos* (human being) but *anêr*, which refers to man in his maleness, man as opposed to woman, and also to a true or "real" man.

[53]   As Leo Strauss observes, man for Timaeus starts out as a "sexless male" (*The City and Man* [Chicago: Rand McNally, 1964], p. 111, note 42).

[54]   An echo of the myth of Er in *Republic* 10: *aitia helomenou, theos anaitios*, "The blame is the chooser's, god is blameless" (617E).

E   whatever was left over of human soul that still had to be added, along
         with all that this entailed—of ruling and steering the mortal animal in
         the most beautiful and best way as far as they were able, except in so
         far as it itself might become a cause of evils for itself.

         And as for him, having ordered all these very things, he proceeded
         to abide in his own proper and habitual state, while his sons, mindful
         of their father's order, proceeded to obey it. Having taken the immortal
         principle of the mortal animal, imitating their own craftsman, they bor-
         rowed from the cosmos portions of fire and earth and water and air, as
         though intending to pay them back again, and went about gluing together
43A   the portions thus taken into the same thing, not with the indissoluble
         bonds with which they themselves were held together, no, but welding
         them with close-packed rivets invisible for their smallness; and fashion-
         ing one individual body out of all the portions, they bound the circuits
         of the immortal soul within a body subject to inflow and outflow.

         And these circuits, as though bound within a prodigious river,
B   neither mastered it nor were mastered, but were forcibly swept along and
         also did sweep, so that the whole animal was moved—moved, however,
         in whatever disorderly way it might happen to progress, and irrationally
         since it had all six motions: it went forwards and backwards, and again
         to the right and to the left, both down and up, wandering every which
         way down all six regions.[55] For as prodigious as was that food-supply-
         ing wave that washed over it and then flowed away, still greater was the
C   uproar that the affections of the bodies produced by attacking each of
         them whenever a body of one of them would collide with fire, having
         met up with it as something alien from the outside, or also with a solid
         chunk of earth or with the liquid glidings of waters, or when it would
         be overtaken by a blast of wind-swept air, and when the motions swept
         through the body by all these properties would attack the soul—which
         is also the very reason why all these motions were then called "sensings"
         and are still called that now.[56]

         And what's more, since these sensings were then bringing about
         the most widespread and greatest commotion then and under those
         circumstances, moving along with the constantly flowing channel of
         nutriment and severely shaking up the circuits of the soul, they com-
D   pletely hindered the circuit of the Same by flowing contrary to it, and
         kept it from ruling and going, while the circuit of the Other in turn they

---

[55] The regions corresponding to the six spatial directions just mentioned: up
      and down, backwards and forwards, left and right.

[56] Timaeus playfully derives the word for sensing (*aisthêsis*) from the word
      for darting or rushing (*aïssein*).

thoroughly shook up so as to twist into all sorts of contortions the three several intervals of the double and triple, as well as in the mean terms and linking bonds of **3:2**, **4:3** and **9:8**, since these were not completely
E dissoluble, except by him who had bound them together,[57] and so as to make all sorts of fractures and disruptions in the circles in as many ways as possible, so that, barely holding together with each other, although they coursed along, they coursed irrationally: now in reverse, now sideways, now upside down. It was as when someone in an upside-down position planted his head on the ground and held his feet above him by pushing them against something; then, given this affection for both the man affected in this way and the people watching him, rights and lefts show themselves as reversed, each party in relation to the other.[58] Now since the orbits suffer with severity this same thing and others like
44A it, whenever they happen to be around something from outside, either from the kind Same or from the kind Other, at that time, by addressing them as "same as" and "other than" what's in fact contrary to their truth, they've become false and unintelligent, and there's not a single circuit among them at that time that either rules or leads. But if certain sensations from the outside, by sweeping along and colliding with these circuits, also draw along with them the entire vessel of the soul, then these circuits seem to master but in fact are mastered.

And so, precisely because of all these affections, both now and in
B the beginning, soul first becomes unintelligent whenever she's bound within a mortal body. But whenever the stream of increase and nutriment comes upon her to a lesser extent, and the circuits, recovering their calm once again, go their own way and are settled down more as time goes by, then from that point on the orbits are set straight with respect to the figure of each of the circles that go according to nature: they address the Other and the Same correctly, and they set the man who has them on his way to becoming thoughtful. And so, if some cor-

---

[57] The double and triple intervals are the two geometric progressions used to generate the soul music at 35B. They are **1:2::2:4::4:8** and **1:3:3::9::9:27**. **3:2**, **4:3** and **9:8** are, respectively, the perfect fifth, perfect fourth and *tonos* or whole tone. See Appendix A.

[58] The Inverted Man is one of many comic moments in the likely story. If I am right side up and you are looking at me, then my left faces your right: we both know that we are mirror images of one another and so correctly identify each other's left and right. But if I am upside down, and neither of us is thinking of the consequences of inversion, we become disoriented with respect to each other's left and right: we use our former principle ("your rights and lefts oppose my lefts and rights") where it no longer applies and so wrongly identify each other's rights and lefts. See Taylor's explanation of the joke (p. 271). Compare what Timaeus says about mirroring at 46A-C.

C

rect upbringing assists in education, the man becomes perfectly sound and healthy, having escaped the greatest disease;[59] but if he was careless in this matter, then, after making his way through a lame living of his lifetime, he comes back to Hades imperfect and unintelligent. These things, however, come about at a later time. But as for what now lies before us, we must go through it with more precision; and as for what came before *that*—everything about the birth of bodies in all their parts and about soul, and the causes and forethought of gods through which soul was born—we must hold on tight to what's most likely and, thus traveling along, go through that too accordingly.

D

Now the divine circuits, which were two, they bound within a spheroform body, thus imitating the figure of the all, which was rounded—the body to which we now give the name "head," which is most divine and dominates all the parts within us. To it the gods also handed over all the body, which they had assembled to be its servant, since they noticed that it would partake of all the motions that were to be. So in order that it not go rolling along on the ground, which has all manner of heights and depths, and be at an impasse when it came to climbing over the one and climbing out of the other, they gave to it the body as a chariot for easy travel, which is exactly why the body acquired length and sprouted four limbs extendable and flexible, since god contrived them as a means of travel, so that by means of these limbs the body, by grasping and being supported, has become capable of traveling through all regions, bearing on high the dwelling of our most divine and most sacred part.[60] In this way, then, and for these reasons, legs and hands sprouted on all of us, and since the gods considered the front more worthy of honor than the back and more fit for ruling, in this direction did they give us most of our traveling. Now it was necessary that a human have the front of his body distinct and dissimilar. That's why they first set down the face on that side, around the vessel of the head, and bound within it organs for all the forethought of the soul; and they ordained that this natural front be that which partakes of guidance.

E

45A

B

And of the organs they first built light-bearing eyes, having bound them in the face by the following cause. All the fire that wasn't able to burn but provides gentle light they contrived to become a body kindred to

---

59 At 88B Timaeus says that the greatest of diseases is *amathia*, stupidity.

60 The verb used to describe the head's quandary is from *aporein*, to be perplexed in the sense of not having a way or *poros*. It is hilarious to think of the bodiless head as actually rolling around, perplexed about how it is to make its way in the world. The body gives the head its proper dignity as well as its means of transport. It is a sort of moving pedestal.

each day.[61] For the unalloyed fire within us, which is brother to this, they made flow smooth and dense through the eyes, having compressed the whole eye but especially the central part, so as to fend off all such other fire as was coarser, while letting filter through only such fire that was itself pure.[62] So whenever the light of open day is all around the stream of vision, then, rushing out like to like and having become compounded with the fire of day, that stream composes with it one kindred body along the eyes' direct line of sight, wherever the stream that rushes forth from inside pushes against any of the objects outside that collide with it. Now as for the entire stream of vision, once it has become similarly affected through its similarity to the outer fire of day, whatever it itself touches at any time or whatever other thing it's touched by, it spreads the motions of these things throughout the entire body until they reach the soul and thus produces that very sensation by which we say that we see. But when the fire that's akin goes off into night, then the stream of vision is cut off; for in going out into the dissimilar, it is itself altered and is utterly quenched, no longer becoming one in nature with the neighboring air, inasmuch as this air doesn't have any fire. So it stops seeing and, what's more, becomes an invitation to sleep, since the gods contrived the nature of the eyelids as a safeguard for vision. Whenever they're closed, they shut in the power of the inner fire, and this power disperses and tempers the inner motions; and when these motions are tempered, peace comes about; and when this peace becomes great, then an all but dreamless sleep comes over us. But if some fairly great motions are left behind, then, depending on what sort they are and in what regions they're left, they produce phantasms of that sort and to that extent, which are copied inside and remembered as outside by those who have awakened.

As for the image-making of mirrors and anything else shiny and smooth, it's no longer difficult at all to observe what happens. For from the communion of the inner and the outer fire, each with the other, and again at that moment when a single fire arises at the smooth surface and is remodeled in various ways, all such images of necessity appear in it—the fire of the reflected face having become compounded with the fire of the vision at the smooth and brilliant surface. And lefts show themselves as right, because contact comes about for contrary parts of the vision with contrary parts of the reflected object, against the established habit of collision, while contrariwise, rights show themselves as right and lefts as left whenever the light, being compounded with that

---

[61] Timaeus is playing on the similarity between *hêmeros* (gentle) and *hêmera* (day).

[62] Here, as elsewhere in his speech, Timaeus follows Empedocles and his doctrine of effluences.

C   with which it is compounded, changes sides; and this occurs whenever the smooth surface of the mirrors, having been curved upwards on either side, drives the right part of the visual stream to the left, and the other part in the other direction. And if the mirror is turned lengthwise to the face, it makes the same entire face appear upside down, since it drives the lower part of the beam up and, conversely, the upper part down.[63]

D   Now all these are among the assistant causes that god uses as his servants in perfecting, as much as in their power, the look of the best.[64] But the opinion held by most people is that they are not assistant causes but causes of all things, by cooling and heating, coalescing and dissolving, and by fashioning all such effects. But none of them is capable of having reason nor any intellect for any purpose at all. For it must be said that the only one of the beings suited to acquire intellect is soul; and this is something invisible, while fire and water and earth and air

E   have all been born visible bodies. And it's a necessity that the lover of intellect and knowledge pursue first the causes that have to do with the thoughtful nature, and second all such things that are moved by others and come to be movers of other things only out of necessity. This is just what we must do as well. Both kinds of causes must be declared: on one side those which, with the aid of intellect, are craftsmen of things beautiful and good, on the other side those which, bereft of prudence, produce on each occasion a disordered, chance effect.

So then, concerning the auxiliary causes that contributed to the eyes' having the power that is their present lot, let it be as stated; but

47A   the greatest work they produce for our benefit, the work on account of which god has given them to us, must next be declared. Now according to my account, sight has come to be the cause of the greatest benefit for us, since none of the accounts we're now giving about the all would ever have been uttered if we had seen neither the stars nor the Sun nor heaven. But as it is now, day and night, once seen, and the months and the circuits of the years, and the equinoxes and solstices, have contrived number and gave us a notion of time and the inquiry into the nature

B   of the all, from which we derived for ourselves a kind of philosophy,[65]

---

[63] For diagrams of Timaeus' explanation of mirror-action, see Cornford, p. 155.

[64] Compare Socrates' disenchantment with Anaxagoras and his inquiry into cause in the *Phaedo* (97B ff.).

[65] Most translators take the phrase *philosophias genos* as referring to philosophy as a whole or in general, but the context seems to be the praise of astronomy in particular. Compare Rivaud's translation of the phrase: "cette sorte de science" ("that kind of science").

than which no greater good either came or ever will come to the mortal kind as a god-given gift. Now this, I say, is the greatest good of eyes. As for the other, lesser goods, why should we sing their praises? The non-philosopher, if made blind to them, "would, in lamenting, sing his dirge in vain."[66] No, for our part let it be said that this is the cause and these the reasons for which god discovered vision and gave it to us as a gift: in order that, by observing the circuits of intellect in heaven, we might use them for the orbits of the thinking within us, which are akin

C   to those, the disturbed to the undisturbed; and, by having thoroughly learned them and partaken of the natural correctness in their calculations, thus imitating the utterly unwandering circuits of the god, we might stabilize the wander-stricken circuits in ourselves.

Concerning sound and hearing, again it's the same account: they've been given to us as a gift from the gods for the same purpose and for the sake of the same things. For not only was speech built for

D   this same purpose and to this end contributes the greatest portion; but moreover, as much of music as, through its sound, is useful for hearing, this much was given to us for the sake of attunement.[67] And attunement, which has coursings akin to the circuits in our soul, has been given by the Muses to him who makes use of the Muses with his intellect—not for the purpose of irrational pleasure (which is what it's now thought to be useful for), but as an ally to the circuit of the soul within us once it's become untuned, for the purpose of bringing the

E   soul into arrangement and concord with herself. Again, because the condition becomes unmeasured in us and deficient in grace for most, rhythm too was given to us by those same Muses as our companion in arms for the same reason.

Now what's gone by so far in what was said, except for a bit, has shown the things that have been crafted through intellect; but one must also set down beside the account the things that come to be through

48A   necessity. For mixed indeed was the birth of this cosmos here, and begot-

---

[66] Timaeus is referring to a line from the *Phoenician Women* by Euripides (1762). The line is spoken by Oedipus, who has just received news that his two sons, Eteocles and Polyneices, have killed each other on the battlefield and that his wife, Jocasta, has killed herself with one of their swords. Banished by Creon, the blind Oedipus at the end of the play says, "But why do I lament these things and sing a dirge in vain? For I must, being mortal, bear the necessities from the gods."

[67] The emphasis here on sound and hearing reminds us that music up to this point had been purely mathematical. For Timaeus there is no audible "music of the spheres."

ten from a standing-together of necessity and intellect;[68] and as intellect was ruling over necessity by persuading her to lead most of what comes to be toward what's best, in this way accordingly was this all constructed at the beginning: through necessity worsted by thoughtful persuasion.[69] So if anyone is to declare how the all was in this way genuinely born, he must also mix in the form of the wandering cause—how it is its nature to

B   sweep things around. In this way, then, we must retreat,[70] and, by taking in turn another, new beginning suited to these very matters, just as in what was before us earlier, so too in what is before us now, we must begin again from the beginning. We must get a view of the nature itself of fire and water, and air and earth, before the birth of heaven, and of their affections before this. For at present no one has yet revealed their birth; but on the contrary, we speak to people as if they knew fire, whatever it is, and each of the others; and we set them down as principles—as elements or "letters" of the all—whereas it would not be at all suitable for them to

C   be likened with any degree of likelihood even to the forms of "syllable," at least not by a man who was even the slightest bit prudent.[71]

But now, let the following at least be held by us. We must not now declare the beginning concerning all things (or the beginnings, or whatever term seems to apply to them), for no other reason than because it's difficult to make plain what seems to be the case according to the present mode of going through things. So, as for you, don't suppose that I must speak of it; and as for me, I in my turn wouldn't be able to

D   persuade my own self that I'd be correct in trying to take upon myself so great a task; but by safeguarding what was declared at the very beginning—the power of likely accounts—I shall attempt to utter an account not less likely but more so, and to speak, as before from the beginning, about things individually and together as a whole. So now too, at the beginning of our speeches, by invoking god the savior[72] to grant us safe

---

[68]   "Standing-together" is *systasis*, elsewhere translated "structure." The Greek word suggests that intellect and necessity stand together in two opposite senses: as allies and as enemies. See Glossary entry, **construct**.

[69]   Whereas the construction of soul required force (35B), the construction of body originates in persuasion.

[70]   The verb for "retreat" here is a form of *anachôrein*, which literally means to go back to one's space or *chôra*. The verb thus anticipates the new principle we meet in this section (52B).

[71]   The word *stoicheion* in Greek means both element and letter of the alphabet.

[72]   The noun *sôtêr*, savior, was a commonly used epithet of Zeus. Drinking to Zeus the Savior, to whom the third cup of wine was consecrated, was supposed to bring good luck. The third cup nicely fits Timaeus' unveiling of a third kind. The word for unusual, *aêthês*, can also mean characterless—yet another foreshadowing of the curiously indefinite nature of space.

E

passage out of a strange and unusual narration to the decree[73] based on likelihoods, let us once more begin to speak.

Now let this new beginning concerning the all have more divisions than the one we made before. For then we distinguished two forms, but now we must make plain another, third kind. Two kinds were sufficient for what was said before: one set down as the form of a model—intelligible and always in the self-same condition—and the

49A

second, an imitation of a model, having birth and visible. A third kind we didn't distinguish at that time, since we deemed that the two would be sufficient; but now the account seems to make it necessary that we try to bring to light in speeches a form difficult and obscure. What power, then, and what nature should one suppose it to have? This especially:

B

that it's a receptacle[74] for all becoming, a sort of wet-nurse. Now truly spoken as all this has been, one must speak about it more distinctly; yet to do so is difficult for various reasons but especially because, for its sake, it's first necessary to raise perplexities about fire and its fellows. For in describing each of these, to say which one should genuinely be called water rather than fire, and which is any one thing rather than all of them individually so as to make use of some word that's trustworthy and stable, is difficult. How then, once we've raised likely difficulties about them, should we speak about this third kind itself, and in what way, and what should we say?[75]

First, the very thing we've now named water we see condensing,

C

thereby becoming, so it seems to us, stones and earth; and this same thing again, by melting and dissolving, we see becoming wind and air; and air, having been heated, becoming fire; and conversely we see fire, having been contracted and quenched, going back once more to the look of air; and air, by coming together and thickening up, going back to become cloud and fog; and when these are compressed still more, we see water flow from them, and from water back to earth and stones—a circle—thus passing on to one another, as it appears, birth. Thus, then, since each of these individually never shows itself as the same, which of

D

them can anyone firmly insist is any one thing and not another without putting himself to shame? There isn't any, but on the contrary, the safest

---

[73]   *dogma*, from *dokein*, to seem. A *dogma* is a seeming or opinion. It refers especially to an opinion of the assembly. The view Timaeus is about to develop is not a mere opinion but an official pronouncement and doctrine. The word reappears at 55D and 90B. See Glossary entry, **seem**.

[74]   The Greek word for receptacle is *hypodochê*. See Glossary under **receptacle**.

[75]   Following Zeyl, I have taken the *tout' auto*, "this itself," as referring to the third kind.

course by far in positing anything about these things is to speak as follows: to address whatever we observe as always coming to be now here, then there (like fire), not as "this"—say, "fire"—but as "of this sort on each occasion," and to address water not as "this" but as "always of this

E   sort," and never to address any other thing as though it had any stability, that is, any of the things we point to with the term "this" or "that," believing that by using such a term, we're making plain a something. For it flees and doesn't abide "this" and "that" and "with respect to this" and every expression that indicts them of being abiding. On the contrary, it's safest not to say these things of any of them individually, but "of this sort" as it always courses around similarly—to call them that, concerning each individually and all of them together, and in particular, to call fire "what is continually of this sort" and everything else whatsoever that has birth. But that *in which* these things individually show themselves

50A   as always coming into being and again *from which* they perish, that alone we must in turn address by using the names "this" and "that"; whereas anything that is "of whatever sort"—whether hot or white, or whatever member of a pair of contraries, or any and every composite of these—that in turn we must call by none of these names.[76]

But one must put one's heart into speaking about this once more and with still more clarity. If someone, having molded all figures out of gold, should in no way stop remolding each figure into all the others,

B   then if someone pointed out one of them and asked "Whatever is it?"—by far the safest thing to say in point of truth is "Gold." But as for the triangle and whatever other figures were being born in it, one must never, ever say that these things *are*, since they shift right in the middle of our positing them. Rather one must be content whenever such a thing is willing to accept being called even "of this sort" with any safety. It's the same account concerning the nature that receives all bodies. One

C   must always call it by the same name, since it never at all abandons its own power. It both always receives all things, and nowhere in no way has it ever taken on any shape similar to the ones that come into it; for it's laid down by nature as a molding stuff[77] for everything, being both moved and thoroughly configured by whatever things come into it; and because of these, it appears different at different times; and the figures

---

[76] Lines 49C7-50B5 have been subjected to minute grammatical analysis by Harold Cherniss, some of whose suggestions I have used in the translation of this obscure passage. See "A Much Misread Passage of the *Timaeus*" in *Selected Papers*, Leiden: E. J. Brill, 1977, pp. 346-363.

[77] "Molding stuff" is *ekmageion*. This is "a uniform mass of wax or other soft stuff on which you can print the different devices of innumerable seals" (Taylor, p. 320).

that come into it and go out of it are always imitations of the things that *are*, having been imprinted from them in some manner hard to tell of and wondrous, and which we'll pursue at a later point.[78]

D

In any case, at present one should keep in mind three kinds: that which comes to be, that *in which* it comes to be, and that *from which* what comes to be sprouts as something copied. And what's more, it's fitting to liken the receiver to a *mother*, the "from which" to a *father*,[79] and the nature between these to an *offspring*, and to notice that if the imprints are going to be sufficiently various with every variety to be seen, then that in which the imprints are fixed wouldn't be prepared well unless it's shapeless with respect to all those looks that it might be going to receive from elsewhere. For if it should be similar to any of the things that come on the scene, on receiving what was contrary to itself or of an altogether different nature, whenever these things arrive, it would copy

E

them badly by projecting its own visage alongside the thing copied. And that's why that which is to take up all the kinds within itself should be outside of all forms, just as with all those fragrant oils, whose makers first artfully contrive this very condition: they first make the liquids that are to receive the scents as odorless as possible. And all those who attempt to make impressions of figures in anything soft in no way allow any figure whatsoever to be manifest in it, but fashion their object by first leveling it out so that it's as smooth as possible.

51A

In the same way, it's appropriate for that which is to receive beautifully over its whole extent, and often, copies of all things that *are* always to be by nature outside of all the forms. For this very reason, let us speak of the mother and receptacle of that which has been born visible and in all ways sensed as neither earth nor air nor fire nor water, nor as any of the things that have been born composites or constituents of these. On the contrary, if we say that it's some invisible and shapeless form—all-

B

receptive, but partaking somehow of the intelligible in a most perplexing way and most hard-to-capture—then we won't be lying. And to the extent that it's possible to arrive at the nature of this form from what was said previously, to this extent someone might speak most correctly if he said that the part of it that's been ignited appears each time as fire; the part that's been liquefied, as water; and both earth and air appear to the extent that it receives imitations of these.

But now, by making more thorough distinctions in speech concerning them, one must examine the following. Is there, then, some Fire

---

[78] An unfulfilled promise.

[79] The father here is not the craftsman god but the form itself (compare 28C, where the god is called "poet and father").

C   Itself on its own, and are there all those things we always speak of in this way, as individuals "themselves all by themselves" that *are*; or are those very things we in fact look at—and the rest that we sense through the body—the only things that are in possession of that sort of truth; and besides them nothing else anywhere in any way *is*, but in vain do we affirm on each occasion that some intelligible form of each thing *is*, whereas such a form was, after all, nothing but a word? Now it wouldn't be worthy to dismiss the present question untried and unjudged and to insist that that's the way it is, nor to tack on another lengthy side-job to a lengthy account; but if some major distinction could be drawn and made

D   to appear with few words—that would really be most opportune.

So here's how I myself cast *my* vote. If intellect and true opinion are two kinds, then these things that are all by themselves—these forms, unsensed by us, only intellected—in every way *are*; but if, as it appears to some, true opinion differs not at all from intellect, then all such things in turn that we sense through the body must be posited as the most stable. Now one must declare both of these kinds as two, because

E   they've both come into being separately and are in a dissimilar condition. For one of them comes to be in us through teaching, the other by persuasion; and one is always accompanied by a true account, while the other is irrational; and one is immovable by persuasion, while the other is alterable by persuasion; and of the one it must be affirmed that every man partakes; while of intellect, only gods and some small kind made up of humans.

Since this is so, it must be agreed that: one kind is the form,

52A   which is in a self-same condition—unbegotten and imperishable, neither receiving into itself anything else from anywhere else nor itself going anywhere into anything else, invisible and in all other ways unsensed—that which is intellection's lot to look upon; and there is a second kind, which has the same name as the form and is similar to it—sensed, begotten, always swept along, coming to be in some region and again perishing from there, graspable by opinion with the aid of sense; and moreover, a third kind—that of Space[80] —which always *is*,

B   admitting not of destruction and providing a seat for all that has birth, itself graspable by some bastard reasoning with the aid of insensibility, hardly to be trusted, the very thing we look to when we dream and affirm that it's necessary somehow for everything that *is* to be in some region and occupy some space, and that what is neither on earth nor

---

[80]   For the extreme difficulty of translating the word *chôra* in this passage, see Glossary under **place, Space**.

C somewhere in heaven is nothing.[81] Under the influence of this dreaminess, we become incapable of waking up and making all these very distinctions (and others that are brother to them)—even in reference to the unsleeping and truly subsisting nature—and of speaking the truth: that in the case of a likeness, since the very thing to which it has come to refer[82] doesn't even belong to the likeness itself, and since it's always swept along as a phantasm of something other, for these reasons it is appropriate that it come to be *in* some other thing, holding fast to Being in some way or other, or else be nothing at all; while the precisely true account, the helper of that which genuinely *is*, holds that so long as something is one thing and another thing another, since neither of the two ever comes to be in the other, neither will simultaneously become

D one and the same thing, and also two.

So then, in summary, let this account be given, proceeding from my vote and reasoned out as follows: Being[83] and Space and Becoming, three in a threefold way, *are* before the birth of heaven; and that wet-nurse of becoming, being liquefied and ignited and receiving the

E shapes of earth and air, and suffering all the other affections that follow along with these, appears in all sorts of ways to our sight. And because she's filled with powers neither similar nor equally balanced, in no part of her is she equally balanced, but rather, as she sways irregularly in every direction, she herself is shaken by those kinds and, being moved, in turn shakes them back; and the kinds, in being moved, are always swept along this way and that and are dispersed—just like the particles shaken and winnowed out by sieves and other instruments used for

53A purifying grain: the dense and heavy are swept to one site and settle, the porous and light to another. So too, when the four kinds are shaken by the recipient, who, being herself moved, is like an instrument that produces shaking, she separates farthest from each other the kinds that are most dissimilar, while pushing together as close as possible those that

---

[81] "Somehow" and "somewhere" are translations of the same Greek word *pou*. At the very beginning of the dialogue, Socrates uses the interrogative form of this word when he asks *where* the missing fourth is (17A). The man in Socrates' simile was gazing at beautiful animals "somewhere" (*pou*, 19B6). And in the *Republic*, Socrates says that the best city is a paradigm or model "perhaps laid up in heaven" for someone who wants to found a regime within himself, and that it makes no difference whether the city is or will be "somewhere" (*pou*, 9. 592B4).

[82] My construal of *eph' hôi gegonen* as "to which it has come to refer" is indebted to Cherniss ("*Timaeus* 52C2-5," ibid. pp. 364-375).

[83] Timaeus switches from the noun *ousia* at 52C to the substantive participle *on* (minus its article). The intent is perhaps to emphasize Being as the ongoing or perpetual state of self-sameness. See Glossary under **Being**.

are most similar—which is exactly why these different kinds also held a different place even before the all was arrayed and came to be out of them. Now on the one hand, before that time, all these things were in a condition that was without ratio and measure; and when the attempt was made to array the all, at first fire and water and earth and air—although they had certain traces of themselves[84]—were yet altogether disposed as is likely for everything to be whenever god is absent from anything; and since this was their nature at that time, god first of all thoroughly configured them by means of forms and numbers. On the other hand, that the god constructed them as far as possible to be beautiful and best, from a condition that was not so before—let this above all be granted by us as that which is always said. So now the attempt must be made to make plain to you, by means of an unusual account, the order of each of these kinds and their birth. But since you partake of the ways of education through which it's necessary to demonstrate what's said, you will follow along.

B

C

First of all, then, that fire and earth and water and air are bodies is plain, no doubt even to everyone; and every form of body also has depth. Moreover, there's every necessity for the nature of a plane to comprehend depth; and the rectilinear nature of the planar surface[85] is constructed out of triangles. And all triangles originate from a pair of triangles, each having one angle right and the others acute.[86] Of these two triangles, the one has, on each side, half a right angle marked off by equal sides, while the other has its right angle distributed into unequal parts by unequal sides. Now this we hypothesize to be the origin of fire and the other bodies, making our way according to the likely account accompanied by necessity, but the origins that are loftier still than these triangles only god knows and whoever among men is dear to god.

D

Now it must be said what would come to be the four most beautiful bodies, dissimilar among themselves, though capable (some of them) of being born out of each other when they dissolve. For if we hit upon this, then we have the truth concerning the birth of earth and fire and their mean proportionals, since we will concede to no one that there are visible bodies more beautiful than these anywhere, each of which corresponds to one kind. So we must put our hearts into this: to join together the four kinds of bodies pre-eminent in beauty, and to affirm that we

E

---

[84]   *ichnê*, literally, tracks or footprints.

[85]   "Surface" here is *basis*, literally, base. It points ahead to the regular "faces" of the regular solids.

[86]   For diagrams of Timaeus' elementary triangles, see Appendix C.

54A have sufficiently grasped their nature.[87] Now of the pair of triangles, the isosceles has been allotted a single nature, but the scalene indefinitely many; so we must choose which among these indefinitely many natures is in turn the most beautiful, if we're to make a proper beginning. If, then, someone could tell of one that's more beautiful that he's selected for the construction of these bodies, then that fellow wins the mastery not as enemy but as friend; so then, passing over the others, we posit for ourselves as the one most beautiful among the many triangles, that which, from the combination of two triangles, the equilateral triangle has been

B constructed as third. Why this is the case requires a fuller account, but if anyone refuted this and discovered that in fact it wasn't so, then the prize is laid aside for him in all friendship. So let there be chosen the following two triangles, from which the body of fire along with the bodies of the others has been contrived: one the isosceles, the other that which always has its greater side three times its lesser side in square.[88]

Now something earlier that was said unclearly must at present be more thoroughly determined: the four kinds all appeared to have birth

C through one another into one another, but they didn't show themselves correctly. For out of the triangles we've chosen, four kinds are born: three come from the one triangle that has unequal sides, while the fourth is the only one joined together from the isosceles triangle. They are therefore not all capable, on being dissolved into one another, of becoming a few large bodies out of many small ones, and the other way around; but it is possible for three. For since by nature they all come from one triangle, when the greater bodies are dissolved, many small ones are constructed from these same bodies and receive the figures that

D are appropriate to themselves; and whenever many small bodies in turn should be dispersed into their triangles, a single number of them that came to be would produce another single, large form of a single mass.

So let all this have been said concerning their birth into one another; but this should be followed by saying what sort of form each of

---

[87] "Join together" here is *synarmosasthai* (see Glossary under **join, fit or tune**). The solids will be "harmonized," that is, composed of parts that fit together like the tones of a melody. Compare Critias' use of the related verb *harmozein*, to fit, back at 26D.

[88] "In square" is *kata dynamin*. *Dynamis*, a technical term in Greek mathematics, can refer to the square of a number or length or to a square root. The *dynamis* as square root is defined by Theaetetus in the dialogue that bears his name (147D). In the present passage, Timaeus is referring to the square figures that could be constructed on the sides of a right triangle such that the square on the greater side is three times the square on the lesser side. In modern notation, the lesser side has length **1**, and the greater side has length $\sqrt{3}$ (the hypotenuse has length **2**). See Appendix C.

them has come to be and how many numbers have combined to make it up.[89] Now the form that's *first*, and is the smallest in structure, shall begin, whose element is the triangle that has its hypotenuse double the length of its lesser side; and when two together of such triangles are put E   together along their hypotenuses, and this has come about three times, the hypotenuses and the lesser sides all tending toward the same point as center, from those triangles (six in number) one equilateral triangle has been born. And when four equilateral triangles are constructed so that three plane angles together meet in a point, they make one solid angle, 55A   which is next in order of birth to the most obtuse of plane angles;[90] and when four such angles are completed, there is constructed the first solid form, which divides the whole surface of a circumscribed sphere into equal and similar parts. The *second* solid form comes from the same triangles, but they combined in groups of eight equilateral triangles and fashioned a solid angle composed of four planes; and when six such solid angles were born, then the second body in turn thus had its end. The B   *third* form comes from twice sixty of the elemental triangles that have been compounded, and from twelve solid angles, each comprehended by five plane equilateral triangles; and it has been born having twenty equilateral triangles for its bases.[91]

And one of the two elementary triangles had acquitted itself once it had begotten these three forms, while the isosceles triangle went on to beget the nature of the *fourth*—the isosceles triangles combining in groups of four, leading their right angles to the center, thus having fashioned one equilateral quadrangle; and six such quadrangles, once C   they've been compounded, produced eight solid angles, each joined together from three plane right angles; and the figure of the constructed body was born cubic, having six plane equilateral quadrangles for its bases. But since there was still one more structure—the *fifth*—the god used it up for the all by depicting various animals on it.[92]

---

[89]   The numbers here perhaps refer to the number of elementary triangles that compose a given solid, or else the number of faces or angles.

[90]   The most obtuse angle is our angle of **180** degrees. The angle "next in order of birth" is produced when this plane angle springs into the third dimension as the meeting of three **60**-degree angles.

[91]   What we call the faces of the various solids are *baseis*, literally, bases on which the figure can stand.

[92]   Timaeus has constructed four of the five regular Platonic solids without naming them. They are, in order of construction, the **tetrahedron** or pyramid, the **octahedron**, the **icosahedron** and the **cube**. They will soon be assigned, respectively, to fire, air, water and earth. The fifth, the **dodecahedron**, has twelve regular pentagonal faces that cannot be constructed out of Timaeus' elementary triangles. The number twelve suggests the "animals"

Now in reasoning about all these things, someone would do so musically[93] if he raised the following point: perplexed as to whether he should say that there are indefinitely many cosmoses or that they're finite in number, he would consider the former decree to be that of someone genuinely inexperienced in matters in which he should be experienced.[94] But as to whether it's appropriate to say that cosmoses are truly by nature one or five—if that's the stand he took, then he'd be more suitably[95] perplexed. So then, in keeping with the likely account, our point of view discloses that the cosmos is by nature one god,[96] while someone else, having looked elsewhere to different considerations, will hold other opinions.

Let this fellow too be dismissed, and let us assign the kinds that have just now been born through our account to fire and earth and water and air. To earth, then, let us give the cubic form, since earth is the most immobile of the four kinds and the most malleable of bodies, and it's a necessity that the body having the most secure bases be this sort of thing most of all. But of the triangles we hypothesized at the beginning, the base of the one with equal sides is by nature more secure than that with unequal sides; and the plane figure put together out of the former triangle—the equilateral quadrangle—is of necessity, in its parts and as a whole, more steadfastly based than the equilateral triangle. That's why, in assigning this form to earth, we are preserving the likely account; and of the remaining forms in turn, the least mobile form to water, the most mobile to fire, and the one in the middle to air; and the smallest body to fire, and the largest in turn to water, and the one in the middle to air; and again, the sharpest to fire, the second in sharpness to air, and the third to water. Now then, with respect to all these forms, it's a necessity for that which has the fewest bases to be by nature the most

D

E

56A

B

---

of the Zodiac, although the decoration of the all no doubt includes all the constellations. In the *Phaedo*, Socrates says that the true Earth "looks just like those twelve-piece leather balls" (110B). Its shape, like the shape of the all in the *Timaeus*, is that of a flexible dodecahedron expanded to form a sphere. Of all the solids, the dodecahedron most closely approximates a sphere in volume. For pictures of the regular solids, see Appendix C.

[93] *emmelôs*, literally, in a way that was in tune. See Glossary under **musically**.

[94] Timaeus is playing on the double meaning of *apeiros*, which means both indefinite (without a *peras* or limit) and inexperienced (without *peira* or experience).

[95] "Suitably" here is *eikotôs*, which is related to the adjective *eikôs*, likely.

[96] Bury and Archer-Hind delete the word *theon*, god, from the Greek sentence. Cornford is reliable here: the *auton* (him) refers to the cosmos itself, which earlier had been called "a happy god" (34B).

mobile, being in every way the most cutting and sharpest of them all; and furthermore, it's the lightest, having been constructed out of the fewest self-same parts; and the second must have these same things to a second degree, and the third third.

Now, in keeping with the correct account—and the likely one—let that solid which was born in the form of the pyramid be element and seed of fire; and the second in order of birth let us call element and seed of air, and the third of water. Now one must think of all these as being so small that none of them, taken singly each in its own individual kind, is seen by us because of their smallness; but when many have been gathered together, then we do see the masses of them. And in particular, with respect to the proportions concerning their quantities and their motions as well as their other powers, one must think that when these had been perfected by the god with precision, wherever the nature of necessity—willingly and upon being persuaded—yielded, there he joined them together everywhere in due proportion.

From all that we've said before about the kinds, here's how it would be according to what's most likely. Earth, when it happens to run into fire and has been thoroughly dissolved by its sharpness, would keep coursing along, whether it might happen to be dissolved in fire all by itself or in a mass of air or water, until its particles, when they happen to have run into each other somewhere and are themselves rejoined with themselves, again become earth—for surely earth would never go into another form. And water, when partitioned by fire or even by air, allows of becoming, once its parts have combined, one body of fire and two of air. And the sections of air that arise out of one particle that's dissolved would become two bodies of fire. And again, whenever fire is surrounded by air and waters, or by some earth—a little of it in a lot—and moving within them as they course along and fighting with them, it is defeated and utterly shattered, then two bodies of fire combine as one form of air. And when air has been mastered and minced up, then from two wholes of air and a half, one whole form of water will be compounded.

Now then, let's reason it all out again in the following way: whenever some one of the other kinds, caught within fire, is cut up by it through the sharpness of its angles and the edge of its sides, then, once reconstructed back into its nature, it ceases being cut. For each kind that's similar and the same as itself is able neither to make some change occur in, nor suffer something from, a kind that's in a self-same and similar condition; but in the process of passing into some other kind, so long as it fights as a weaker with a stronger, then it doesn't cease being dissolved. Again, when a few of the smaller bodies are surrounded by many larger ones and are thoroughly broken up and quenched, then, if

C

D

E

57A

B   they're willing to be reconstructed into the look of the mastering kind, they've ceased being quenched, and from fire is born air, and from air water. But if these smaller bodies go up against air or water[97] and one of the other kinds engages them and fights, then they don't cease to be dissolved until either they're altogether driven out and thoroughly dissolved and seek refuge with their kindred, or else, having been conquered, they become one out of many and, similar to the mastering kind, abide with it as a fellow countryman. Furthermore, in accordance with

C   all these affections, they all exchange their places; for while the bulks of each kind stand apart in their own private region through the motion of the receiver, yet those that from time to time become dissimilar to themselves and similar to others are carried, because of the shaking, toward the region of those to which they've been made similar.

Through such causes, then, have all the unmixed and primary bodies come to be; but for the implanting of other kinds within their forms, one must hold responsible[98] the structure of either of the elemen-

D   tary triangles, each such structure having implanted at the beginning not a triangle having only one size, but triangles of both lesser and greater sizes, whose number is as great as that of the kinds within the forms.[99] Which is exactly why these triangles, when mixed together with themselves and one another, are indefinite in their variety; and it's of just this variety that those who are to use a likely account concerning nature must become observers.[100]

As for what relates to motion and rest, unless someone's going to give his thorough agreement about the manner and conditions in which

E   these two come about, much would get in the way of the reasoning to come. To be sure, some of what relates to them has already been talked about, but there's the following in addition: motion is never willing to be present in uniformity. For it is difficult, or rather impossible, for that which is to be moved to be without that which is to move, or for that which is to move to be without that which is to be moved: there is

---

[97]   Reading, with Cornford, *tauta* for Burnet's *t'auta*, where *tauta*, these, refers to air and water.

[98]   "One must hold responsible" here is *aitiateon*, which is related to *aition*: cause, blame or accusation. See Glossary under **cause**.

[99]   See Cornford for a detailed account of this gradation in the size of the elementary bodies (pp. 230-239).

[100]   "Observers" is *theôrous*, from *theasthai*, to view, behold or be a spectator. A *theôros* is a spectator or, more specifically, an ambassador entrusted by the city to visit the oracle and bring back an accurate report. A *theôria* can be the embassy itself (see *Phaedo* 58C). It is also the activity of philosophic contemplation (as in Aristotle).

no motion if these are absent, and it's impossible for these ever to be uniform. In this way, then, let us always put rest in uniformity, but motion in non-uniformity; moreover, the cause of the non-uniform nature is inequality. And we've gone through the birth of inequality, but we didn't say how it is that these several bodies have never been completely separated off according to their kinds and ceased their motion and coursing through one another. So we shall go back and declare the following. Since the circuit of the all embraced the kinds, and since it's circular and by nature wants to come together upon itself, it squeezes them all together and allows no empty place whatsoever to be left. Which is exactly why fire most of all has permeated all things; and to a second degree air, since it sprouted as the second in fineness; and so on with the others, for those born from the largest parts have left remaining in their structure the largest void, and those with the smallest parts the least. Now the coming-together that results from the compression pushes the small bodies into the gaps in the large ones. So when small bodies are put next to large ones, and the lesser disintegrate the greater, while the greater integrate the lesser, then they're all carried up and down into their own regions, for by changing size each also changes the position of its region. Thus, precisely for these reasons, the birth of non-uniformity, which is continually being preserved, constantly provides that the continual motion of these bodies both *is* and *shall be*.

Now after all this, one must note that there have come to be many kinds of fire: flame, for example, and that which emanates from flame and doesn't burn but provides light for the eyes, and that which is left over among its embers, when flame's put out. And likewise for air, there's the most unpolluted kind called by the name "aether," and the murkiest, "fog" and "gloom," and other forms that are nameless and have been born through the inequality of their triangles. And the kinds of water are primarily twofold: the one its liquid kind, the other its molten. Now the liquid kind, because it partakes of the kinds of water that have small particles and that are unequal, has been born with a tendency to move, both in itself and by the action of some other, through its non-uniformity and the look of its figure; but the other kind, constructed out of large and uniform particles, is more steadfast than the former as well as heavy, having been compacted by its uniformity. And when fire comes in and thoroughly dissolves it, then the water casts off its uniformity; and, once it loses this uniformity, it partakes more of motion; and having grown more mobile, it's pushed by the air nearby and extends itself over the ground. It has taken on a name for each affection: "melting" for the breaking down of its masses, "flow" for its spreading over the ground. And again, when fire rushes out from the water, since it doesn't go out into a void, the air

58A

B

C

D

E

59A

nearby is pushed by it and in turn pushes together the liquid mass (which is still mobile) into the seats of the fire and mixes it together with itself; and the liquid mass, being thus pushed together and again taking back its uniformity, settles down into self-sameness, inasmuch as the fire—the craftsman of its non-uniformity—goes off. The departure of the fire has been termed "cooling," while the coming-together that arises when fire leaves is the kind that's termed "congealed."

B   Now of all the kinds of water we called "molten," that which is densest and born from the finest and most uniform particles, unique in its kind, imparted with a glittering and yellow color, and yes, the most highly prized possession is "gold," which has been sifted through rocks and has congealed there; and the offshoot of gold, which is very hard because of its density and has been blackened, has been called "adamant." Then there's the kind that's close to gold in its parts but has more forms than one; in density, it's denser than gold, and it's harder

C because it partakes of a small and fine portion of earth, but it's lighter by virtue of its having large interstices inside itself. This one kind of the brilliant and congealed waters, once constructed, has become "bronze"; and the portion of earth that's been mixed with it, whenever the two become old and again separate from each other, becomes manifest all by itself and is called "rust."

    As for the rest of this sort of thing, it's not at all complicated[101] to reason it out further—that is, for one who pursues the look of likely stories. And whenever, for the sake of a rest, a man puts down[102] accounts about things that always *are* and peruses likely accounts about becoming, thereby gaining a pleasure not to be repented of, then he would make within his life a temperate and prudent sort of play. So now too, giving

D free rein to this very play, we shall proceed as follows to the likelihoods next in order about these same things.

    The water that's been mixed with fire—all of it that's fine and fluid—is called "fluid" because of its motion and the way it rolls along on the ground;[103] and moreover, it's soft by virtue of the fact that its bases give way, since they're less sedentary than those of earth. Whenever this

E kind has been separated off from fire and deserted by air, it has become more uniform, but it's been pushed together into itself by them when they leave; and once congealed in this way, the part of it that's *above* the

---

[101]   "Complicated" here is *poikilon*, which means various, colorful or intricate.

[102]   The verb Timaeus uses here (*katathemenos*) can mean put aside, store in a safe place, or bury.

[103]   Timaeus derives *hygron* (moist or fluid) from the phrase *hyper gên rheon* (flowing over the earth).

ground and has most suffered all this is called "hail"; and the part that's *on* the ground is called "ice"; and the part that's less congealed and is still only semi-solid is in turn called "snow" when it's above the ground but "hoarfrost" when it's congealed on the ground and has been born from dew.

60A As for most forms of water that have been mixed with one another, those that have been sifted through earth-grown plants take the name of the kind as a whole and are called "saps." But since each has taken on dissimilarity because of the mixings, they've provided many various, unnamed kinds; but four of them—the forms that are fiery and have become especially apparent—have taken on names. One, which is capable of heating the soul along with the body, is "wine"; another, which is smooth and capable of dividing the visual stream and for that reason shows itself as brilliant to look at and glistening and shiny, is the form of "oil," which includes pitch and castor oil and olive oil itself

B and all the rest that have the same power. And the kind that is capable of relaxing the contracted parts around the mouth back to their natural condition, and by means of this power brings forth sweetness, has taken on a general term that covers all cases: "honey." Then the foamy kind, which is capable of dissolving the flesh by burning it and is separate from all the other saps, has been named "verjuice."[104]

Of the forms of earth, the one that's been filtered through water becomes a stony body in some such manner as this. Whenever the

C water that's mixed with it has been broken up in the process of mixing, it changes into the look of air; and having become air, it rushes back up into its own region. But no void whatsoever surrounded it, so it pushed the neighboring air; and the air, insofar as it's heavy, having been pushed and poured around the mass of earth, pressed it hard and pushed it together into the seats from which the new air was going up; and when earth's been pushed together like this by air so as to be indissoluble by water, it composes stone, the more beautiful of which is the transparent earth that comes from equal and uniform parts, and the baser earth is the opposite. And the kind from which all the moister part has been snatched away by swift fire, and which is more brittle in its

D structure than the first kind, has become that which, in kind, we've given the name "earthenware." But sometimes, whenever some moisture's been left over, once earth has become fused by fire and then cooled, it becomes the stone that has a black color. Then again, there are the two kinds which, after the mixture, are isolated in the same way from a lot of water. These are salty, being made of finer parts of earth, and have

---

[104] Bury conjectures that this is a kind of fig-juice. See Archer-Hind's note (page 218).

become semi-solid and again soluble by water. And one of them is the kind capable of purging oil and earth—"lye"—while the other, which fits nicely with the combinations of taste-sensations in the mouth, has become the body which, as the customary saying goes, is "dear to the gods"—"salt."[105]

As for the combined bodies that are made of both earth and water and are dissoluble not by water but by fire, they become thus compacted in the following way. Fire and air do not melt masses of earth, for inasmuch as their particles are by nature smaller than the gaps in the structure of earth, the particles go through a lot of free space without forcing their way; and so, in having left earth undissolved, they allow it to be unmelted. But since the parts of water are by nature larger, they make a forced path for themselves and, in dissolving earth, melt it. For earth, when it's not held together by force, is dissolved in this way only by water; and when it has been held together, it's not dissolved by anything except fire, for no entrance has been left for anything except fire. Again water's most forcible cohesion is dispersed by fire alone, while its weaker by both, by fire and air: air acting by way of water's gaps, and fire by acting also on the triangles; and air that's held together by force is in no way dissolved, except according to its element; and air that's unforced is melted down by fire alone.

As for the bodies that are mixed together out of earth and water, so long as water occupies the gaps in earth that are compressed by force, the parts of water that come in from the outside and have no entrance and so flow around the whole mass, leave it unmelted; but the parts of fire that enter into the gaps left by the parts of water produce in water the very effects that water produces in earth; and these parts of fire turn out to be the only causes for the flowing of the combined body once it's been melted. These combinations of earth and water happen to be the following. Those that have less water than earth are the entire kind relating to "glass," and as many forms of stones that are called "molten"; while those that have more water are in turn all those bodies that are congealed as wax and incense.

And so, the forms, which have been embellished with a variety of figures, combinations and transformations into each other, have pretty much been displayed; but one must attempt to bring to light the causes through which their affections have been born. Now first of all, it's necessary that sensing must always belong to the things being talked about, although we haven't yet gone through the birth of flesh and

---

[105] In Homer salt is called divine (*Iliad* 9.214). I have retained the *nomou* (of convention) bracketed in Burnet's text.

D   whatever relates to flesh, nor of soul, however much of her is mortal. But it happens that these things are not capable of being adequately spoken about apart from the affections related to sensing, nor is it possible for these affections to be spoken about without those other things, while to speak about both at once is hardly possible.[106] So one or the other of these must be set down as a hypothesis first, and then we'll go back once more to what's been hypothesized. Therefore, so that the affections may be spoken of in order after the births, let the things that *are* concerning body and soul be what we set down first.

E   First of all, then, let's see why we call fire "hot," investigating as follows—by having noted the dividing and cutting that arises from it in relation to our body. That fire's affection is somehow sharp, all of us pretty much sense; but as for the fineness of its sides and the acuteness of its angles and the smallness of its portions and the swiftness of its

62A course, for all of which reasons fire is intense and keen and always acutely cuts what it encounters—all this must be reasoned out by recollecting the birth of its figure, how that nature most of all, by dividing up our bodies and mincing them up minutely, provides, as is likely, both that affection we now call "heat" and the name.[107]

And the affection contrary to this is quite plain; but, nevertheless, let it in no way lack an account. Now when the larger particles of fluids that surround our body come into it, they push out the smaller particles,

B   but since they're not able to go into their seats, they compress the moisture within us and congeal it by making out of what was non-uniform and moved something unmoved through uniformity and compression; but that which is being contracted against nature fights, in accordance with its nature, and itself pushes itself back in the contrary direction. To this very fighting and shaking the names "trembling" and "shivering" were assigned; and this entire affection, as well as what acts to bring it about, has the name "cold."

And "hard" is assigned to all those things to which our flesh gives way, and "soft" to whatever gives way to our flesh, and the terms are thus used relative to one another. And whatever gives way stands on a small

C   base, but when it's made of quadrangular bases, since it's firmly based, it is most obstinate in form as is anything that's especially resistant because of its contracting to maximum density.

---

[106]   This is one of many points at which Timaeus grapples with the difficulty of establishing a strictly linear progression in his account of the cosmos.

[107]   Another of Timaeus' many name-games like the ones we find in the *Cratylus*. Here the word for heat (*thermon*, which resembles *kermon*) is playfully derived from *kermatizein*, to mince up.

And "heavy" and "light" would be most plainly revealed if examined along with the nature of so-called "above" and "below." Now it is in no way correct to think that there are by nature two definite and contrary regions that have divided the all in two—one the "below," toward which all things that have some bodily mass are born; and the other the "above," toward which everything goes unwillingly.[108] For

D   since the entire heaven is spheroform, its extremities, which have all taken their stand equally from the center, should themselves be by nature similarly extreme; and the center, which has stood apart from the extremes in the same measure, must be thought to be directly opposite to all of them. Now since the cosmos is this way by nature, which of the points just mentioned could someone set down as "above" or "below" and not seem in any court of law to utter a name that's in no way suitable? For the inner, central region of the cosmos is justly called neither "below" nor "above" by nature but rather "at the center"; and surely the circumference is neither central nor does it have any

E   one part of itself that's different from another with respect to the distance either to the center or to parts directly opposite to it. And since the cosmos is by nature everywhere similarly disposed, what sort of contrary names could someone apply to it anywhere and still consider himself to speak beautifully? For if, furthermore, there should be some solid body equally balanced at the center of the all, then, because of

63A   the similarity of the extremes everywhere, this body would never be carried to any of those extremes; on the contrary, if someone were to travel around it in a circle, he'd often call the same part "below" and "above" when he stood at antipodal positions. For since the whole, as was said just now, is spheroform, to say that it has a certain region below and another above just doesn't hold for anyone who's thoughtful.[109]

B   But as for where these names have come from and in what circumstances we've been habituated to use them when we speak about even the heaven as a whole by dividing it into these two regions—this we must thoroughly agree on by hypothesizing the following. Suppose someone were to step up onto that region of the all which the nature of fire most of all has been allotted, even to that region where the fire

---

[108] The sentence begins with *physei* (by nature) and ends with *nomizein* (to acknowledge), which can mean "adopt as one's custom" (from *nomos*, law or custom). Timaeus is telling us not to avoid all customary accounts of cosmic place, but to be careful that we adopt the *right* customs of thought.

[109] In his discussion of heavy and light in *On the Heavens*, Aristotle defends the use of the terms "above" and "below" (4.1). To deny that there is an up or down in the heaven, he says, paraphrasing this very sentence from the *Timaeus*, is *atopon*, placeless or absurd (308A17).

to which all fires are carried has been gathered in the greatest amount, and suppose, if he had the power to do this, he could stand there and separate parts of the fire and put them on scales, then when he raises

C   the beam and forcibly drags the fire into dissimilar air, I suppose it's plain that the lesser amount will be more easily forced than the greater; for if a pair of masses are lifted up at the same time by a single thrust, it's a necessity, I suppose, that the lesser one follow along with the force more, and the greater one less, because it strains against the force; and the one there's a lot of is called "heavy" and is carried "down," while the one that's small is called "light" and is carried "up." Now this same thing is what we must catch ourselves in the act of doing in this region here. For walking as we do upon the earth, when we detach various kinds of earthy chunks, and sometimes even earth itself,[110] we drag them into dissimilar air by force and against nature, since both these

D   kinds cling to their kindred; and as we force it into what's dissimilar, the smaller amount follows us along more easily and sooner than the larger; and therefore we refer to it as "light," and the region into which we force it "above," and the affection contrary to these we call "heavy" and "below."

It's a necessity, then, that these affections are differently disposed in their relation to one another, because the bulks of the different kinds occupy regions contrary to one another. For when we compare what's

E   light in one region with what's nimble in the contrary region, and the heavy with the heavy, the below with the below, and the above with the above, it will be discovered that they all become, and are, contrary and skewed and totally different in their relation to one another. There is, however, at least one thing to be noticed about them all: that the path of each of the kinds toward its kin makes the carried body "heavy" and the region to which such a body's carried "below," while contrary conditions make for contrary results. So, concerning these affections in turn, let these be stated as their causes.

Again, of the affections "smooth" and "rough," I suppose every-

64A   one, on seeing the cause, might be able to tell it to another, for hardness mixed with non-uniformity produces the one, and uniformity mixed with density the other.

As for the affections common to the body as a whole, the greatest topic still remains to be discussed, that is, the cause of the pleasures and pains among the affections we've gone through and all the affections that have attained to sensations throughout the body's parts and have within themselves pains and pleasures that simultaneously attend

---

[110]   In excavation.

these sensations. Therefore, let's take up the causes in connection with every sensed, as well as unsensed, affection in this way: by recollecting how, in what was said before, we distinguished between the nature of what's easy to move and that of what's hard to move, for this is exactly how everything we have in mind to grasp must be tracked down. Now as for what's by nature easy to move, whenever even a slight affection invades it, its particles keep producing the same effect by transmitting it, the one to the other, in a circle, up to the very point that they reach the prudent part[111] and report the agent's power. But the contrary sort of thing, since it's steadfast and doesn't at all go in a circle, is only passive, and it doesn't move anything among its neighbors, so that, since the particles don't transmit the first affection among themselves, one to the others, they make the affection unmoved in the animal as a whole, and the animal in this way becomes insensible. This is the case concerning bones and hair and all the other parts in us that are mostly earthy, whereas the former description especially applies to the organs of vision and hearing because they contain within themselves the greatest power of fire and air.

Now one must think of pleasure and pain in the following way. An affection that's against nature and forceful and that arises in us suddenly is painful, while the sudden going back again to nature is pleasant; and an affection that's mild and gradual is unsensed, and the contrary sort is sensed. And the affection that arises with the greatest ease is sensed in the greatest degree but doesn't partake of pain and pleasure, for example, the affections that have to do with the visual stream itself, which was said in the previous discussion to arise in the daytime as a body one in nature with ourselves. For in this case, cuttings and burnings and whatever else the stream suffers do not produce pains in it, nor pleasures either when it goes back again to its same form; but its sensations are strongest and clearest according to what it's affected by and whatever it itself touches on somewhere and strikes, since there is no force at all either in the vision's dilation or in its contraction. But bodies made of greater parts, since they yield only with difficulty to the agent and transmit their motions to the whole, do have pleasures and pains—pains when the bodies are estranged from their self-sameness, pleasures when they are settled back into it. And all bodies that have suffered gradual withdrawals from themselves and voidings, but refills that are intense and large-scale, becoming insensible of the voiding but sensible of the refilling, do not provide pains for the mortal part of the soul, but only the greatest pleasures; this is especially clear in the case of perfumes. But all bodies that undergo sudden estrangement from

---

[111] *to phronimon.*

B   themselves and are settled back into sameness with themselves gradually and with difficulty, render all the effects contrary to what was said
before; and again, it's quite plain that this is what happens in the case
of the body's burns and cuts.

Now the affections common to the entire body, as well as all the
names that have arisen for their agents, have pretty much been discussed.
But the attempt must be made, if we are in any way able, to describe what
comes about in our particular parts—both the affections and again the
causes of what does the affecting.

C   First, then, all the affections having to do with tastes (which we left
out of our previous discussion), that is, affections which are particular
to the tongue, must be brought to light as far as possible. It appears that
these too, like many other things as well, arise through certain contractions and dilations and, in addition, have more to do with roughness
and smoothness than the other sensations. For when all the earthy parts
D   that enter the area around the small veins (which act just like probes for
the tongue and have stretched all the way to the heart) impinge on the
moist and soft particles of flesh, as they're melted down, they contract
and dry up the small veins; and these parts, when more rough, appear
as "sour," and when less rough as "tangy." And as for the parts that are
capable of acting on the veins like cleaners by washing off the whole area
around the tongue, when they do this beyond measure and lay hold of
E   the tongue so as to melt away its nature (like the power of soda), they are
all thus named "bitter," while those parts that are less strong than the
soda-like condition and bring about the cleansing within measure are
"salty" without the rough bitterness and make a more friendly impres-
sion on us. As for those parts that have shared in the heat of the mouth
and are made smooth by it, when they're fully fired up and themselves
burn back in turn the thing that heated them, they're carried upward
due to their lightness toward the senses of the head, and they cut all the
66A   particles on which they impinge. On account of these powers, all such
things have been called "pungent."

Again, there are particles that have been worn thin by putrefaction
and slip into the narrow veins, being proportionate to the earthy parts
there within and also to whatever parts of air are in that same place,
so as to make them churned and to move around one another; and, in
being churned in this way, they surround one another and, as parts of
one sort slip into parts of others, produce hollows that stretch around
B   the incoming particles—which hollows, once a moist film (sometimes
earthy, sometimes pure) has been stretched around air, become moist,
hollow, round and watery reservoirs of air; and the ones enclosing
transparent reservoirs of pure moisture have been called by the name

"bubbles," but those of an earthy moisture, which moves and rises all at once, have been spoken of with the surnames "fizzing" and "fermenting," and the cause of these affections has been termed "acid."[112]

C   An affection that's contrary to everything that's been said about these previous things comes about by a contrary explanation. Whenever the structure of the entering particles in liquids is by nature kindred with the condition of the tongue, these particles lubricate and smooth over the rougher parts, sometimes constricting, sometimes relaxing parts that are unnaturally dilated or contracted; and they settle everything as much as possible in accordance with nature. And every such remedy for the forceful affections, becoming pleasurable and dear to everyone, has been called "sweet."

D   So that's how it is with tastes. But now, as for the power of the nostrils, there aren't any forms in it. For the entirety of smells is a sort of half-breed, and it turns out that in no form is there a proportionality for having any smell; but on the contrary, our small veins around these parts had too narrow a construction for the kinds earth and water, and too wide a construction for the kinds fire and air, which is why no one has ever sensed any smell at all from any of these, but smells arise only

E   from bodies that are either moistened or putrefied or melted or evaporated. For when water is changing into air and air into water, smells arise during the intermediate state, and all these smells are either vapor or mist—mist in going from air into water, vapor when it's from water into air. Whence it follows that all smells taken together have come to be finer than water but thicker than air. This is made plain whenever anyone who's had some blockage in his breathing forcibly draws breath into himself, for at that time no smell at all filters through along with it, but the breath itself follows alone bereft of smells.

67A   For these reasons, then, the varieties of smells have been born nameless, since they don't come from forms either definite in number or simple. But let them be spoken of here in a twofold way—the "pleasant" and the "painful"—the only pair of terms that applies to them with any clarity, the one roughening and acting forcibly on the whole cavity that lies between our head and navel, the other softening this same area and restoring it with contentment to its natural condition.

---

[112]   On the difficulty of construing this long, convoluted sentence, see Taylor, pp. 467-9. Language here seems to be churning along with the physical process being described. Here, as in many other places in his speech, Timaeus lays particular stress on the human act of assigning conventional names to natural things and processes. To the man on the street, a bubble is just a bubble; to the natural philosopher, it is understood technically (and somewhat comically) as *a transparent reservoir of pure moisture formed when particles of water enclose particles of air.*

B   And a third sensory part that's within us, and which has to do with hearing, must be spoken of, as we examine the causes through which the affections related to this sense come about. On the whole, therefore, let us posit sound as the blow transmitted through the ears by the action of air upon brain and blood and reaching all the way to soul; the motion produced by this blow beginning in the head and ending around the seat of the liver is *hearing*; and insofar as the blow is swift, the sound is high-pitched, and insofar as it's slower, lower; and even motion produces a uniform and smooth sound, but the contrary motion a rough sound;

C   and a big motion produces a lot of sound, but insofar as it's contrary to this, a small one. And as for the concords of sounds, it's necessary that they be spoken about at a later point in our account.

Now a fourth sensory kind is still left for us, which must be divided up, since it's acquired a great many variations[113] within itself, all of which collectively we've called "colors"—color being a flame that flows from individual bodies and having parts proportionate to our vision so as to produce sensation. At an earlier point, the causes of the birth of vision

D   had been addressed. Here, therefore, in the case of colors, it would be most suitable and fitting to go through them too with a reasonable account.[114]

Of the parts that are carried off from the rest and impinge on the visual stream, some are less than, some greater than, and some equal to the parts of the visual stream itself. Now the ones that are equal are unsensed; and we in fact call these parts "transparent," while the greater and lesser parts (the former contracting and the latter dilating the visual stream) are brothers[115] of the hot and cold particles that pertain to flesh, and of the sour particles that are tongue-related, and of all the

E   heat-producing particles that we've called "pungent." These brothers are "white" and "black," affections born of contractions and dilations and the same as those other affections we mentioned, although they belong

---

113   "Variations" here are *poikilmata*. A *poikilma* is anything wrought in various colors or embroidered. Earlier, Timaeus had used similar color-related words to describe the receptacle as something capable of taking on imprints "sufficiently various with every variety to be seen" (50D). And at 59C, we are told that an explanation of physical phenomena is no longer "complicated" or "colorful" (*poikilon*) so long as one sticks to likely stories. Do likely stories in some way take the color out of the world? Compare Rule 12 of Descartes' *Rules for the Direction of the Mind*, where Descartes replaces white, blue and red with arrangements of straight lines.

114   "Suitable" here is *eikos*, and "reasonable" is *epieikei*. See Glossary under **likeness**.

115   Timaeus had used this language of brothers earlier at 45B, also in reference to the visual stream.

to a different kind and, on account of that cause, are different in how they show themselves. So here's how they must be addressed: that which is able to dilate the visual stream is "white," while that which is able to do the opposite is "black."

68A

And when the more piercing course of a different kind of fire attacks and dilates the visual stream all the way to the eyes, and forces its way to the very passages within the eyeballs and melts them, it pours out from there a mix of fire and water—what we call a "tear." This piercing motion, which is itself fire, encounters fire coming from the opposite direction; and as the one fire leaps forth from the eyes like a lightning-flash and the other enters them and is quenched in the surrounding moisture, all manner of colors are born through this melee; and we call this affection "dazzling," while to that which produces it

B

we give the names "brilliant"[116] and "glittering." Again, when the kind of fire that's between the extremes of white and dazzling reaches to the moist part of the eyes and is blended with that part, then it isn't glittering; but, because the fire's ray shines through the moisture it's mixed with, it produces a bloody color, which we call by the name "red." And "brilliant" mixed with "red" and "white" becomes "yellow-orange."[117] But to say in what proportions these have been mixed, even if someone knew, doesn't make sense, since one wouldn't be able, even moderately, either to state any necessity for it or give the likely account.

C

Now red blended with black and white is "purple," but "violet" when the mixture's burnt more and blended together with black. And "tawny" is born from the blending of yellow-orange and gray; and "gray" from white and black; and "amber" from white mixed with yellow-orange. And when white goes together with brilliant and is steeped in intense black, a "steely blue" color is produced; but when steely blue is

D

blended with white, then "light blue"; but when tawny is blended with black, then "green."[118] As for the rest of the colors, it's fairly plain from

---

[116] This is the word Socrates had used to describe the feast of speech outlined by Critias (27A-B).

[117] Yellow-orange here (*xanthos*) "is an epithet of ripe corn, of gold, of honey, of wines, and of hair" (Taylor, pp. 483-4). It is a golden yellow or even auburn. For a full account of early theories of color-vision, see Taylor, pp. 485-491.

[118] Taylor calls this account of the color green "the most puzzling of all Timaeus' statements." He goes on to say: "Why [green] should be supposed to be produced by a combination of a kind of red with black is a mystery" (p. 485). As Taylor observes, this unlikely explanation comes right before Timaeus' unusually strong emphasis on "the merely conjectural character of his color-equations."

these cases with what mixtures they're to be portrayed if one is to preserve the likely story. But if, in investigating these matters, someone were to make a test of all this through experiment, he would only show his ignorance of the difference between the human and the divine nature: that it is god who is sufficiently knowledgeable, and also able, to blend together the many into a one and again in turn to dissolve a one into a many, but no one among humans either is now or ever will be in the future sufficient for either of these.[119]

E   Once all these things had by nature come to be in this way from necessity, the craftsman of the most beautiful and best within things born then proceeded to take them over when he was begetting the self-sufficient and most perfect god, using their relevant causes as his servants, while he himself was building the good[120] in all things born. For this very reason one should mark off two forms of cause—the necessary
69A   and the divine—and seek the divine in all things for the sake of gaining a happy life, to the extent that our nature allows, and the necessary for the sake of those divine things, reasoning that without the necessary it isn't possible to discern on their own those things we seriously pursue, nor again to apprehend them, nor to partake of them in any other way whatsoever.

So then, now that the kinds of causes have been sifted out and lie ready to hand for us, like wood[121] for builders, out of which we must weave together the account that remains, let us go back again briefly to the beginning and make our way swiftly to the same point from which
B   we arrived here; and let us now attempt to add to our story a finish and a head that's joined to what has gone before.[122]

So just as was said also at the beginning, since these things were in a condition of disorder, the god introduced proportions in them,

---

119   "Experiment" here is simply *ergon*, deed. "Test" is *basanos*, which is a touchstone by which gold is proved. In general, it is any test to determine whether something is or is not genuine and can also refer to trial by torture, that is, to inquisition. We are reminded of Bacon's exhortation to "vex" and "constrain" Nature in order to torture the secrets out of her (*Novum Organum*, translated and edited by Peter Urbach and John Gibson, [Chicago: Open Court, 1994], p. 25). Timaeus (Plato too?) warns us against such violence and presumption by reminding us of our inevitable human limits. But why should *color*, in particular, provoke so strong a warning? Why is color any more mysterious or problematic than other affections?

120   *to d'eu*. This is not the Good of the *Republic* (*to agathon*) but rather a condition of well-being.

121   The word for wood is *hylê*, Aristotle's term for matter or material.

122   The metaphor suggests that the likely story is not only a speech but also in some way a *statue*.

making each thing proportional both to itself and to the others, that is, to whatever extent and in whatever way it was possible for them to be commensurable and proportional. For at that time, things partook of none of this, except insofar as it happened by chance, nor was there

C anything at all whatsoever that was worthy of the names we now use to name things, such as "fire" or "water" or any of the others; but all these things he first put in array and only afterwards constructed out of them this all—one animal that holds within itself all animals both mortal and immortal. And he himself becomes craftsman of things divine, but the birth of things mortal he ordered his own offspring to craft. Imitating him, and having taken over the immortal principle of soul, they next sculpted around it a mortal body and gave it all the

D body for its chariot; and they housed within this entire body another form of soul, the mortal form, which has within itself affections terrible and necessary: first pleasure, evil's greatest lure; then, pains, deserters of goods; and yet again, rashness and fear, thoughtless counselors the pair of them; and anger, difficult to appease; and hope, easy to seduce; and having blended them all together with irrational sensation and all-venturing love, they put together the mortal kind, as was necessary.

And for these very reasons, they, in reverential fear of defiling the divine, and doing so only if this was an utter necessity, go about

E settling the mortal kind separate from it and in another dwelling of the body, having walled off an isthmus and boundary for the head and the chest by putting a neck in between, so that they might be separate. Now within the chest region or so-called thorax they proceeded to bind the

70A mortal kind of the soul. And since one part of it is by nature better and another worse, they build the cavity of the thorax in turn in sections, as though marking off one dwelling for women and a separate one for men, by putting the midriff between them as a partition.[123] The part of the soul, therefore, that partakes of courage and spirit, because it's a lover of victory, they settled closer to the head, between the midriff and neck, so that it might hearken to reason and, making common cause with it, forcibly keep down the class of desires, whenever they might in

B no way wish to give willing obedience to the command and word from the citadel.[124] Now the heart, which is the junction of the veins and wellspring of the blood that vigorously sweeps around through all the limbs, they positioned in the guardhouse in order that, whenever the

---

[123] Timaeus adopts the three-part soul described in the *Republic* (4. 435B ff.).

[124] The citadel is, in Greek, the *Acropolis* or "heights" of the city. Aristotle makes the *heart* the citadel because it supplies the animal with heat (*Parts of Animals* 3.7.670a24). "Word" here is *logos*, which also means reason. See Glossary under **speech**.

ferocity of spirit might boil up, as soon as reason sends word that some unjust action is arising that involves these limbs, either from outside or even some action from the desires within, then, by way of all the narrow vessels, every sense-faculty in the body might grow acutely sensible of both the exhortations and threats and in all ways give heed to them, thus allowing the best part among them all to be leader.

C   Now for the leaping of the heart in anticipation of terrors and for the awakening of spirit, the gods, knowing beforehand that all such swelling of the impassioned parts[125] comes about through fire, contrived assistance for it and implanted the look of the lungs, which, in the first place, is soft and bloodless, and then in addition is perforated and has within it caverns like a sponge, in order that, when it receives the breath and the drink, it might have a cooling effect and offer a "breather" and
D   relief in the burning heat. For just this reason they cut conduits from the windpipe to the lungs and placed them around the heart like padding, in order that, when spirit is at its peak, the heart, by leaping into something that yields and being cooled off, might strain less and be more able to go along with spirit in being subservient to reason.

As for that part of the soul that's desirous of food and drink and all those things it needs because of the nature of the body, they settled
E   it in between the midriff and the boundary in the navel area, building a sort of trough in that entire region for the feeding of the body; and such a thing as this they bound down there as though it were a wild beast which, because it had been tied to the rest, they were compelled to feed if indeed the mortal kind was ever going to *be* at all. In order, then, that this part, while grazing at its trough and settling as far away as possible
71A   from the counseling part, and offering the least possible clamor and roar, might let the most masterful part take counsel in peace concerning what's beneficial to all in common and to each privately—for these reasons, it was here that they gave it its post.

And since they knew that it wasn't going to understand reason, and that even if it did somehow partake of some perception of reasons, the care for any of them would not be inborn in it, but it would, at night
B   and by day, fall readily under the spell[126] of images and phantasms—god, having planned for this very thing, constructed for this part the look of

---

125   "Impassioned parts" is *tôn thymoumenôn*, which is related to *thymos* (spirit or anger).

126   *psychagôgêsoito.* This verb means, literally, would have its soul [*psychê*] led away. The verb means conduct souls to the underworld and, with respect to the living, lead away, delude or seduce. Recall the curious reference to Hades at 44C. Taylor notes that *psychagôgein* also means call up spirits, and that a *psychagôgos* was a professional ghost-raiser (p. 510).

the liver and placed it in that part's dwelling, having contrived it to be dense and smooth and brilliant and sweet and having some bitterness, in order that the power of our thoughts that courses from the intellect, moving in the liver as in a mirror, when the liver receives patterns and offers images to be looked at, might frighten this part of soul, whenever this power bore down on it with harsh threats by using a part of the liver's bitterness akin to bitter thoughts, swiftly mixing this throughout all the liver, and made bilious colors appear in it, and, by contracting it, made it all shriveled and rough. And as for the lobe and the receptacles and "gates" of the liver, by bending back the first of these from its correct position, compressing it, and by blocking up and closing the others, the thought-power provided pains and bouts of nausea. And when, in turn, some breath[127] of gentleness coming from thought painted on the liver the contrary sort of phantasms and provided peace from its bitterness by being willing neither to set in motion nor to touch the nature contrary to itself, and used on the liver the sweetness inborn in it and straightened out again all its parts, making them correct and smooth and free, then the power of thought might make the portion of soul that's settled in the area of the liver serene and cheerful, keeping to moderate pastimes at night by applying itself to divination while asleep, since of reason and prudence it had no share.

For our constructors, remembering the command of their father when he commanded them to make the mortal kind as excellent as possible, in this very way also rectified the base part of us by establishing within it the divining part,[128] in order that this part might somehow touch on truth. And a sufficient sign is that god has bestowed divination on human thoughtlessness; for no one has contact with true and inspired[129] divination when in his right mind, but only when the power

---

[127] "Breath" here is not the ordinary *pneuma* but rather *epipnoia*, a breathing upon or inspiration. True inspiration, for Timaeus, comes from reason. In the upcoming passage, the inspired utterances of divination must be rationally interpreted if they are to be of any use.

[128] *to manteion.* The word for diviner or soothsayer, *mantis*, is related to the verb *mainesthai*, to rage or be mad. Recall that the Egyptian priest in Solon's account boasted of his city's prudent study of divination and medicine (24C). At *Phaedrus* 244B ff., Socrates playfully derives the word *mantikê* (divination) from *manikê* (the art of madness). He proceeds to give an extended defense of divine madness, the highest instance of which is philosophy. The reader is strongly encouraged to compare the praise of divine madness in the *Phaedrus* with the praise of sound-mindedness here in the *Timaeus*.

[129] "Inspired" here is *entheou.* To be *entheos* is to have a god (*theos*) inside you, to be filled with a god. The noun that refers to this condition is *enthousiasmos*, from which we get our "enthusiasm."

of his prudence has been fettered in sleep, or when it has been deranged by disease or by some inspiration. But it is for one who is thoughtful to reflect on and recollect what's uttered in a dream, either while asleep or awake, under the influence of a divining and inspired nature, and to determine, by reasoning about all the phantasms seen, in what way and for whom they signify bad or good that's future, past or present; but it is not the job of one who's been raving and still remains in this state to judge the apparitions and utterances by himself. On the contrary, that saying of old puts it well: "To act and to know one's own actions and oneself befit only a sound-minded man." Whence custom too has set up the class of interpreters as judges over these inspired divinations, who are themselves given the name "diviners" by some who are totally ignorant of the fact that these men are expounders of the riddling voice and vision[130] and are not diviners at all, and that they would be most justly named "interpreters of things divined."[131]

So that's why the nature of the liver is what it is, and why it's by nature in the region that we're describing: for the sake of divination; and while each animal is still alive, such an organ contains signs that are very lucid, but when deprived of life it becomes blind and contains divinations too faint to signify anything plainly. And again, the structure of the organ that neighbors the liver, and its seat on the left, has come about for the liver's sake: to keep it always brilliant and pure, like a napkin[132] laid next to a mirror, always prepared and ready to hand. And for just this reason, whenever certain impurities arise around the liver through diseases of the body, the loose texture of the spleen purifies them all and receives them, insofar as the spleen has been woven hollow and bloodless; which is why, when it's filled up with the impurities that have come off the liver, it swells to great size and becomes festered, and

72A

B

C

D

---

[130] *phêmês kai phantasias.* Timaeus repeats the alliteration of the previous *phanenta kai phônêthenta* ("apparitions and utterances"). This may be a playful mimicry of inspired, prophetic speech.

[131] Timaeus is here playing on the literal meaning of the word *prophêtês*, which means, one who speaks for another. Cornford construes the *manteuomenôn* at the end of the sentence as referring not to the things divined but to those who practice divination (p. 288). Both readings make sense. The gods in their wisdom know better than to try to educate the low part of the soul. By giving us the gift of divination, a kind of madness, they gratify this part's tendency to be bewitched by phantasms (71A-B), at the same time making sure that the witchery ultimately leads to sobriety and reason. In divination, the divine descends to the level of the irrational in order to lift man toward the rational.

[132] *ekmageion.* Here used with a different meaning, this word had been used earlier to describe the receptacle as a molding stuff (50C).

why, conversely, whenever the body has been purified, the spleen shrinks and settles back down to the same size.

So then, as for what has to do with soul—what part of her is mortal and what divine, and where and in what company and through what reasons these have been housed separately from one another—only if god gave his consent, only then, could we insist that the truth has been spoken; but the claim that what we've said is at the very least likely must be utterly risked, both now and even more so as we continue to investigate further, and let that be our claim.

E   What comes next in order right after all this must be pursued along the same lines: the way in which the remainder of the body has come to be. Now it would be most of all fitting for it to be constructed on the basis of such reasoning as this. Those who were putting our kind together knew of the incontinence that was going to be in us over food and drink, and that because of our gluttony we would use much more than was temperate and necessary. So in order that quick destruction through diseases might not arise, and an immediate end to the still imperfect mortal kind—foreseeing this, they put in place the "lower belly," as it is named, as a receptacle[133] for the holding of superfluous food and drink;

73A and round about they coiled the growth of the intestines, so that the nourishment might not pass through swiftly and swiftly again compel the body to need other nourishment, and, by producing insatiableness through gut-gluttony, fashion the entire kind unphilosophical and uncultured—disobedient to the most divine of the things within us.[134]

B   As for what had to do with bones and flesh and everything of such a nature, here's how it was. The origin of all these things was the birth

---

133 *hypodochên.* See 49A.

134 Throughout the sentence, Timaeus uses words related to *telos*, end, in the sense of both perfection and death or destruction. Were it not for the gods' foresight, gut-gluttony (*gastrimargia*) would have been the end of us: it would have led to swift death. It would also have permanently distracted us from our true end and perfection. Recall the "food-supplying wave" that contributed to our irrationality at 43B. "Compel" here is *anankazoi*. The belly, perhaps more than any other organ, reminds us that to be mortal is to be subject to the cause and power of *anankê*, necessity. In the *Odyssey*, a poem filled with eating and being eaten, Odysseus tells King Alkinoös that "there is no other thing more dog-like than the loathsome belly, and she urges me with necessity [*anankêi*] to remember her" (7.216-17). And later in the story, Odysseus speaks of his "wretched belly, that accursed thing, who bestows many evils on humans" (17.473-4). In Timaeus' poem, the belly and intestines are providentially devised as a means of safeguarding man from this infinite desire. The anger Odysseus shows toward his lower nature in these passages is characteristic of *thymos*. To live according to the demands of necessity is to be a slave.

of the marrow, for it was in this that the bonds of life (as long as the soul's bound up with the body) gave the mortal kind its roots; but the marrow itself was born from other things. For of the primary triangles, all those that were unwarped and smooth and, through their precision,

C   especially able to produce fire and water and air and earth, these the god discriminated as separate, each apart from its own kind, and mixing them with one another in due proportion, he contrived a universal seed-stuff[135] for every mortal kind and fashioned the marrow out of them; and right after this, he planted within the marrow the various kinds of souls and bound them down; and according to how many and what sort of shapes soul in turn was going to have in her particular forms, into so many and of such sorts did he divide the marrow itself in the distribution at the beginning. And the field, as it were, that was going to

D   hold within itself the divine seed—having molded it as rounded on all sides, he bestowed on this portion of the marrow the name of "brain," intending that, when each animal had been completed, the vessel surrounding this would become the head. But that portion of the marrow that was in turn going to keep in the remaining and mortal part of the soul he divided into figures at once rounded and elongated, and all these he designated[136] "marrow," and from these, as from anchors, he cast forth bonds for all the soul, and around this stuff he proceeded to fashion our whole body, having first compacted around the whole marrow a bony shelter for it.

E   And he proceeds to construct bone in the following way. After he'd sifted earth pure and smooth, he kneaded it and soaked it with marrow; and after this, he puts it in fire; and after that, he dips it in water, and back into fire, and once more into water; and by thus transferring it often

---

[135]   *panspermian.* "The word is an old fifth-century one for a medley or 'concourse' of minute 'molecules' of different kinds" (Taylor, p. 522). Aristotle uses it in reference to the elements of Anaxagoras (*On Coming to Be and Passing Away* 1.314A29).

[136]   *epephêmisen.* The basic meaning of *epiphêmizein* is utter words ominous of the event, or give the name of a god to something (cf. *Laws* 6.771D). More generally, it means call or name and can also mean appoint. The verb appeared at 36C where the divine craftsman appointed the outer celestial circle to be the circle of the Same. Perhaps the verb in both cases indicates, simultaneously, a blessing and a curse. Positively, it refers to the privileged nature of the thing made; negatively, to the destined fall of this nature into the necessary distortions of divine circularity: just as the most authoritative circle becomes warped in the act of mortal birth, so too the marrow must accommodate not only the spherical brain but also the non-spherical shapes of every mortal kind. It contains the divine seed of intellectual activity but, in its literal fall from the brain down along the spinal column, also becomes the seed emitted in the male's sexual frenzy (91A ff.).

from the one into the other, he fashioned it to be insoluble by both. So by making full use of just this stuff, he sculpted a bony sphere out of it around the brain, and in this sphere he left a narrow passageway; and out of this bony stuff he molded vertebrae around the marrow of both the neck and back area and propped them under one another like pivots, starting from the head and extending through the entire length of the trunk. And he preserved all the seed by thus fencing it in with a stony enclosure, into which he inserted joints, applying to them the power of the Other as a mean between them for the sake of moving and bending.

But once he considered that the condition of the bony nature was, in turn, more brittle than was needful and inflexible, and that if, moreover, it became fired and cooled back down, it would gangrene and swiftly destroy the seed within itself—for these reasons, he thus went about contriving the kind of the sinews and that of the flesh, in order that, by binding together all the limbs with sinews, which tighten and relax about the pivots, he might render the body capable of bending and stretching itself out; while flesh he contrived as both a block against burning heat and a barrier against the winter cold, and furthermore, in the case of falls, so that it might gently and easily give way to bodies, just like the woolen goods we wear; and since it has a warm moisture within itself, in summer, by its sweating and wetting, it might provide a congenial coolness over the entire body; and alternately, in winter, it might in turn, by means of this fire, defend the body temperately against the frost that attacked and surrounded it from outside. With all this in mind, our wax-modeler mingled and joined together water and fire and earth; and by putting together a ferment out of acid and brine and mingling this with the previous mixture, he composed flesh, sappy and soft, while the nature of the sinews he blended together from a blend of bone and unfermented flesh, thus making a single nature out of both and intermediate in power, and he used yellow for its color. That is why sinews acquired a power that's stretchier and tougher than that of flesh, yet softer and moister than that of bone. With these the god enveloped bones and marrow; and, having bound them together with sinews, he then, from above, overshadowed[137] them all with flesh.

---

[137] The verb Timaeus uses here is *kataskiazein*, to overshadow or cover over. It is a poetic expression for the act of burial. (For the curious use of *anôthen*, from above, see Cornford's note, p. 297.) The metaphor reminds us that to be born is to have one's originally divine nature buried and imprisoned in the mortal realm of becoming. Flesh, like the earth placed over a corpse, is the shroud of our skeletons. It is ironic, to say the least, that the gods' conscientious effort to protect us from bodily harm, while keeping us as intelligent as possible, is an act that in giving us life also makes our lives death-like. The indirect reference to *skiai*, shades or shadows, suggests that the realm of becoming in which we "live" is a Hades or underworld (compare the reference to Hades at 44C).

E   All the bones, then, that had the most soul, he packed in least flesh,
while those that had the least soul inside, in the most and the densest.
And in particular, at the joints of the bones, where reason didn't show
any necessity for them to need it at all, he made grow only a little flesh,
in order that flesh, in being an impediment to the bendings of bodies,
might not render them unwieldy, inasmuch as they'd be hard to move,
and again, in order that many layers of really dense flesh, when packed
close to one another, might not make our thought-related parts more
unretentive and blunted by introducing the insensibility that results
75A   from solidity. Which is exactly why the thighs and calves, and the area
around the nature of the hips, and the bones of both the upper and lower
arm, and all other parts of us that are jointless, as well as all the bones
that are void of prudence owing to the scarcity of soul in the marrow,
have received their full complement of flesh, but why all the thoughtful
parts have less flesh, except, I suppose, where he so composed some
flesh to be in itself for the sake of sensing, as is the case with the form
B   of the tongue. But for most parts, it is as we've described it, for the
nature that comes to be from necessity and is nourished along with us
in no way allows dense bone and abundant flesh to go together with
acutely attentive sensation. For if indeed these two had been willing
to coincide, the structure around the head would have possessed them
most of all, and the human kind, having on itself a head fleshy and
sinewy and strong, would have acquired a life that was twice, indeed
many times, as long as the one we have now, and healthier and more
free from pain.

But as it was, it seemed good to the craftsmen who concerned
themselves with our birth, when they were reckoning whether they
C   should fashion a kind that was more long-lasting but worse or less
long-lasting but better, that everyone must in all ways choose a life that
was shorter but superior over one that was longer but inferior; whence
they covered the head closely with thin bone but not with flesh and
sinews (since it had no joints). So in accordance with all these reasons
the head that was attached to the body of every man was made more
D   sensitive and prudent than it would otherwise have been, but far weaker.
It was for these reasons and in this way that the god set the sinews in

---

138   *homoiotêti.* Similarity (*homoiotês*) is a power akin to that of the Same. It is
here enlisted as "itself the solder by which the [sinews] are fastened round
the neck at the base of the head" (Taylor, p. 534). The power of the Other,
by contrast, had been employed at 74A to accommodate the jointed, flexible nature of the spine.

139   *hoi diakosmountes.* The mouth is an especially good example of *kosmos* as
the cooperation-in-conflict of intellect and necessity (47E-48A).

a circle at the lowest part of the head, around the neck, and glued them there with similarity;[138] and by means of them he bound the ends of the jawbones below the nature of the face, while the rest of the sinews he dispersed throughout all the limbs, attaching joint to joint.

Now the arrayers[139] of the power of our mouth arrayed it in the way it's now ordered, with teeth and tongue and lips, for the sake of things that are necessary and things that are best, contriving this power

E   as an entrance for things that are necessary but an exit for things that are best; for all that goes in and gives nourishment to the body is nec-essary, while the stream of speech that flows out and is subservient to prudence is of all streams the most beautiful and best.

Again, it wasn't possible to let the head consist only of bare bone, in view of the excessive heat or cold in the seasons; nor again, to allow it to be all shrouded up[140] and to become dull and insensitive due to its

76A   mass of flesh. And so, from the fleshy nature that wasn't completely dried up, there grew in excess a larger film that was separated off—"skin," as it is now called.[141] By coming together with itself on account of the moisture around the brain and budding, this clothed the head all around in a circle; and the moisture, rising up under the sutures, watered the skin and closed it up at the crown by drawing it together as in a knot.[142] And the form of the sutures has come to be extremely varied because of the power of the soul's circuits and nourishment: the more these two powers fight one another, the more sutures there are; the less they do so, the fewer.

Now the divine part kept piercing this entire skin in a circle with fire;[143] and when it had been bored through, and the moisture

B   had coursed out through it, all the unadulterated wetness and heat went off, while all that was mixed with the stuff that also composed

---

[140]   *syskiastheisan*, another shadow-word (see 74D and note). The ordinary meaning of *skia* as shade appears at 76D. The head must be protected and shaded without being overshadowed and buried. We are, in other words, buried in flesh only from the neck down.

[141]   "More skin is formed on the fleshy parts of the face than these require, and it grows over the cranium forming the scalp" (Cornford, p. 299).

[142]   The analogy with the growth of plants is striking. (Compare 45A, where our limbs are said to have "sprouted" from our torsos, and 76B-C, where hair "sprouts" in the skin.) Throughout this whole passage, "the operation of 'Necessity' comes to the front and Plato speaks as if skin, hair, and nails had been developed by the blind action of the primary bodies, unconsciously subserving a useful purpose" (Cornford, p. 300).

[143]   Cornford explains that this happens because of the fire in the brain, "forcing its way upward to seek its like" (p. 300).

the skin was lifted up by the coursing and stretched into a long strand outside, being equal in fineness to the size of the puncture; but due to the slowness with which this happened, and since it was pushed back by the surrounding air outside, it was huddled back inside under the skin and there took root; and in accordance with these very processes the kind *hair* sprouted in the skin—akin to skin and thread-like, but harder and denser on account of the cooling involved in the felting

C   process by which each hair, having cooled upon separation from the skin, got felted together.[144] With this very stuff the maker fashioned our head bushy, using the causes just described and intending that, for the

D   area around the brain, hair instead of flesh should be, for safety's sake, a roof, since it was light and adequate to provide shade in summer and shelter in winter, but it wouldn't become an obstacle that got in the way of the head's sensitivity.

And where sinew and skin and bone were woven together around the fingers there was mixed a combination of the three, which, upon drying, came to be one hard skin compounded of them all—crafted by these accompanying causes, but fashioned by thought, the superlative cause, for the sake of those who were to come afterwards.[145] For they

E   who were constructing us knew that out of men some day women and the rest of the wild animals would be born; and they saw, in particular, that many of these nurslings would, for many reasons, require the use of nails; whence they sketched out the origin of the nails in human beings right from their birth. So on this very account and with these explanations, they made skin, hair, and nails sprout at the extremities of our limbs.[146]

---

[144] The felting process, *pilêsis*, gives rise to a natural *pilos*—a hat. Now we have a hat to go with our cloak of flesh (74B-C).

[145] "Superlative cause" is my attempt to capture the adjective *aitiôtatêi*, literally, most responsible or causal in the highest degree. Thought here, *dianoia*, also means intent or purpose.

[146] Benardete offers a helpful comment on this passage: "Timaeus, the commentators believe, refers to women fighting with nails; but it is hard to see how that serves a divine end. If, however, one thinks of skin, hair, and nails together, one comes to think of the ritual of mourning, in which men and women cut their hair and women rake their cheeks. Death would thus come to light along with natural becoming; and the unwritten law of burial would have its source in nature" ("On Plato's *Timaeus* and Timaeus' Science Fiction," *Interpretation*, [Summer, 1971], pp. 58-59). This reading goes well with Timaeus' earlier references to overshadowing and shrouds (74D, 75E). Of course, the lower animals, according to Timaeus, need nails "for many reasons." This no doubt includes fighting.

And when all the parts and limbs of the mortal animal had been made to grow together by nature, and it turned out that the life it had 77A was in fire and air and for this reason wasted away when it was melted and left empty by them, the gods contrived help for it. They engender a nature akin to human nature, though blending it with different looks and sensations so as to be another kind of animal. These are precisely our current cultivated trees and plants and seeds that are trained by the agricultural art and domesticated for our use; but formerly there were only the wild kinds, since these were elder to the cultivated ones. For everything that partakes of living may justly and most correctly B be called an animal; and this animal we're talking about now surely partakes of the third form of soul, that which the account has seated between midriff and navel, and which shares in no way at all in opinion and reasoning and intellect, but only in sensation, pleasant and painful, accompanied by desires. For since it persists in being entirely passive, its birth did not bequeath it a natural ability to reason about any of its C own affections and observe itself by turning within itself around itself, fending off motion from outside, while making use of its own indwelling motion. For this reason, it lives indeed and is none other than an animal; but because it has been deprived of self-motion, it stays firmly fixed and rooted down.

When our superiors had engendered all these very kinds as nourishment for us inferior beings, they channeled through our body D itself, just as if they were cutting channels in gardens, so that the body might be refreshed as though from an inflowing stream. First they cut two veins—hidden channels just under the natural junction of the skin and flesh—to go down either side of the back, on the right and on the left, since the body happens to be twofold with a right side and a left. These they brought down alongside the spine, having placed between them the fecund marrow in order that this might flourish as much as possible, and that the stream of nourishment, by running downhill and E flowing freely over the rest of the body, might make the irrigation uniform. After this, having split the veins around the head and interwoven them, they drove them through in directions contrary to one another, inclining those on the right of the body to go left and those on the left to go right, so that they, along with the skin, might be a bond that attaches the head to the body, since the head wasn't encompassed in a circle by sinews at the crown, and, moreover, in order that the affection of the senses coming from either side of the body might be made plain to the body as a whole.[147]

78A   At this point they now prepared the irrigation system in the following sort of manner, which we'll observe more easily if we agree beforehand on the following: that all things that are constructed out of lesser parts shut in the greater, while those constructed out of greater parts aren't able to shut in the smaller; and fire is the smallest of all the kinds, which is why it makes its way through water and earth and air and everything that's constructed out of these, and nothing's able to shut it

B   in. One must think that this very same thing also applies in the case of our belly. Whenever food and drink rush down into it, the belly shuts them in; but it isn't able to shut in the air we breathe and fire, since these are smaller in their parts than the structure of the belly. These bodies, therefore, the god used for the irrigation from the belly to the veins, having spun together a network of air and fire, like a fish-trap that had two inner funnels at its entrance,[148] one of which he again unraveled and divided in two; and it was from these inner funnels that he stretched

C   reeds, as it were, all over the trap in a circle up to the extremities of the network. Now all the parts on the inside of the basket he constructed entirely out of fire, but the funnels and the shell were aeroform.

And having taken up the whole thing, he set it around the fabricated animal in the following way.[149] The funnel part he inserted into the mouth; and, since it was twofold, he dropped one part down into the lungs by way of the windpipe, and the other alongside the windpipe into the belly; and having split the former, he assigned to both a common outlet by way of the channels of the nose, so that when the

D   other passage wasn't working by way of the mouth, all its currents might be replenished from this passage as well. But the rest of the trap (that is, the shell) he made grow around all the hollow part of our body; and he made the whole of it at one time flow together into the funnels (gently,

---

[147]   "The passage is most easily understood, not as a grossly inadequate account of the circulatory system, but rather as formulating the mechanical problem of hydraulics. The blood can easily flow downhill through branches in all directions. But some force is needed to raise the blood from the belly to the top of the hill" (Cornford, p. 306). Such force is supplied by the respiratory process, which Timaeus now proceeds to explain. As Cornford notes: "In this process the lung itself appears to play as little a part as the heart plays in circulation. The mechanism is to consist of currents of air and fire" (p. 306).

[148]   Cornford gives a helpful discussion (along with diagrams) of the fish-trap (pp. 308-315).

[149]   The animal is surrounded by a sort of atmosphere or "sphere of breath," which is rhythmically taken into the body and then pushed out.

since they were air), while at another time he made the funnels flow back into it. And since the body is porous, he made the network slip into and through it and to slip back out; and the rays of fire that were bound within the shell he made follow the air as it went one way and

E then the other; and so long as the mortal animal maintains its structure, this doesn't come to a stop. To just this kind of process the Assigner of Names, we say, assigned the names "inhaling" and "exhaling."[150] Now all this work and affection has come about for the sake of our body, so that by being refreshed and cooled, it might be nourished and live; for

79A whenever the inner fire, which is attached to the breathing that goes in and out, should follow this breathing, and, in its perpetual swaying back and forth, should enter in through the belly and lay hold of food and drink, it melts them and, by dividing them up into small pieces, drives them through the outgoing channels in the direction of its advance, drawing them into the veins like drawing water into channels from a spring, and it makes the currents of the veins flow through the body as though through a pipe.

But let's look again at the affection of breathing—at the causes

B employed by which it's come to be what it is now.[151] Here's how it was. Since there's no void into which anything coursing along might be able to go, and since the breath from us courses outward, it's at once plain to everyone what happens after that. The breath doesn't go into a void but pushes what's next to it from its seat, and what's pushed always drives out what's next to it; and in keeping with this necessity, everything is driven around toward the seat from which the breath went out and, upon entering there, also follows the breath and fills up the seat; and this happens all at once, like a potter's wheel that goes round and round,

C because there's no void whatsoever. Which is exactly why the area of the chest and lungs, as it's letting out the breath, comes to be filled again by the air surrounding the body, which slips inside through the pores of the flesh and is driven around; and again, when the air is turned back and goes out through the body, it pushes around the air that's been breathed in by way of the passageway of the mouth and nostrils.

And the cause of the principle for all this must be set down as follows. Every animal has its inward parts hottest around the blood and

D veins—a sort of fount of fire that resides within itself. This is exactly

---

[150] In the *Cratylus*, Socrates speaks of "the one who first assigned names" (436B), a being who is "some demon or god" (438C).

[151] Work and affection (*ergon* and *pathos*) at 78E here become simply *pathos* or affection, a *being done to*. See Glossary under **affection**. As Timaeus' account makes clear, breathing is a purely mechanical process. Strictly speaking, it is something we suffer rather than do.

what we also likened to the netting of the fish trap, which, as we said, was all woven out of fire in the part that was extended down its mid-section, while all the other, outer parts were made of air. Now it must be agreed that according to nature the hot goes out into its own place to its kindred; and since there are two passageways—one out by way of the body's pores, the other in turn by way of the mouth and nose—whenever the hot rushes for the one passageway, it pushes the air around to the other; and the air, having been pushed in this way, is heated upon its encounter with the fire, while the outgoing air is cooled. As the heat changes and the air-particles around the other passageway become hotter, the hotter body of air is in turn more inclined to go back the way it came and, coursing along toward that which has the same nature as itself, pushes around the air at the other passageway; and the air—by continually suffering the same thing and paying back the same thing, just like a wheel fashioned to roll this way and that under a double impulse—makes inhaling and exhaling come about.

E

Furthermore, one must in the same way pursue the causes of the affections having to do with medical cuppings, and of swallowing, and of all projectiles which, once let go, keep coursing along either aloft or over the ground;[152] and one must investigate all the sounds which, being either swift or slow, appear either shrill or deep, sometimes dissonant as they course along because of the dissimilarity of the motion they produce in us, sometimes consonant because of their similarity. For in this case the slower sounds catch up with the motions of the sounds that are earlier and swifter, as these are already coming to a stop and have reached the point of similarity with the motions applied to them by the sounds that came later; and when the slower sounds catch up with the swifter, they don't provoke disorder, even though they impose a different motion; but on the contrary, by attaching to the course of the swifter sound, which is dying away, the beginning of a slower one that bears a similarity to it, out of shrill and deep they blended together a single affection; whence pleasure is provided for the thoughtless and good cheer for the thoughtful through their imitation of the divine concord born within mortal coursings.[153]

80A

B

And what's more, when it comes to all flowings of waters, and the falling of thunderbolts, and all that's wondered at in the attraction of amber and lodestones, there's never the slightest bit of attraction in

C

---

152   For the ancient physicists, there was no such thing as inertia. Why a body in motion continued in its motion was a problem that had to be explained. See, for example, Aristotle's account of projectile motion in the *Physics* (8.10.266B ff.).

153   For a helpful explanation of this discussion of sound, see Cornford, pp. 320-326.

any of them.[154] But the fact that there's no void at all, and that these bodies push themselves around into each other, and that they move by exchanging their respective seats as they separate or combine—it is by means of these complex and reciprocal affections that such wonders are worked, as will be plain to anyone who inquires in the proper way.

D   And what's more, the affection of breathing (from which our account took its impetus) came about in accordance with and through these means, as was said earlier. The fire cuts up the food and sways this way and that inside us as it follows the breath; and in this swaying to and fro it fills up the veins from the belly by pumping into them from there the cut-up bits of food; and for just these reasons, the streams of nourishment in all animals have thus become free-flowing throughout the whole body. And since the bits of food are freshly cut and come from things kindred to themselves—some from fruits and others from herbs,

E   which god made sprout for us for just this reason, to serve as food—they come to have all manner of colors because of their intermingling; but the hue that runs through them most is *red*, a nature crafted by the cutting and staining action of fire upon moisture. Whence the color of what flows through the body comes to have the sort of aspect that

81A   we've described. We call it "blood," which feeds the flesh and the entire body, from which source the various parts of the body are irrigated so as to fill up the base of what's been left void. The mode of the filling and withdrawing comes about in just the way the course of everything in the all has come about: all that is akin courses to its own kind. In fact, everything that surrounds us from without is always melting us away and distributing us by sending off each particle to the form that's of the same tribe, while our blood-particles in turn, having been minced up inside us and encompassed by the structure of each animal, as though

B   by a heaven, are compelled to imitate the course of the all; so when each

---

154   Amber in Greek is *êlektron*, the origin of our "electron." The lodestone is *lithos Hêrakleios*, which refers either to "the stone from Heraclea" or "the Herculean stone." The general point here is that, from the standpoint of mechanics, pushes make sense (because there is direct physical contact) whereas pulls do not: there is no action at a distance. We are reminded of gravitational attraction, regarding the cause of which Newton famously said: *Hypotheses non fingo*, "I feign no hypotheses" (*Principia Mathematica*, the General Scholium). Timaeus' implicit critique of *thauma*, wonder, is yet another echo of the modern temperament: "That is why, even though it is good to be born with some inclination to this passion [wonder], because it disposes us to the acquisition of the sciences, we must nevertheless try to free ourselves from it as much as possible" (Descartes, *The Passions of the Soul* 2.76).

of the particles divided up inside us courses toward its kin, at that time it fills back up again the place that's been left void.

Now whenever more is leaving than is flowing in, everything withers; but whenever the outflow is less, then everything grows. So when the structure of the entire animal is new, having the triangles of its kinds still, as it were, fresh from the workshop, then it's possessed of a strong C interlocking of triangles with one another, and the entire mass of the structure has a pliant texture, inasmuch as it's newly born from marrow and nourished on milk. And since the triangles encompassed within the structure, which have invaded it from without and constitute its food and drink, are older and weaker than its own triangles, the structure gains mastery over them by cutting them with its own, fresh triangles, and D thus makes the animal large by nurturing it from many similar bodies. But whenever the root of the triangles grows slack through their having contended against many for a long time in many contests, they're no longer able to cut up the incoming food-triangles and reduce them to similarity with themselves, but they themselves are easily divided by the triangles that invade them from the outside; in fact, every animal that's mastered in this way withers, an affection that goes by the name "old age."[155] And in the end, when the bonds of the triangles fitted together in the marrow-area no longer hold out under the stress but come apart, E they let slip in turn the bonds of the soul; and thus released in accordance with nature, she flies out with pleasure, for all that is contrary to nature is painful, while that which happens naturally is sweet. So too, in accordance with the same rule, death that comes about through diseases or by wounds is painful and forced, while that which comes with old age at an end that's in accordance with nature is the least distressing of deaths and comes about more with pleasure than with pain.

Whence diseases are constructed is, I take it, plain to everyone. 82A For since there are four kinds of which the body is compacted (earth, fire, water and air), when, contrary to nature, either an excess, or a deficiency, of these kinds arises; or else when there's a shift from their familiar place to one that's alien; or again, since the kinds of fire and the rest happen to be more than one, when a particular bodily part takes in an additional something that's not suited to it—when all such things happen, they provide factions and diseases. For when any one B kind arises or shifts its place contrary to nature, parts that previously were cooled become heated, and parts previously dry afterwards become moist, and so too with particles that are light or heavy; and they receive

---

[155] The "root" of the triangles is presumably the perpendicular dropped from the right angle. Decrepitude and natural death are literally the erosion and eventual collapse of a structure.

all changes in all ways. For, as we claim, only when that which arrives at or departs from a bodily part is the same as that part—in the same condition, consistent and in the right proportion with it—only then will it allow that part to remain safe and sound in its sameness with itself; but whatever is unmusical[156] and steps outside of any of these conditions upon leaving or arriving will produce alterations of any and every variety and indefinitely many diseases and corruptions.

C   Moreover, since secondary structures have by nature been constructed, a thorough noting of secondary diseases arises for one who wants to take note of them. For inasmuch as marrow and bone and flesh and sinew are compacted from the elements (and blood too has come to be from the same elements, though it's compacted in a different way), most diseases arise in just the manner previously stated; and the greatest and most dangerous diseases are contracted in the following way. Whenever the birth of these secondary bodies proceeds in the reverse direction, at that time these bodies are corrupted. For in accordance with nature

D   flesh and sinews are born from blood—sinew from the fibers because of its kinship with them, flesh from the coagulated blood, which coagulates upon separation from the fibers; and the sticky and oily part that in turn comes from the sinews and flesh not only glues the flesh to the nature of the bones but also feeds and augments the bone itself that encloses the marrow, while the purest part, which is made of the smoothest and oiliest kind of triangles, filters through the density of the bones and, as it oozes and drips from the bones, waters the marrow. And when they

E   are severally born in this way, then health for the most part results.

But diseases arise whenever this goes in the contrary direction. For whenever flesh wastes away and sends its waste back again into the veins, at that time there is much blood in the veins of every sort along with air, and this blood is mottled by colors and bitternesses, as well as by acidic and salty powers, and contains bile and serum and phlegm of all sorts. For when all these things have become reversed and thereby corrupted, they first destroy the blood itself; and they themselves, providing no further nourishment for the body, course through the veins in every direction,

83A   no longer abiding by the order of their natural circuits, becoming hateful

---

[156] *plêmmelêsêi*. Recall that before the god made the cosmic order, everything moved "unmusically" (*plêmmelôs*, 30A). See Glossary under **musically**. Just as health is a form of musicality, disease is the absence of musicality. Account-giving too may be healthy or diseased, musical or unmusical. See 55C-D, where the tuneful raising of perplexities has to do with acknowledging limits. As the likely story now descends to the topic of disease, *nosos*, it is important to recall that Timaeus' very first word in the dialogue is *astheneia*, debility or illness (17A).

to themselves because they have no enjoyment of themselves and hostile to whatever in the body stands together and stays in its assigned place, thus destroying and wasting everything.[157] Now when all the oldest flesh wastes away, it becomes resistant to concoction, and it blackens under the action of the burning that's been going on for a long time, and, being

B bitter from having been eaten away on all sides, it attacks with severity every part of the body that hasn't yet been destroyed. Sometimes, when the bitter stuff becomes more thinned out, the black color takes on an acidity in place of its bitterness; again, at other times the bitterness takes on a redder color when steeped in blood; and when the black stuff is blended together with this, it turns greenish; and furthermore, a yellow color is mixed together with the bitterness whenever the flesh that disintegrates under the inflammation of fire is new. Now to all these the common name "bile" has been given—I suppose either by certain doctors

C or else by someone who was able to look at many and dissimilar things and see one inherent kind among them that was worthy of a name; and as for all the rest that are said to be forms of bile, each has taken on its own special definition depending on its color.[158]

Then there's serum. One sort is the benign, watery part of the blood, while the other, from acidic black bile, is malignant whenever it gets mingled with a saline power through the action of heat; and this sort of thing is called "acid phlegm." Again, there's the part that

D comes from the wasting away of new and tender flesh accompanied by air; and when all this gets inflated and encompassed by moisture and there arises from this affection bubble-structures (which, taken one at a time, are invisible because of their smallness but taken together yield a visible mass, and which have a white look to them because of the birth of foam), all this waste-matter that comes from tender flesh entangled with air we say is "white phlegm." And again phlegm that's

E newly constructed has a watery part: "sweat" and "tears" and whatever other such stuff that's purged from the body every day. And indeed, all these things have come to be instruments of disease, whenever blood

---

[157] "Assigned place" here is *chôra* in the sense of one's station or post. Note that this long sentence on disease contains many terms central to Timaeus' cosmology: order (*taxis*), circuit (*periodos*), construct or stand together (*synistanai*), and place (*chôra*). The context is a powerful reminder that the concerns of the physicist for Timaeus, like those of the statesman and general, are war and peace. The cosmologist and the statesman-general literally speak the same language.

[158] "Kind" (*genos*) is what we would call a genus, of which the "forms" (*eidê*) would be species.

isn't replenished from food and drink in accordance with nature but takes its mass from contraries, against the laws of nature.[159]

84A

Now when each bit of flesh is being dissolved by diseases but the foundations of flesh stand their ground, the power of the disaster is only half of what it would otherwise be, for it still has an opportunity for ready recovery; but whenever the stuff that binds together flesh with bones becomes diseased and now no longer separates itself from them and from the sinews, so as to provide food for bone, while also becoming a bond that attaches flesh to bone, but instead of being oily and smooth and slippery becomes rough and briny, having been dried out by a bad regimen—at that time, all such stuff that suffers this itself

B

crumbles away under the flesh and the sinews and stands apart from the bones; while the flesh that falls away with it from the roots leaves the sinews bare and full of brine and, itself falling back into the bloodstream, aggravates the diseases described earlier.

But dangerous as these body-related ailments are, still more serious are those that are prior.[160] These arise whenever bone, through density

C

of flesh, doesn't get sufficient air and, getting all heated up by mold, gangrenes, fails to receive its nourishment, and crumbles, itself going back again into that nourishment, contrary to what it should do; and the nourishment goes into flesh; and this flesh, by falling into the blood, renders harsher all the diseases mentioned before. The most extreme case of all, which arises whenever the nature of the marrow becomes diseased from deficiency or from some excess, brings about the greatest and lordliest diseases that end in death, since the whole nature of the body flows backwards by necessity.

D

Again, a third form of diseases must be thought to arise in a three-fold way: from air, from phlegm, and from bile. Whenever the lungs, the dispenser of air to the body, are blocked up by humors and do not keep the passageways clean, then air in some places doesn't get in, so that

---

[159] The phrase "laws of nature," so familiar to our modern ears, is rare in Plato. The only other appearance is in the *Gorgias*, where Callicles, after drawing a sharp distinction between nature and custom (or law), at one point merges the two in the phrase "law of nature" (483E). Cornford warns against the translation "laws of nature" and opts for "established use of nature" (p. 339). But these laws for Timaeus are precisely nature's established habits and customs, which, like humanly established laws, can be violated. They are not laws in the modern sense of what always happens without exception.

[160] Prior in the sense of afflicting the more fundamental parts of the animal structure: bone and marrow. The most grievous diseases in this way acquire the greatest dignity, as Timaeus soon indicates by calling them *kyriôtata*, lordliest (84C).

the parts that don't happen to get refreshment rot; while in other places there enters more than the appropriate amount of air, so that the air forces its way through the veins and, twisting them together like strands and wasting away the body, is hemmed in by the body's middle region,

E   which holds the diaphragm; and for this very reason countless painful diseases are thus produced, accompanied by a profusion of sweat. And often, when flesh has been dissolved, air that's come to be enclosed in the body and is unable to pass to the outside brings about the same intense pains that are brought about by air that comes from without; and the greatest arise whenever the air, by settling around the sinews and the veins, there swells up and thus stretches backwards our "back-stays" and the sinews attached to them;[161] and it's also from this very condition of stretching that the diseases of tetanus and opisthotonus have gotten their names. Dangerous too is the remedy for these diseases, since what in fact does the most to relieve such things are bouts of fever.

85A   And white phlegm, when hemmed in, is dangerous because of the air in the bubbles it contains; but when it has vents to the outside of the body, then it's milder, though it mottles the body all over with white, leprous spots and also brings forth diseases that are their kin. When this phlegm has been blended with black bile and is scattered over the head's circuits, which are most divine, and throws them into confusion,

B   then the effect is rather gentle during sleep, though harder to shake off for those awake. And since this is a disease of our sacred nature, it is most justly called the "sacred disease."[162] And phlegm that's acidic and saline is the wellspring of all diseases that arise from catarrhs; and these have taken on all manner of names because the regions into which they flow are of all sorts.

As for the diseases that are "inflammations" of the body, so-called because the body is burned and enflamed, they have all arisen through

C   bile. Now when bile has gained a vent to the outside, by seething it sends up all sorts of boils; but when it's confined within, it introduces many "fiery" diseases. The greatest occurs whenever bile is blent with pure blood and wrenches the fibrous kind out of its own order, which fibers are dispersed throughout the blood in order that the blood might have the right measure of thinness and thickness, and neither flow out from the porous body through heat that liquefies it, nor again be hard

D   to move because of its excessive thickness and circulate with difficulty

---

[161]   The adjective *epitonos* means stretched or strained. The noun *epitonoi* refers to the back-stays of a ship's mast. Here the back-stays are probably the tendons in our shoulder and neck area. The names for tetanus or lockjaw and opisthotonus both derive from *teinein*, to stretch.

[162]   Epilepsy.

in the veins. Now the fibers guard the due amount of these contraries through the birth of their nature. Even after death when the blood is in the process of cooling, whenever anyone collects the fibers together with one another, the rest of the blood goes all runny; but if the fibers are left alone, they swiftly congeal the blood with the aid of the surrounding cold. Now since the fibers have this power, bile, which has arisen by nature from old blood and has melted back again into blood

E   from flesh, falling hot and moist into the blood at first little by little, is congealed through the power of the fibers; and as it's being congealed and having its heat forcibly quenched, it produces internal cold and trembling. But when bile flows in more copiously, mastering the fibers by its own heat, it boils up and shakes the fibers into disorder; and if ever it should become sufficient to mastering them to the end, it penetrates all the way to the marrowy kind and, by burning, cuts loose from that place the bonds of the soul, as cables from a ship, and sets her free. But whenever the bile's less plentiful and the body resists dissolution, then the bile itself, having been mastered, either is banished over the entire body or pushed through the veins into the lower or upper belly, being

86A   banished from the body like exiles from a city in civil war; and it makes for diarrhea and dysentery and all diseases of that sort.

Now when a body is diseased mostly from an excess of fire, this produces continual burnings and fevers; when from air, fevers that recur daily; when from water, fevers that recur every third day (because water's more sluggish than air and fire); and when from earth (which is the fourth and most sluggish of all and is purged in fourfold periods of time), it makes fevers that recur every fourth day and is shaken off only with difficulty.

B   That's how the body-related diseases happen to be born, while the soul-related ones that arise through the body's condition are born in the following way. Now it must be granted that folly is a disease of the soul, and of folly there are two kinds: one is madness, the other stupidity. So when anyone suffers at all from either of these, it must be termed disease; and pleasures and pains that are excessive must be set down as the greatest of diseases for the soul. For when a human is overjoyed

C   or suffers in a contrary way from pain, and hastens inopportunely to seize the one while fleeing the other, he can neither see nor hear anything correctly, and he goes crazy and at just those times is least able to partake of reasoning. And when the seed from a man's marrow-area grows copious and free-flowing, just like a tree whose nature makes it fruitful beyond measure, he brings on himself again and again many

D   intense pains and many pleasures amid his desires and their offspring; and he comes to be raving mad for the greater part of his life through those greatest pleasures and pains; and although he has a soul that's diseased and thoughtless under the influence of the body, people hold the opinion that he's not diseased but willingly bad. But the truth is that sexual incontinence has come about as a disease of the soul, due for the most part to the condition of a single kind which, because of the porosity of the bones, flows freely in the body and irrigates it. In fact, just about all such things that are spoken of as lack of mastery in pleasures on the part of the bad and as a reproach, as if they were willingly bad, are not correctly reproached, for no one is willingly bad; but it's rather through

E   some corrupt condition of the body and an uneducated upbringing that a bad man becomes bad, and this is hateful to everyone and comes upon us against our will.[163]

Again, as for pains, the soul in just the same way comes to have lots of badness through body. For whenever the humors from acidic and briny phlegms and those that are bitter and bilious, wandering

87A   throughout the body, have no vent to the outside but remain huddled up inside, and mingle the vapor that comes from them with the coursing of the soul and get thoroughly blended with it, they introduce all manner of soul-diseases, some more intense and widespread than others; and once they've penetrated to the three regions of the soul, in whatever region each of these attacks, they mottle her with diverse forms of bad temper and melancholy as well as of recklessness and cowardice, and also forgetfulness together with slowness in learning. In addition to this, whenever people are stuck in this bad condition, and when their

B   regimes are bad and their speeches uttered in cities privately and publicly are bad, and furthermore when no studies that might cure them are in any way learned from childhood, in this way all of us who are bad become bad—through two utterly involuntary causes. And for this bad condition one must always put the blame on the planters more than the planted and the nurturers more than the nurtured; still, one must put one's heart into fleeing the bad and seizing its contrary in whatever way one is able, both through upbringing and through one's pursuits and studies. But that of course goes with a different mode of speech.

---

[163] Socrates argues that no one knowingly desires the bad at *Meno* 77B-78B. And in the *Protagoras* we hear: "all those who do ugly and bad things do them unwillingly" (345E). A very similar passage occurs in the *Laws* (5. 731B-C). Timaeus' argument, however, relying as it does on the condition of the body, makes us wonder how anyone could be held responsible for his actions. A. E Taylor has an interesting discussion of this passage (pp. 610-614). The whole context for Timaeus' remarks underscores the connection between the two senses of *aitia*: cause and blame.

C   And it is likely and fitting that we deliver in turn the counterpart that answers to all this, which has to do with the treatment of our bodies and thought-processes, as well as the causes by which these are preserved, for it is more just that good things have their account rather than bad. Now all the good is beautiful, and the beautiful is not disproportionate;[164] so one must posit that an animal too, if it is to be beautiful, must have due proportion. And while we thoroughly perceive and reason out the minor proportions, concerning those that are lordliest and greatest, we are unreasoning. For with respect to health

D   and diseases and virtues and vices, there isn't a single proportion or lack of proportion greater than that of soul herself in relation to body itself; but we don't examine them at all, nor do we notice that when a soul strong and in all ways great rides a bodily form that's too weak for her and puny, or again, when the two of them get put together in the contrary way, then the animal as a whole—disproportionate with respect to the most important proportions—is not beautiful; but an

E   animal in the contrary condition, for him who has the power to see, is of all sights the most beautiful and loveliest. For example, a body that's too long in the legs or somehow disproportionate with itself because of some other excess is not only ugly: it's also the cause of countless evils for itself, and when its parts have to share in any common tasks, it often gets tired and brings on itself many sprains and falls because it courses this way and that.

One must also think the same thing about the duality of body and soul, which we call an animal. Whenever the soul within the body

88A   is stronger than it and becomes enraged, she thoroughly shakes it all up from the inside and fills it with diseases; and whenever she strenuously goes after certain studies and inquiries, she wears down the body utterly; and again, when she makes teachings and word-battles for herself in public and in private, by making the body enflamed, she rocks it to and fro because of the strife and contentiousness that have arisen, and she brings on discharges, by which she deceives most so-called physicians and makes them put the blame on what is in fact blameless.[165] And again, when a large body that's too much for its soul[166] comes to be naturally joined with an intelligence that's small and weak, then, since humans

---

[164]   Timaeus' maxim is very musical-sounding in Greek: *pan dê to agathon kalon, to de kalon ouk ametron.*

[165]   That is, the soul deceives physicians into laying the blame on the body. The sentence resounds with forms of the verb *poein*, do or make. Soul here is presented as a productive or demiurgic cause.

[166]   "Too much for its soul" is *hyperpsychon.* The word echoes the *hyperskeles* at 87E: "too long in the legs."

B   by nature have a double desire—for food because of the body, and for prudence because of the most divine of the parts within us—the motions of the stronger part gain mastery and augment their own power; but they make that of the soul dull, slow to learn and forgetful, thereby producing the greatest of diseases—stupidity.[167]

The one safeguard from both these conditions is this: never to set the soul in motion without body nor body without soul, so that both C   of them, by defending themselves, may become equally balanced and thereby healthy. And so, the student of mathematics or one who works intensely at some other exercise in intelligence must render to the body the motion that is its due by attending to gymnastics; and again, he who is diligent about molding his body must in turn render to the soul the motions appropriate to her by also applying himself to the liberal arts and all philosophy,[168] if he is justly to be called beautiful along with being correctly called good.[169]

The various bodily parts must also be treated in the same way, D   in imitation of the form of the all. For since the body is burned and chilled within by what enters it, and again dried up and moistened by what comes from the outside, and suffers everything that follows from this by both motions, it happens that whenever anyone surrenders his body, which has been in a state of peace, to these motions, the body is overpowered and utterly destroyed. But if someone imitates what we have called the nurturer and wet-nurse of the all,[170] and for the most part never allows the body to be at peace but keeps it in motion and, by always inducing certain shakings in it, provides a constant natural E   defense against the inner and outer motions and, by temperate shaking, arrays the affections and particles that wander around the body and puts them in order with one another according to their various kinships, as in the previous account we gave concerning the all, then he will not allow foe to be set next to foe to breed wars in the body and diseases as well, but rather he will have friend set next to friend so as to produce health.

89A   And again, of motions, that motion which is brought about in oneself by oneself is the best, for this is most akin to the motion of thought

---

[167]   Timaeus had alluded to this greatest of diseases back at 44B.

[168]   Compare the phrase "all philosophy" with Socrates' praise of Timaeus for having reached the peak of "all philosophy" (20A). The word for "liberal arts" here is *mousikê*, music.

[169]   The words *kalos* (beautiful, fine or noble) and *agathos* (good) combine in Greek to form *kalos kagathos* (or *kalokagathos*), a word used to describe a gentleman. Timaeus here gives a natural basis for the proper use of this term.

[170]   The wet-nurse was first mentioned at 49A.

and the motion of the all; but motion that comes about by another is worse. And worst of all is that which, when the body is just lying there and at peace, moves it part by part by means of other things. Which is exactly why the best motion for the purging and bracing[171] of the body comes about through gymnastics, and second best that which comes about through swaying like that of boats and whatever vehicles aren't

B   exhausting. And a third form of motion is useful for anyone who must occasionally resort to it under dire necessity; but in other circumstances it must in no way be accepted by anyone who is sensible—the medicinal sort of motion that arises from purging through drugs. Diseases that don't involve great dangers must not be aggravated with drugs. For the whole structure of diseases in some manner resembles the nature of animals. And the formation of these animals is so ordered as to have definite time periods for the entire kind, and each animal by itself sprouts

C   having a destined life span, that is, apart from affections that come from necessity, for the triangles of each one, right from the beginning, are constructed having the power to last up to a certain time, beyond which limit of life no one could ever continue to live. So the same mode of construction also applies to diseases. Whenever anyone tries to destroy them with drugs, contrary to what has been destined for their time, then many and great diseases just love to arise from those that are small and few. That's why one must, as far as leisure permits, guide all such diseases by a healthy regimen rather than aggravate a temperamental

D   evil by using drugs.

As for the composite animal and the bodily part of it—how a man, both guiding and being guided by himself should live most in accordance with reason—let it be as was said; and indeed, one must no doubt give an even higher priority to preparing, as far as possible, that which guides the animal, so that it may be as beautiful and as good as

E   it can for its task of guidance. Now to go through all this with precision would in and of itself be work enough; but if someone were to follow it up as a side-job, along the lines of what was said before, then it wouldn't be out of character to examine the matter in the following way and bring the account to its conclusion.

As we've said often, there are three distinct forms of soul housed within us, and each happens to have its own motions. So now too it must likewise be said, as briefly as possible, that whichever of these forms remains in a state of idleness and keeps its own motions at peace neces-

90A   sarily becomes weakest, whereas the one that engages in gymnastics is the most vigorous, which is why one must be on guard and make sure

---

[171]   On the medical use of *systasis* in this passage, see Taylor, p. 626.

that they all have their motions in due proportion with one another. And as for that lordliest form of soul within us, one must think of it in this way: that god has given it to each of us as a divinity[172] that dwells at the peak of our body and lifts us up toward our kindred in heaven and away from the earth, since we're not an earthly but a heavenly plant. And we say so most correctly, for it is from *there*, whence the soul's first birth sprouted, that our divine part, by suspending our head and root, would keep the entire body upright.

B   So then, when a man has fallen in with desires or contentions and labors away at them intensely, all his decrees necessarily grow mortal, and, as far as it's possible for a man to grow utterly and completely mortal, he falls little short of this, since that's the part of himself he has made great; but, on the contrary, when a man devotes himself to the love of learning and to true prudence, and has exercised himself in these things above all others, then there is every necessity, I suppose, that he think thoughts that are immortal and divine (if in fact he touches on truth); and again, to the extent that human nature admits to a share in

C   immortality, he does not fall short of this; and since he's always caring for his divine part and keeping well-arrayed the divinity[173] that dwells within him, he is supremely happy. Now, the treatment of every part for everyone is one: to render to each part its congenial foods and motions. And the motions within us that are akin to the divine are the thinkings and coursings of the all: these each must follow, rectifying the circuits in

D   our head that were destroyed at birth by a thorough study of the attunements and orbitings of the all, thereby making the part that understands similar to that which is understood, in keeping with its ancient nature; and, having made them similar, he will possess the end of that best life set out for humans by gods both for the present and for the time to come.

E   Now then, at this point, that which we were commanded to do at the beginning, to go through an account of the all down to human birth, seems just about to have reached its end. For how the rest of the animals in turn were born must be recalled only briefly: there is no necessity for someone to speak at length. In that way, he would seem to himself to be more temperate in his accounts of these things. So let what is said be as follows.

Among those who were born men, all that were cowardly and lived an unjust life were, according to the likely account, transplanted in their second birth as women; and it was at that very time and for that

---

[172]   *daimona.* See 40D and note.

[173]   Timaeus here plays on the word *daimôn*. Happiness, *eudaimonia*, consists in keeping one's guardian spirit or *daimôn* well-ordered, *eu kekosmêmenon*.

91A   reason that gods built the love of sexual intercourse by constructing one
sort of ensouled animal in us and another sort in women, in either case
having made them in some such manner as this. From the passageway
by which drink goes out, where it receives the liquid that comes through
the lungs down into the kidneys and on into the bladder and ejects it with
the air that presses on it, they bored a hole into the compacted marrow
B   that extends from the head down along the neck and through the spine
(what in our previous accounts we called "seed"); and since this marrow
was ensouled and had found a vent, it instilled in that very part where
it found a vent a lively desire for emission and thus produced a love of
begetting.[174] Which is exactly why the nature of the genitals in men has
grown unpersuadable and autocratic, like an animal that won't listen to
C   reason, and attempts to master all things through its stinging desires.[175]
Again, for the same reason, there's the matrix or so-called womb in
women, which is an indwelling animal desirous of childbearing; and
whenever this comes to be fruitless long beyond its due season, it grows
difficult and irritable; and, wandering[176] everywhere throughout the
body, it blocks up the breathing-passages, and, by not allowing breathing,
throws one into the most extreme frustrations and brings on all sorts
of other diseases until the desire of the one and the love of the other[177]
D   bring the sexes together; and, as if plucking the fruit from trees, they
sow in the womb, as though in a field, animals invisible for their smallness and not yet formed; and these animals they again make distinct in
their parts; and they nourish them to great size within the womb and
afterwards, by bringing them into the light of day, complete their birth
as animals.

So that's how women and the entire female sex were born; and
the tribe of birds was the result of a remodeling: sprouting feathers
instead of hair, it comes from men harmless but light-minded, and
E   studious of the heavenly bodies yet believing, in their naivete, that the
firmest demonstrations about such things come through sight. Again,
the beastly form that goes on foot has been born from those who neither
applied themselves at all to philosophy nor at all pondered the nature

---

[174]   Sexual climax for the male is literally the loss of his brains. See 73B ff.

[175]   Compare *Republic* 9. 573B, where Socrates says that love "has of old been
called a tyrant." There too erotic desire is characterized as a stinging.

[176]   Timaeus' language connects the nature of the female with the wandering
cause (48B).

[177]   Timaeus attributes erotic longing (*erôs*) to the male but only desire (*epithymia*) to the female. (See Cornford's note on page 357.) He is playing on
the fact that in Greek, the word *erôs* is masculine and the word *epithymia*
feminine.

of the heavens, because they no longer made use of the circuits in their head but followed as their leaders those parts of the soul that are in the area of the chest. So from these pursuits their forelimbs and their heads were dragged down toward earth by their kinship with it and there supported; and their crowns became elongated and took on all sorts of shapes, depending on whichever way the inner orbits of each had been squeezed together by idleness; and this was also the explanation for why their kind grew up four-footed, and even many-footed, since god placed more supports under the ones that were more thoughtless, so that they might be more dragged down toward earth. And since there was no further need of feet for the most thoughtless among these same animals, which had their whole body stretched along the earth, they[178] begat them footless and crawling around on the ground. And the fourth kind, which lives in the water, was born from the absolutely most unintelligent and stupidest men of all, whom their remolders considered no longer worthy of pure breathing, since their soul was in an impure condition because of her total lack of musicality;[179] so instead of letting them have a fine and pure breathing of air, they pushed them down into water for a breathing murky and deep; whence was born the clan of fish and shellfish and of all such animals that live in the water, all those that were allotted the most extreme dwellings as retribution for their extreme of stupidity. And that's just how all animals, then and now, turn into one another as they change through the shedding and gaining of intellect and folly.

And so, let us now declare that our account of the all at last has its end; for by having acquired animals mortal as well as immortal and having been all filled up, this cosmos has thus come to be—a visible animal embracing visible animals, a likeness of the intelligible, a sensed god; greatest and best, most beautiful and most perfect—this one heaven, being alone of its kind![180]

---

[178] "Gods" is the implied subject of the verb "begat." Having referred to plural "gods" at 91A, Timaeus momentarily refers to the singular "god" and then switches back. This is one of the most striking shifts from singular "god" to plural "gods" in the likely story.

[179] *plêmmeleias*, literally, out-of-tune-ness. The extreme unmusicality of these souls recalls the unmusical motion of pre-cosmic becoming at 30A. See Glossary under **musically**.

[180] The final phrase repeats what Timaeus had said at 31B. In his translation of the final sentence, Archer-Hind adopts the variant *eikôn tou poiêtou* (likeness of the maker or poet) in place of *eikôn tou noêtou* (likeness of the intelligible). So does Apelt ("ein Bild des Schöpfers"). See A. E. Taylor's note (pp. 646-649).

GLOSSARY

This glossary has two aims: to introduce the reader to the Greek of the *Timaeus* and to convey a sense of the dialogue's central philosophic themes. My hope is that the reader will use the glossary not only for reference but also as a source of reflection on the thought and spirit of the dialogue as they are revealed in Plato's artfully chosen words.

affection (*pathos, pathêma*). Next to *chôra* (see **place**, **Space**), *pathos* and *pathêma* are the most difficult words in the dialogue to translate adequately. Both nouns derive from the verb *paschein*, which means to suffer or undergo something (the opposite of *poiein*, do or make). A *pathos* is anything that happens to or befalls one. It can be a feeling or passion (compare our English "pathos"), a passive condition, a misfortune, or just a quality that something necessarily has or happens to have. Socrates makes *pathos* a central theme in the dialogue when, in his long speech at 19B, he confesses to an affection or feeling that leads him to want to see the best city in motion. *Pathêma* is similar to *pathos* in its range of meanings and can refer, in addition, to the symptoms of a disease (compare our "pathological"). So that the reader may track this recurring emphasis on passivity in the dialogue, *pathos* and *pathema* are translated by the unfortunately colorless word "affection" throughout.

art (*technê*). A *technê* is any teachable, specialized and publicly acknowledged know-how (compare our "technique"). It does not have the aesthetic overtones of our word "art" but refers to any craft or trade. It is not opposed to science. Examples of arts or *technai* include fishing, farming and tool-making as well as sculpture, rhetoric and mathematics. A *technitês* is the practitioner of an art, while someone without an art is an *idiotês* or layman. An *idiotês* lacks a specialized know-how that connects him with other human beings and thus remains *idios* (on his own or private). To do something with art, in Greek, is to do it with method and cunning.

beautiful (*kalos*), **temperate** (*metrios*). Beauty and beautification are central to the *Timaeus*. The encomium of the best city that Socrates desires is, in effect, the longing for a beautification. Critias' story is about an Athens grown young and beautiful. And the likely story presents the all as a *kosmos* or beautifully arranged whole. The adjective *kalos* means beautiful, fine or noble (its opposite, *aischros*, means both ugly and base). Although it appears as "beautiful" throughout, the reader must keep in mind the strong suggestion of nobility. *Metrios* (rendered "temperate" throughout) is related to the noun *metron*, measure or rule. The attempt to combine mathematics and moral virtue (especially moderation) is typical of Timaeus.

Being, substance (*ousia*), **what *is*** (*to on*), **the things that *are* or the beings** (*ta onta*), **genuinely** (*ontôs*). The origin of all these words is *einai*, to be. *To on*— rendered "what is"—is the neuter participle made into a substantive by the article *to*. The plural, *ta onta*, has been translated as either "the things that *are*" or "the beings." Here and in other dialogues, the Forms are sometimes called *ta onta auta kath' hauta*, the things themselves all by themselves. (At 51B ff., Timaeus asks whether there are such purely eidetic counterparts, "things themselves all by themselves," for the four elements of body.)

Ousia derives from the feminine form of the participle (*ousa*) and appears as "Being." (At 52D "Being" also appears as a translation of the neuter participle, *on*.) In ordinary Greek it refers to wealth in the form of property or real estate. It appears in the dialogue with this meaning in Socrates' praise of Timaeus and has been rendered "substance" (20A), as in the phrase "a man of substance." The adverb *ontôs* means something like "in its very being," and has been rendered as "genuinely."

cause (*aition, aitia*), **responsible** (*aitios*), **blameless** (*anaitios*), **put the blame on, hold responsible** (*aitiasthai*). The word for cause in Greek (which appears as either the feminine *aitia* or the neuter *aition*) occurs frequently in the dialogue. An *aitia* is a cause, origin, ground or occasion. It also means blame, charge or accusation. (Latin *causa* has a similar range of meaning). It is in general that which is to be held responsible for something. The adjective *aitios* (which can mean blamable or guilty) appears as "responsible," and the adjective *anaitios* appears as "blameless." The verb *aitiasthai* means charge, accuse or blame. It has been rendered as "put the blame on" or "hold responsible." There is no verb in Greek that simply means to cause.[1]

chance (*tychê*), **happen** [used as an auxiliary verb], **happen to run into, happen to meet with** (*tynchanein*). The word for chance in Greek is *tychê*, which comes from the verb *tynchanein*, which means hit upon, light upon, meet by chance, or fall in with. *Tychê* can refer to the fortune someone is dealt by the gods, whether for good or evil. In the translation, *tychê* appears as "chance," and *tynchanein*, which occurs quite often in the dialogue, is either "happen," "happen to run into" or "happen to meet with." *Tynchanein* sometimes comes up in odd contexts, for example, when Socrates announces how he happens to feel with respect to the city in speech (19B), or when Timaeus says that the model after which the cosmos was fashioned *happened*, that is, *chanced* to be eternal (37D1-3).

---

[1]   Heidegger offers the following derivation of the noun "cause": "*Causa, casus*, belongs to the verb *cadere*, 'to fall,' and means that which brings it about that something falls out as a result in such and such a way" ("The Question Concerning Technology," [*The Question Concerning Technology and Other Essays*, tr. William Lovitt, New York: Harper Torchbooks, 1977], p. 7).

come to be, be born, happen, arise (*gignesthai*), **becoming** or **birth** (*genesis*), **class, kind, race** (*genos*), **beget** (*gennan*). Forms of the verb *gignesthai* appear with great frequency in the dialogue. The verb has been rendered in a variety of ways, including "come to be," "become," "arise," "happen" and "be born." (At 56A5-6, the expression *gignomenon eis* has been rendered "passing into.") The noun *genesis* (as in the book of *Genesis*) has been rendered either "becoming" or "birth." "Becoming" is capitalized when it is opposed to Being (for example, at 29C) or when it is listed as one of the three kinds: Being, Space and Becoming (52D).

Related to *gignesthai* and *genesis* is the noun *genos*, which means race or descent and refers to a group of human beings related by blood (compare our "genus" and "gene"). It too occurs with great frequency in the dialogue and has been rendered "class" in Socrates' political summary (and once at 70A-B for the "class of desires") and "kind" for the remainder of the dialogue. At one point it appears as "race" (23B). The verb *gennan* is rendered "beget" throughout. It derives from *genna*, an alternate form of *genos*. *Gennan* can refer either to the siring that the father does or the childbearing that the mother does. To beget is to produce another of one's own kind (*genos*).

congeal, be compounded (*sympêgnunai*). A combination of *syn* (with or together) and *pêgnunai* (plant, fix or make firm), *sympêgnunai* occurs often in the likely story and means put together, frame, make solid, become frozen together. It has been translated as either "congeal" or "be compounded."

construct, compose, combine, stand together (*synistanai*), **structure, construction, standing-together, composition** (*systasis*). The verb *synistanai* literally means "make stand together." It is the origin of our word "system." In the translation it appears most often as "construct" and occasionally as "compose" or "combine." The craftsman god is sometimes called *ho synistas*, the constructor. The noun *systasis* (literally, a standing together) occurs with great frequency in the dialogue. It has been rendered for the most part as "structure" and less often as "composition" or "construction." (It appears as "bracing" in the medical sense of the term at 89A.) A *systasis* can also refer to a political constitution and to either a compact or a conflict. At the crucial occurrence of this word in the dialogue, where Timaeus says that the cosmos originated in a *systasis* of intellect and necessity (48A), I have rendered it "standing-together" to preserve the double sense of opposition and alliance. And at 83A a form of the verb *synistanai* appears as "stands together."

cosmos or adornment (*kosmos*), **arrangement** (*diakosmêsis*), **array or put in array** (*kosmein, diakosmein, katakosmein*), **order** [verb] (*epitattein*), **order** [noun] (*taxis*), **disorder** (*ataxia*). Words in Greek for order and putting things in order tend to have a martial meaning. They fit nicely with Socrates' desire for a war story (19B). The verb *kosmein* means order or arrange, and especially, marshal troops for battle. Likewise, *taxis* has the general meaning of order but refers more specifically to an array of soldiers ready for battle. The noun *kosmos*, in one of its meanings, is the world or universe. More generally, it suggests beautiful arrangement and decency. In Homer, *kosmos* can also refer to a contrivance or stratagem, as in the *Odyssey*, when Odysseus exhorts the singer Demodicus to recount the *hippou kosmon*, the contrivance of the horse (8. 492). The adjectival form, *kosmios*, refers to anyone who is orderly and well-behaved. Whereas the all (*to pan*) is the world as a totality, *kosmos* is the world as a beautifully ordered whole. A *kosmos* is also an ornament, decoration or adornment (as in our word "cosmetic"). The verbs *kosmein*, *diakosmein* and *katakosmein* have been rendered as either "array" or "put in array" to suggest both beautification and war. *Diakosmêsis* appears as "arrangement."

The verb *epitattein* appears often in the dialogue, especially in the early conversation between Socrates and his hosts. It means enjoin or order and has been rendered throughout as "order." Socrates is like a commander issuing military orders to his hosts. And although the word *ataxia*, disorder, occurs in the dialogue, the word *chaos* (infinite space, chasm or abyss) does not.

course or sweep (*pherein*), **circuit** (*periodos*), **course** [noun] (*phora*), **orbit or orbiting** (*periphora*). An important motion-word in the dialogue is *pherein*, which means bear, bring, lead, carry or carry off. In the passive it means rush, or be borne or swept along. It has been rendered as either "course" or "sweep." The noun *phora* derives from *pherein* and appears as "course." A *periphora* is a being-swept-around. It appears as either "orbit" or "orbiting." A *periodos* is literally a way or path (*hodos*) around. My hope was that translating it as "circuit" would, to modern ears, suggest circuitry. The cosmic soul is an elaborate sort of wiring. It is the great *transmitter* of periodic motion and Timaeus' mathematical "soul music." We are the *receivers* of its signal.

craftsman (*dêmiourgos*), **craft** [verb] (*dêmiourgein*). The Greek word is a combination of *dêmos* (the people) and *ergon* (work). A *dêmiourgos* is thus one who works for the people. The word "demiurge" has passed into English usage and has acquired an exalted status. But the Greek word is quite humble and refers to any ordinary worker or craftsman. (Timaeus' craftsman god is thus something like a public servant.) More restricted in meaning than *technitês*, a *dêmiourgos* is anyone who has a method for making something. In Book 10 of the *Republic*, when Socrates takes up his second critique of poetry, it is the poets as *dêmiourgoi* that he is attacking (makers do not know the proper use of what they make). The noun *dêmiourgos* and forms of its corresponding verb *dêmiourgein* occur frequently in the dialogue, sometimes in unusual contexts. Earth, for example, is at one point said to be the *craftsman* of Night and Day (40C), and fire is called a *craftsman* of non-uniformity (59A). In the translation, the noun is always "craftsman," and the verbal forms are always some variation of "craft."

desire [noun] (*epithymia*), **spirit, anger** (*thymos*), **heart** (*prothymia*), **heartily** (*prothymôs*), **put one's heart into** (*prothymein*), **love, erotic love** (*erôs*), **yearn for** (*pothein*). *Epithymia* refers to any bodily desire or longing such as the desire for food and drink. In *Republic* 4, where Socrates outlines the three-part soul, the lowest part is called *alogon te kai epithymêtikon*, irrational and desirous (439D7-8). It is opposed to the calculating or rational part of the soul. In his long speech near the beginning of the *Timaeus*, Socrates compares himself to a man who had an *epithymia* to see animals in motion (20B7).

Thymos, a word related to *epithymia*, covers a wide range of meanings in Plato and refers to the emotional or passionate part of the soul. It can refer to spiritedness and courage and also to anger. In the tripartite soul of the *Republic*, the middle part is characterized by this spiritedness, which can ally itself either to the lower, desirous part or to the higher, rational part that is by nature fit for ruling. The most distinctive thing about *thymos*, Socrates tells us, is that it is the source of the love of "victories and honors" (*Republic* 8. 548C). Timaeus describes *thymos* at 70A, where he calls it a lover of victory. *Prothymia*, another *thym*-word, refers to a ready willingness, zeal or enthusiasm. It has been rendered "heart," its adverbial form *prothymôs* as "heartily," and the verbal form *prothymein* as "put one's heart into." (Heart in this sense is not to be confused with the bodily organ, which is *kardia*.) In the prologue the characters all take turns using either the noun or the adverb (17B, 20B, 20C, 23D and 26C). Spiritedness, whether as *thymos* or *prothymia*, is the reigning passion and animating principle of the *Timaeus*, which emphasizes honor, praise, feasting, war, music and the control of potential disorder. Spiritedness in the dialogues seems, furthermore, to be deeply related to mathematics and the mathematical temperament of problem-solving.[2] The mathematical education in the *Republic* must be suited to those who are to be warriors as well as philosophers (7. 525B, 527C). And in the dialogue that bears his name, the young geometer Theaetetus expresses confidence that he can answer Socrates' question about knowledge if it's a task requiring spiritedness or heart, *prothymia* (*Theaetetus* 148D).

Like *epithymia*, *erôs* is desire, especially sexual desire. But unlike *epithymia* it can be directed to something non-bodily like power, honor or wisdom. It appears in the translation as either "love" or "erotic love." In the *Symposium* philosophy, in its longing for the transcendence of the bodily and the human, is presented as a form of *erôs*. In the *Republic* we are told that love has of old been called a tyrant (9.573B6-7). Timaeus echoes this opinion when he calls love "all-venturing" (69D) and identifies the love of begetting with the lust for dominance (91B). *Erôs* appears in a positive light only once in the dialogue, when Timaeus praises the *erastês* or lover of intellect and knowledge (46D).

At the end of his political summary, Socrates uses the verb *pothein* (yearn for), thereby suggesting that the summary might be humanly unsatisfying as well as theoretically incomplete: "Are we yearning for something further in what was said, my dear Timaeus, something that's being left out?" Timaeus has no such yearning. He responds, "Not at all."

---

2   The *thymos* of modern mathematics is evident in the closing sentence of François Viète's *Introduction to the Analytical Art*: "Finally, the analytical art ... appropriates to itself by right the proud problem of problems, which is: TO LEAVE NO PROBLEM UNSOLVED" (Appendix to Jacob Klein's *Greek Mathematical Thought and the Origin of Algebra*, tr. Eva Brann, New York: Dover Publications, Inc., 1992, p. 353).

district (*nomos*). See **law**.

everlasting (*aïdios*), **eternity** (*aiôn*), **eternal** (*aiônios*). Both adjectives convey the sense of eternality or endurance in time and are derived from *aei*, always. An *aiôn* is a period of time (compare our "aeon") and can refer either to an era or to an infinitely long stretch of time—an eternity. It appears in the famous definition of time at 37D5. Although *aïdios* and *aiônios* appear, respectively, as "everlasting" and "eternal," it is difficult in the dialogue to distinguish their meanings. The intelligible model is said to be everlasting (*aïdion*) at 29A, but at 37A ff., where the god proceeds to construct time, the intelligible Animal is said to be both *aïdion* and *aiônion*. It is worth noting that *aiôn*, the origin of *aiônios*, has a strong connection with the soul or vital force—that by which we endure and live.[3]

form (*eidos*), **look** (*idea*), **figure** (*schêma*), **shape** (*morphê*). These renderings are kept consistent throughout the translation. *Eidos* and *idea* both derive from the stem [w]id, to see (compare our "video"). *Eidos* can mean beautiful appearance. In the *Odyssey*, Odysseus praises Calypso for her *eidos* (5.217). As a philosophic term, the *eidos* or form of something is its purely noetic or intelligible "whatness"—what a thing most deeply and truly is. It is the objective counterpart to philosophic insight or intellection (see **intellect**). As the kind-character of a thing, the *eidos* is intimately related to *genos* (see **kind, class or race**).

habit (*ethos*, *êthos*), **usual** (*eiôthôs*), **unusual** (*aêthês*). An *ethos* is a custom, usage or habit. It has been translated "habit." The word *eiôthôs* (a participle used as an adjective) comes from *ethein*, be accustomed or in the habit of. It appears as "usual." The words for "unusual" and "unusualness" (*aêthês* and *aêtheia*) are related to the Greek word *êthos* (with a long "e"), which also means custom, usage or habit but can also refer to someone's character. Socrates refers to the unusualness (*aêtheia*) of his city in matters pertaining to child-production (18C), and Timaeus calls his account of place unusual (*aêthês*, 48D).

hearsay (*akoê*). *Akoê* is related to the verb *akouein*, hear. It refers not only to hearing but also the thing heard, to a report or even the fame of something. It also means hearsay. In Critias' speech, which has numerous references to *akoê*, hearsay seems to be virtually a form of wisdom. The Greeks are naïve, says the Egyptian priest to Solon, because they lack "ancient hearsay" (22B). The Egyptians, by contrast, are wise because they are old and because they record the hearsay of the cosmos.

heaven (*ouranos*). The *ouranos*, here translated as "heaven," is the vault or firmament of the sky. It is also the word for the roof or "vault" of the mouth. The likely story is largely devoted to a radical revision of the gods as we find them presented in Homer and Hesiod. In Hesiod's *Theogony*, first to be born was Chaos, then "broad-bosomed Earth" (116-117). The firstborn of Earth and Erebus was Ouranos or Sky, "an always

---

[3]   See *aiôn* in Pierre Chantraine, *Dictionnaire Etymologique de la Langue Grecque*, Paris: Editions Klincksieck, 1968, p. 42.

unfailing seat for the blessed gods" (128). Hesiod goes on to say that Ouranos buried his children, the Titans, as soon as they were born. One of them, Kronos, is goaded by his mother to exact vengeance on Ouranos by castrating him. Kronos in turn becomes the devourer of his children (459). In the Battle of Gods and Titans, Kronos and the other Titans are ultimately defeated and hurled into Tartarus by Zeus and the other children of Kronos (713ff.). Timaeus presents an expurgated version of all this at 40D.

image (*eidôlon*), **imitation** (*mimêma*), **phantasm** (*phantasma*). An *eidôlon* is a diminutive *eidos*, literally, a little form. *Mimêma*, imitation, is related to *mimêsis* (the act of imitating), which has passed into English "mimesis." A *phantasma* (from *phantazein*, see **seem**) or phantasm is a ghostly, fleeting sort of image. In the *Sophist*, the Eleatic stranger sharply distinguishes between *eikones*, which preserve the proportions of their originals, and *phantasmata*, which do not (235D ff.). In the likely story, phantasms are connected with dreams and dreaminess (45E, 52C).

intellect, mind (*nous*), **make sense, be sensible** (*noun echein*), **intellection** (*noêsis*), **intelligible** (*noêtos*), **unintelligent** (*anoêtos*), **folly** (*anoia*), **stupidity** (*amathia*), **thought, intelligence** (*dianoia*). The word *nous* has been rendered as "mind" for the expression *kata noun* ("to one's mind," for example, at 17C and 36D). Elsewhere it appears as "intellect." *Nous* in its highest sense is that by which rational beings—whether humans, gods or spirits—are immediately in touch with the highest and unchanging objects of thought. It is that by virtue of which we "see" something in the sense of experiencing an insight into its "whatness" or nature. The divine craftsman embodies nous in that he seems to have direct, intuitive access to his intelligible model. *Noêsis*, intellection, is the activity of nous or intellect. *Nous* does not always have an exalted meaning in Plato. Sometimes it simply means good sense (*Meno* 88B)—a meaning that may be hinted at in certain appearances of the word in the *Timaeus* (for example, 89B, 92C, or even the famous passage about *nous* persuading necessity at 48A).

The idiom noun *echein*, literally, to have mind or intellect, has been rendered "make sense" or "be sensible." The adjective *noêtos* means intelligible. *Anoêtos* means not to be thought, unheard of, unintelligible, and unintelligent or silly. It has been rendered "unintelligent." *Amathia* is the condition of being without learning but also refers to stupidity or coarseness. The word *dianoia*, which appears as either "thought" or "intelligence," refers to discursive intelligence but can also mean thought in the sense of purpose or intent. At one point in particular, this latter meaning is strongly suggested (76D).

join, fit or tune (*harmottein*), **build** (*tektainein*), **mold or fabricate** (*plattein*), **sculpt** (*torneuein*). The *Timaeus* bristles with words for doing things in an artful way. Next to *synistanai*, to construct, Timaeus' favorite "doing" word is *harmottein*. It means join, as in the joiner's or carpenter's art. The main idea here is that the things joined have a perfect fit, like the dovetail joints in well-made wooden cabinets. It can also mean marry or wed, or tune a musical instrument, and is related to the noun *harmonia* (see **tuning**). Throughout the translation *harmottein* and *synarmottein* have been rendered either by "join," "fit," or variants of "tune."

The verb *tektainein* always appears as "build." (The most striking occurrence is at 91A where we are told how the gods *built* sexual desire.) *Plattein* is either "mold" or "fabricate." The verb also means counterfeit or forge. The verb *torneuein* means turn neatly with a chisel and lathe (a *tornos* was the tool used by carpenters to draw circles). It appears as "sculpt."

law, custom, song, district (*nomos*), **distribute** (*nemein* and *dianemein*). The noun *nomos* derives from the verb *nemein*, which means both deal out and pasture. *Nemein* and its variant *dianemein* occur regularly and have been translated as "distribute." The noun *nomos* is notably absent from Socrates' political summary at the beginning of the dialogue but occurs frequently in the speeches of Critias. *Nomos* as custom (or convention) is opposed to *physis* or nature. (Socrates reminds his hosts repeatedly in his summary that his city is based on *physis* or nature.) Solon hears the tale about Athens and Atlantis in the nome or district, the *nomos*, of Sais (21E). And in the most interesting use of the word in the dialogue, Socrates at 29D calls the speech of Timaeus a *nomos* (which here means both law and song). *Nomos* as law is present not only in the Egyptian priest's display of his laws (which are also longstanding customs) but also in the likely story, which refers to laws of destiny (41E) and laws of nature (83E).

life (*bios*), **animal** (*zôon*). Whereas the noun *zôê* refers to life in the sense of being alive (from *zan*, live), *bios* means the span of one's life, one's lifetime. (Compare English words like "zoo," "zoology" and "biology.") An animal in Greek is a *zôon*, that is, a living thing. Plants for Timaeus are "animals" insofar as they are animate or alive (77B). "Animal" is capitalized when it refers to the intelligible Animal or Animals (30C-31A).

likeness (*eikôn*), **model, example** (*paradeigma*), **likely, suitable** (*eikôs*), **reasonable** (*epieikês*). The noun *eikôn* has been translated "likeness" throughout (compare our "icon"). The adjective *eikôs* is translated mostly as "likely" and once as "suitable" (24D). The adverbial form, *eikotôs*, appears as "suitably" (55D4). Noun, adjective and adverb derive from the verb *eoikenai*, be like. When something is *eikôs*, it is like the truth: likely, probable or reasonable. It also means fair or equitable. The adjective *epieikês* (from *eikôs*) occurs once (67D). Like *eikôs*, it means fitting, suitable, fair, reasonable or probable. It has been rendered as "reasonable."[4] The artist-god fashions the cosmic likeness after an intelligible paradigm or *paradeigma* (from the verb *paradeiknynai*, show alongside of). A *paradeigma* is an example, original or model. It appears as "model" throughout the likely story and once, in Critias' long speech, as "example" (24A).

---

[4]   See Aristotle's discussion of *epieikeia*, equity, in the *Nicomachean Ethics* 5. 10.

manner, fashion, mode (*tropos*), **proper, in the proper way** (*kata tropon*). The noun *tropos*, from the verb *trepein*, to turn, refers generally to a direction, way, manner or mode (compare English "trope"). It can also refer to a habit or one's customary way of life, as well as to someone's temperament or turn of character. In Greek music, a *tropos* (like *harmonia*, see **tuning**) refers to one of the musical modes (it is something like our musical term "temperament" in reference to the tuning of keyboard instruments). At 35A, just before the god makes the cosmic soul out of music, Timaeus refers to the *tropos* in which the soul was ordered, no doubt referring to the Dorian mode, which gives the soul a warlike temperament (see Appendix on Music). The phrase *kata tropon* has been rendered as either "proper" (42E) or "in the proper way" (80C). The phrase *apo tropou* has been rendered "out of character" (89E).

master [verb] (*kratein*), **mastery** (*kratos*), **mistress** (*despotis*), **dominate** (*despotein*). The translations in the heading are used consistently throughout. *Kratos* (mastery) and *Bia* (force) are characters in Hesiod's *Theogony*. They are children of Styx and dwell with Zeus (385-403).

motion (*kinêsis*), **move** (*kinein, kineisthai*), **rest, faction, civil war** (*stasis*), **peace** (*hêsychia*). *Kinêsis* in Greek can cover all forms of change, not just local motion. In the *Timaeus*, the principal form of motion is local, and so *kinêsis* has been translated throughout as "motion" (except for one rendering as "commotion" at 43C). The corresponding verbs, *kinein* (transitive) and *kineisthai* (intransitive), are translated "move." *Stasis*, "rest," also means faction or civil war. The word *hêsychia* refers to stillness, rest, peace or quiet. It is central to the dialogue and its strong political overtones as the opposite of war. It appears as "peace" throughout the translation.

musically (*emmelôs*), **unmusically** (*plêmmelôs*), **lack of musicality** (*plêmmeleia*), **be unmusical** (*plêmmelein*). A *melos* in Greek is a limb. It is also the word for a song or strain of music and is the origin of our "melody." To be *emmelês* is literally to be in tune and, by extension, refers to someone who is "in tune" or "in step" with the demands of modesty, right judgement and decorum. To be *plêmmelês* is, by contrast, to be immodest, poor in judgement, and ignorant of one's proper place—to strike the wrong human note. *Plêmmeleia*, then, is any impropriety or transgression. In the *Apology*, Socrates accuses the craftsmen of *plêmmeleia* for thinking that they know everything just because they know something (22D). The likely story is framed by two references to the lack of musicality (30A, 92B).

nature (*physis*), **sprout** (*phyein*). *Physis* or "nature" covers a wide range of meanings in Greek. It can refer to a thing's innermost quality, power or disposition. It can also refer to a thing's outward appearance or look, or to the kind of thing something is (a lion, ox or man). *Physis* can be the indwelling order or constitution of something, the internal principle by which that thing grows and does what it does. In sum, *physis* embraces a thing's being, appearance and becoming. The verb *phyein* is translated "sprout." It is related to the Greek word for a tribe (*phylê*) and a plant (*phyton*, see 90A).

necessity (*anankê*), **compel** (*anankazesthai*), **force** [noun] (*bia*), **force** [verb] (*biazein*). *Anankê* or necessity is of course the second of Timaeus' two great cosmic principles. The corresponding verb, *anankazesthai*, has been rendered "compel." At one point a variant of this verb (*eisanankazesthai*) is rendered "make necessary" (49A). The various cases of the word *bia* appear as forms of "force," and the verb *biazein* is always "force." The most famous instance of *bia* occurs when the god mixes Same and Other (35B).

old (*palaios*), **young** (*neos*), **elder** (*presbyteros*), **ancient** (*archaios*). Nothing is more characteristic of the *Timaeus* than its preoccupation with age. *Timaeus* and *Critias* both seek to take us back in time, to the time of a "first and best condition" (42D). By retrieving the oldest things, their mythic time-travel recovers what those things were in the freshness of their youth. The word *palaios* (which occurs often in the speech of Critias) has been consistently rendered "old" (compare English "paleontology.") The word *neos* means both new and young (it appears as "young" throughout). Compare our "neophyte," which literally means newly planted (from *phyein*, sprout) and refers to a recent convert or novice. I have tried to keep the adjective *presbyteros* "elder" wherever possible (for example, the cosmic soul is the body's "elder" at 34C). *Archaios* has been rendered "ancient" throughout (compare our "archaeology"). It is related to both *archê* (beginning) and *archein* (begin). See **rule**.

persuasion (*peithô*), **persuade** (*peithein*), **trust** [noun] (*pistis*), **trust** [verb] (*pisteuein*). The words for "persuasion" and "trust" are related to the verb *peithein*, persuade. The central occurrence of *peithô* is at 48A, where Timaeus says that the cosmos came about when necessity yielded to "thoughtful persuasion." The noun *pistis* (related to the verb *pisteuein*) means trust or belief. It is used in Timaeus' proportion, "Just as Being is to Becoming, so is truth to trust" (29C). It is also the word Socrates uses for the next-to-lowest segment of the divided line (*Republic* 6. 511E).

place, Space (*chôra*). This ordinary Greek word defies translation once Timaeus breathes new meaning into it. A common enough word, *chôra* refers to a place, space or field. It is the room or expanse in which something is or belongs. It can be the country or land, or a position that one occupies (one's proper place). The word occurs for the first time in the dialogue in the context of Socrates' political summary (19A). But as Timaeus' third kind (52B), the *chôra* (or receptacle) is neither mere place (since it is constantly in motion) nor empty space (because it is full of "powers" and "traces" of the four elements). In spite of the extreme difficulty involved in translating this word at all,[5] I have rendered *chôra* as "Space" when it refers to the third kind (without a

---

[5]   On the difficulty of translating *chôra*, see John Sallis, *Chorology: On Beginning in Plato's Timaeus*, Bloomington: Indiana University Press, 1999, pp. 113-124. See also Jacques Derrida, *Khora*, in *On the Name*, tr. Ian McLeod, ed. Thomas Dutoit, Stanford: Stanford University Press, 1995, pp. 89-127. In his entry for *chôra*, Chantraine notes that *chôra* is "distinct from *kenon*, which is void and unoccupied, and from *topos*, which is a more restricted place and can even refer to a point" (ibid. p. 1281).

capital at 52B4) and as "place" everywhere else. At one point, it appears as "assigned place" to convey the sense of a station or post (83A). The word "Space" conveys the appropriate indeterminateness of the *chôra* and also suggests the extension or three-dimensionality of the geometric solids used to construct the four elementary bodies. Nevertheless, it is abundantly clear from what Timaeus says about the *chôra* that no name seems capable of doing justice to this deeply mysterious non-being.

poet (*poiêtês*), **do or make** (*poiein*). The word for poet means maker. It is related to the verb *poiein*, do or make. The craftsman god is the world's poet as well as its father (28C). At the beginning of the *Critias*, Socrates calls Timaeus "the previous poet" (108B6). See **affection**.

power (*dynamis*), **be able** (*dynasthai*). The word *dynamis*, translated as "power," occurs with great frequency in the dialogue. At one point, we even hear of "the power of likely accounts" (48D). *Dynamis* derives from the verb *dynasthai*, which means be able. It is the term in Aristotle that is commonly translated as "potentiality" (compare English "dynamic" and "dynamite"). It can refer to the quality or even the meaning of something. It also has the technical mathematical sense of either the "square" of a magnitude or a "square root" (see *Theaetetus* 147D, where the young geometer defines *dynamis* in the sense of "square root"). At 54B the mathematical expression *kata dynamin* has been rendered as "in square." One of the best jokes in Plato occurs in the *Statesman*, where the stranger, combining the ordinary and the mathematical senses of *dynamis*, defines humankind in terms of "the 'power' of two feet" (266A ff.).

pretext, explanation (*prophasis*). This highly interesting word occurs four times in the *Timaeus*.[6] It often has the negative sense of pretext or excuse and is used in this way when it first appears (in the mouth of Hermocrates at 20C). It appears near the end of the *Critias* at the pivotal moment when Critias recounts the degeneration of the Atlantians (120D8). *Prophasis* comes from *phainein*, show or make apparent (or *phanai*, say) and *pro*, before. A *prophasis* is a cause, reason or motive that one shows or says "up front," either in order to reveal the true reason behind something or to conceal it behind a merely alleged or professed reason. It has been translated as either "pretext" or "explanation." It is not clear why Timaeus sometimes uses *prophasis* instead of *aitia* or *aition* (66C1, 76E5, 92A3).

prudence (*phronêsis*), **prudent** (*phronimos*), **thoughtful** (*emphrôn*), **thoughtless** (*aphrôn*), **thoughtlessness** (*aphrosynê*). The noun *phronêsis* has an interesting range of meanings in Greek. It comes from the verb *phronein*, which means think, intend or take heed. It can also mean be high-minded, and be arrogant. *Phronein* is related to *phrên*, the word for the midriff or diaphragm, the Homeric seat of

---

[6] *Prophasis* is a central word in Thucydides. An excellent explanation of its various meanings is given by Lionel Pearson, "*Prophasis* and *Aitia*," in *Transactions and Proceedings of the American Philological Association* (*TAPA*) 83, 1952, pp. 205-223.

feeling, mind and reason. *Phronêsis* takes its meanings from the verb *phronein* and can mean purpose or intent, high-mindedness, and arrogance. It is also good sense, judgement and practical intelligence. Throughout the translation *phronêsis* appears as "prudence" and the corresponding adjective, *phronimos*, as "prudent."

The adjective *emphrôn* is very close in meaning to *phronimos* and has been rendered "thoughtful." *Aphrôn* is "thoughtless," and *aphrosynê* is "thoughtlessness." Aristotle carefully distinguishes between *sophia* as theoretical wisdom and *phronêsis* as prudence or practical wisdom.[7] And while *phronêsis* has a wider and less specific meaning in the dialogues generally, here in the *Timaeus* it has a definite practical emphasis. When the Egyptian priest of Critias' tale refers to the wisdom of his city, his examples are prophecy and medicine (24C), and the wisdom that Timaeus praises is the sort that orders the soul and makes it healthy.

The word *sophia*, which also means wisdom, is absent from the dialogue except for its appearance within the word for philosophy (*philosophia*, love of wisdom). Its adjectival form, *sophos*, appears twice and then only as an epithet of Solon in Critias' speech, both times in the superlative (20E, 21C).

random (*eikê*). At one crucial moment in his speech (when body is mistakenly constructed before soul), Timaeus uses the word *eikê*, which means without plan or purpose (34C). It closely resembles the word *eikôs* or likely. The origin of *eikê* is uncertain but may be *a-hekôn*, unwillingly or unintentionally. The word appears here as "random."

receptacle (*hypodochê*), **receive** (*dechesthai*). "Demiurge" and "receptacle" are the two most famous words from the *Timaeus*. A *hypodochê* is any hospitable reception or refuge. It can also refer to a presupposition or assumption. It comes from the verb *hypodechesthai* (literally, receive under), which means receive under one's roof or welcome, undertake, admit or allow, withstand an attack, and conceive or become pregnant. The verb's range of meaning is well-suited to the role of the receptacle in Timaeus' account. The verb *dechesthai*, receive, occurs often in the dialogue. It sets the tone for the entire drama of hosts who entertain or "receive" their guests. Socrates in this dialogue is uncharacteristically defined by his extreme receptivity (20C).

region (*topos*), **strange** (*atopos*), **seat or site** (*hedra*). Topos (compare our "topic" or "topology") appears as "region." The Greek word translated throughout as "strange" is *atopos*, which also means absurd. Critias and Timaeus both use it to describe their accounts (20D, 48D). To be strange or absurd is, literally, to be placeless or "out of place" (*a-topos*). *Hedra* can be something ordinary like a seat or bench, or else exalted like the seat or abode of the gods. It has been rendered "seat," except in one place, where it appears as "site" (53A).

right (*themis*). Themis is the goddess of custom and of law and order. She appears in Homer and Hesiod. The noun *themis* refers to law or right, something established and

---

[7]   *Nicomachean Ethics* 6.5 ff.

sanctioned by custom. Early in the likely story, Timaeus rejects certain alternatives on the grounds that they would be *ou themis*, not right, in the sense of not allowed or permitted—blasphemous (29A, 30A).

rule, begin (*archein*), **beginning, origin or principle** (*archê*). The words *archê* and *archein* are strongly political. The verb *archein* in its political sense means rule. The noun *archê* is rule, sovereignty or empire. The political sense of these terms must be born in mind as we hear the likely story. We must remember that *archê* in the sense of beginning, origin or principle is also that which *rules*. Throughout the *Timaeus* there is a play on the different meanings of *archê*, which can refer to a beginning in the temporal sense or to a non-temporal origin or principle. Indeed, the likely story may be defined as the attempt to reveal eternal origins through the language of time. (A similar thing happens in Socrates' myth of recollection in the *Meno*, 81A ff.) Going back to a beginning is thus a going *into* the (timeless) origin of something. When Timaeus says at 48A that he must go back to the beginning of his talk, he is playfully alluding to the fact that he is revising his account of cosmic principles. The two beginnings of the likely story point to the fact that the cosmos has not one principle but two. The verb *archein* has been rendered throughout as either "rule" or "begin."

seem, seem good, seem so, suppose (*dokein*), **opinion** (*doxa*), **hold [an] opinion** (*doxazein*), **decree** (*dogma*), **shine forth, come to light** (phainein), **appear** (*phainesthai*), **show itself (as)** (*phantazesthai*). The verb *dokein* means think, suppose, imagine, seem, or seem either good or true. It has been rendered "seem," "seem good," "seem so" and "suppose." In the dramatic prologue to the *Timaeus*, this verb has a distinctly official ring to it and suggests the political process of deliberation and decree (20D, 27A).[8] The related noun, *doxa*, refers to an opinion, sentiment or judgement. It can also mean reputation or glory. It has been translated "opinion," although the reader must bear in mind that a *doxa* is not merely an inner, psychological state but is always in reference to the way something seems. (Our word "orthodoxy" is literally the right or correct opinion about something—the correct "seeming.")

Doxa is like a refrain that runs through the whole prologue of the *Timaeus*. Socrates stresses the opinion-nature of his estimation of the poets and of Timaeus (19D, 20A), and the old priest in Solon's story chides modern Athens for not having any ancient opinion (22B). *Doxazein*, another *doxa*-related verb sometimes translated "opine," is also rendered "hold [an] opinion." At a crucial point in the dialogue (48E), just before he embarks on his account of the third kind, Timaeus uses the noun *dogma* (related to *doxa*), which is a publicly accepted opinion, decree, or ordinance. It has been rendered

---

[8] "The classic example of the formula is that most familiar from the decrees of the Athenians as the introduction of the assembly's decision, *edoxen têi boulêi kai tôi dêmôi* ['it seemed good to the council and to the people'] (or simply *edoxen tôi dêmôi* ['it seemed good to the people')." A. G. Woodhead, *The Study of Greek Inscriptions*, 2nd Edition, Cambridge: Cambridge University Press, 1981, p. 38. Critias alludes to this formula when he uses the expression *edoxe hêmin*, "it seemed good to us," at 27A.

"decree." The sense of *dogma* as decree or ordinance fits with Timaeus' curious reference to accusations and indictments (49E), trial and verdict (51C), and voting (51D).

The verbs *phainein, phainesthai* and *phantazesthai* are all related to the Greek word for light: *phaos* or *phôs* (compare our "photon" and "photograph"). They all have the basic sense of coming to light or shining forth and have been translated as shown in the heading.

similar (*homoios*), **copy, portray** (*aphomoioun*), **copy** [noun] (*aphomoioma*), **imprint** [verb] (*ektypoun*), **imprint** [noun] (*ektupoma*). *Homoios* always appears as "similar." *Aphomoioun*, "copy or portray," is the act by which one thing is made similar to another. The result is a copy or *aphomoioma*. *Ektypoun* means work or model in relief. It has been rendered "imprint." The result is an imprint or *ektypoma*.

speech, account, word, reason, ratio (*logos*), **irrational** (*alogos*), **proportion** (*analogia*), **calculation or reasoning** (*logismos*), **calculate or reason out** (*logizesthai*), **converse** (*dialegesthai*). The distinction between *logos* as speech or account and *mythos* or story has been strictly preserved throughout (see **story**). The noun *logos* is related to the verb *legein*, which means say or speak. Its root meaning is gather or select. *Logos* has a wide range of meanings in the dialogue and is most often rendered by "speech," "account," "reason" or "word." (It appears as "definition" once, at 83C.) Perhaps the most important meaning of *logos* in the dialogue is "ratio" since Timaeus tends to identify the rational with the mathematical. Just as number (*arithmos*) for the ancients was always "a multitude composed of units," so a ratio was not a fraction but "a sort of relation in respect of size between two magnitudes of the same kind."[9] The sameness of two ratios is an *analogia* or proportion (compare our "analogy").

Logismos, "calculation" or "reasoning," occurs regularly in the dialogue. *Logizesthai* can mean count or compute as well as reason or reason out. It appears as either "calculate" or "reason." The verb *dialegesthai* does not occur in the dialogue. It means converse but also suggests the dialectical activity of the philosopher in his effort to move from opinion to knowledge. Dialectic in this sense is completely absent from the *Timaeus*. Indeed, even the opening series of interchanges is hardly a conversation.

story (*mythos*), **tell stories** (*mythologein*). The Greek word for story, *mythos* (the ancestor of our "myth"), is related to the verb *mytheisthai*, say, speak or tell. A *mythos* is anything conveyed by word of mouth—a word, speech, message or command. The verb *mythologein* combines *mythos* and *logos*. It occurs once and has been rendered "tell stories." Although *logos* and *mythos* are for the most part complementary in the dialogues, Timaeus uses both words to describe his account of the all. It is far from clear what it means for a speech to be both an account and a story.[10]

---

[9]   The definitions cited are those found in Euclid's *Elements*. The definition of number is Def. 2 from Book 7; that of ratio is Def. 3 from Book 5.

[10]   A highly interesting passage that combines *logos* and *mythos* occurs at the end of the *Gorgias*. Just before he presents his concluding story to Callicles, Socrates says: "You will consider it a *mythos*, I imagine, but I consider it a *logos*" (523A).

time (*chronos*). The Greek word for time is familiar to us from English words like "chronological" and "chronic." It is a commonplace to connect *chronos* or time with the Titan Kronos, who seems to resemble time in the devouring of his offspring.

tuning, attunement (*harmonia*). The word *harmonia* derives from the verb *harmottein* (see **join, fit or tune**). It is a fitting together, connection or joint, as in the Heraclitus fragment, *harmoniê aphanês phanerês kreittôn* ("The non-apparent connection is better [or stronger] than the apparent one," 54). The word does not mean harmony in our sense of the term and has nothing to do with chords or the simultaneous sounding of different pitches (although that, to be sure, is a modern instance of *harmonia* in its most general sense). In music a *harmonia* is a tuning or scale. The Greek modes, which Socrates discusses and critiques in *Republic* 3 are *harmoniai*. To be "harmonized" in Greek, therefore, means to be tuned. It means that the parts of a whole are arranged in the proper order from top to bottom (a Greek scale is thought of as going down instead of up) such that they acquire their right and precisely defined relation to one another. The cosmic soul is the paradigm of such ordering. The noun *harmonia* has been rendered as "tuning" or "attunement." For more on *harmonia* in relation to scale, mode and scale-building, see Appendix A.

In *Republic* 4, Socrates calls the virtue of moderation a *harmonia*. It is the principle according to which the parts of the ideal city are made to keep their proper place and be in a condition of unanimity (431E-432A). In the *Phaedo*, in order to defend the immortality of the soul, Socrates attempts to refute the Pythagorean notion that the soul is a *harmonia* or attunement (92A-95A).

work, job, deed, task (*ergon*). An *ergon* in Greek (compare English "energy") can refer to anything done or made—to works of art and deeds of war. It can be someone's job or business. It may, but need not, imply something laborious. *Ergon* as deed is often opposed to *logos* or speech. Socrates plays on this duality throughout his long speech at 19B ff. The word *parergon* (from *para*, beside or alongside of, and *ergon*) appears several times in the dialogue and has been rendered "side-job." See **craftsman**.

APPENDICES

The purpose of the following appendices is to give a brief and basic introduction to the musical, astronomical and geometrical constructions of the dialogue. Readers who want a more detailed treatment of these topics are encouraged to consult the commentaries of Taylor and Cornford.

Each of the impressive technical accomplishments of Timaeus has buried within it a deep problem that the technical construction in part copes with and in part conceals. The musical problem, that of building a scale, is the so-called Pythagorean comma; the problem of astronomy is the disjunction between being and appearance; and the problem of building the solids is that these most perfect of plane-sided, three-dimensional figures have irrational lines as a necessary feature of their internal structure. Each of these problems will be described in the appropriate appendix.

APPENDIX A—MUSIC

The two greatest architectural feats of the *Timaeus* are the construction of soul and the construction of body. Soul is constructed in three separate stages. First, the god mixes Same, Other and Being to make a sort of soul-stuff (35A-B). Second, he takes this stuff and makes a musical strip out of it (35B-36B). Third, he cuts and pastes this strip to form the two circuits according to which the all moves (the circles of Same and Other) and cuts one of these circles (the circle of the Other) into seven strips to form the paths of the Sun, Moon and planets (36B-D). These paths are then mythically interpreted as "revolutions" of thought and opinion (36E-37C). Here we take up the second stage of the soul's construction: the tuning of the cosmic scale. In the next appendix, we shall take up the third.

The musical ordering of soul is based on the Pythagorean discovery that musical intervals can be represented by ratios of string lengths.[1] The monochord is a single-stringed instrument with a moveable bridge. If you move this bridge to

---

[1] Boethius (c. 480-524 AD) recalls the story according to which Pythagoras first made his famous discovery when he heard consonant sounds produced by the hammers of blacksmiths. Having experimented with weights attached to strings and glasses filled with different weights of water, he proceeded to examine the ratios of string-lengths (*De institutione musica*).

the halfway point and pluck one of the half-lengths, then the parts of the string will be to the whole in the ratio of **2:1**, and the interval you hear will be the **octave** above the pitch of the undivided string. If the bridge is moved to the point where the string is divided into a two-thirds part and a one-third part, then the two-thirds part will divide the string into the ratio of **3:2**, and the interval will be a **perfect fifth** above the original pitch. The 4:3 ratio yields the **perfect fourth**. The 5:4 ratio yields the **major third**. And the 9:8 ratio yields the **major second** or **whole tone** (what the Greek musicians called the *tonos*).[2]

Here a problem arises. When you try to construct a scale or *harmonia* out of successive perfect fifths, you end up overshooting the octave by a small amount.[3] The scale refuses to close. This notorious small amount is called the **Pythagorean comma** (a *komma* is something cut or chopped off, a chip, from *koptein*, chop off). Its ratio is **531,441:524,288**. It can be shown similarly that if you try to construct an octave by putting together six **9:8** whole tones, you get this same amount of difference, this time as an excess.[4] The Pythagorean tuning used by Timaeus gets around this famous problem in a thoroughly ingenious way. It tunes the scale such that the octave, perfect fifth, perfect fourth and whole tone retain their mathematical perfection (**2:1, 3:2, 4:3, 9:8**) at the expense of the thirds. The major third's nice, small-number ratio of **5:4** becomes **81:64**, the combination of two **9:8** whole tones. It also introduces the ugly ratio **256:243** (ugly, that is, to a Pythagorean) as a mathematically necessary feature of the system.

The god begins with two sets of numbers. These numbers can be thought of as corresponding to subdivisions of a single string length. The two sets are **1, 2, 4, 8** and **1, 3, 9, 27**. Each set constitutes a *tetraktys* or "quaternary"—a mystic Four in which the Pythagoreans saw inscribed such things as the ages of man, the seasons, the elements, and more.[5] The two quaternaries form two continuous or geometric

---

[2] The *tonos* is defined as the *difference* between a perfect fourth and a perfect fifth.

[3] Building a scale through fifths amounts to adding as many perfect fifths as you need to come full circle to the starting pitch (subtracting octaves to get all the degrees of the scale within a single octave). The ancients did this mathematically through a process called "the compounding of ratios." Our modern equivalent is the multiplication of fractions.

[4] The failure of six whole tones to add up to an octave appears as Proposition 14 in Euclid's mathematical work on music. The work goes by the Latin name *Sectio Canonis* (*Kanonos Katatomê* or "The Cutting of the Canon or Rod"). The goal of Euclid's little treatise is the same as that of Timaeus' god: to build a scale in Pythagorean tuning.

[5] See Theon of Smyrna, *Mathematics Useful for Understanding Plato*, tr. R. and D. Lawlor, San Diego: Wizards Bookshelf, 1979, pp. 62-66. Greek scales ordinarily spanned two octaves. As we shall see, the numbers used in the two original proportions yield a scale that spans four octaves and a major sixth. Theon tells us that Plato "extends the calculation up to the solid numbers (8 and 27) and joins the terms by two means, in order to be able to embrace completely everything that the solid body of the world is made up of; and he extended harmony [that is, the scale] to this point, which by nature, can go on to infinity" (ibid., pp. 42-43).

progressions: **1:2::2:4::4:8** and **1:3::3:9::9:27**. Timaeus used such progressions in his initial arrangement of body (31B). When simply arranged in series, the terms are **1, 2, 3, 4, 8, 9** and **27**. (Note that the first six numbers add up to give the seventh.)

If we translate the number-lengths into actual pitches and rank them from highest note to lowest, as was the practice for Greek musicologists, we then get a musical span of four octaves and a major sixth. To preserve the order of intervals in this scale, and to avoid sharps and flats, we start on an E. The deeper significance of this starting-pitch will appear after we get a complete scale.[6]

Having used the **geometric mean** to get the original lengths, the god now uses the so-called **harmonic** and **arithmetic means** to fill in the gaps. These two means are easiest to grasp if we look at them in the case of numbers. The harmonic mean is that number which has the same proportional difference with respect to both extremes. **8**, for example, is the harmonic mean between **6** and **12** because its difference from **6** (that is, **2**) is *one third* of **6**, and its difference from **12** (that is, **4**) is *one third* of **12**. The arithmetic mean is simply the average of two numbers. **9** is the arithmetic mean between **6** and **12** because its numerical difference with respect to both extremes is the same.

The harmonic division of the octave is the string length that is the harmonic mean between an original string length and its double length. Given two strings of lengths **6** and **12**, the length that corresponds to the harmonic mean between them is **8**. The ratio of this length to that of the shorter of the first two strings is **8:6** or **4:3**. Thus the harmonic division of the octave yields the *perfect fourth* down from the pitch produced by the shorter string. Similarly, the arithmetic division of the octave is the arithmetic mean between an original length and its double. It yields the *perfect fifth*. Here's what the god's scale looks like after the two means are inserted:

The numbers below, remember, correspond to ever increasing subdivisions of a single string length. The fractions **4/3** and **3/2** in the first measure correspond, respectively, to the harmonic and arithmetic mean between **1** and **2**; the fractions

---

[6] All illustrations in this section are by Tina Davidson.

8/3 and **3** in the second measure to the harmonic and arithmetic mean between **2** and **4**; and so on. Notice all the perfect fourths that remain unfilled (for example, from the highest E in the first measure down to the neighboring B) and the final unfilled perfect fifth (from the lowest D down to G). The god fills *them* with **9:8** whole tones. This completes the musical order, leaving, as we have seen, the gaps corresponding to the ratio **256:243**. Rather than look at the complete range of four octaves and a major sixth, we confine ourselves to one octave (this time starting at the bottom). We also ignore the string lengths at this point and concentrate on the *ratios* involved in the resultant scale.

This gives us an octave of the so-called **diatonic order** ("diatonic" meaning *dia tonou* or "through the whole tone") in Pythagorean tuning. The diatonic order is a fixed recurring pattern of steps. In modern terms, the recurring pattern is "two whole steps, half step, three whole steps, half step" and corresponds to the white keys of the piano. The Greeks thought of the scale as consisting of two so-called **tetrachords**, that is, two perfect fourths (E to A, and B to E in the example above) joined by a whole tone. Note, however, that Timaeus' scale, unlike the scales with which we are familiar, is not constructed *so that* it will have whole steps and half steps. The whole tone or *tonos* is the true step or degree of the scale, while the interval that approximates our familiar semitone or half step is no more than an inconvenient *leimma* or left-over with an unwieldy ratio of **256:243**.[7]

To insure the proper order of intervals in Timaeus' scale (the left-over in a perfect fourth comes *after* the two whole tones), and to avoid sharps and flats, we started the scale on a high E and went *down*. To determine the so-called **mode** of Timaeus' scale, we rewrite it from the bottom up. E becomes the *lowest* pitch. Then the half steps occur between the first and second, and between the fifth and sixth degrees. This is the formal definition of the Greek Dorian mode.[8] Now the Greek modes were always associated with a certain character or temperament. The Dorian mode was associated with the war-like temperament.[9] It and the Phrygian mode are the only two modes

---

7   "The ancients took the tone [whole tone] as the first interval of the voice, without taking into account the half-tone … the voice, in reaching this interval, gives the ear a sensation of something fixed and well determined" (Theon, ibid., p. 44).

8   Cornford thinks, mistakenly, that the starting pitch and the mode of Timaeus' scale are undetermined and unimportant (p. 69). Archer-Hind gets the scale right (*The Timaeus of Plato*, [New York: Arno Press, 1973], pp. 108-11). He also makes the highly interesting point that Timaeus' entire scale, in its second half, does not seem to be in any recognizable mode. As the scale goes on—that is, descends into its lower regions—it becomes modally, "temperamentally," unstable.

9   Socrates discusses the modes in *Republic* 3. 398D-399E. Aristotle takes them up at the end of his *Politics* (8. 5-7).

that Socrates permits in the just city of the *Republic* (3.399A). Here in the *Timaeus*, the Dorian, warlike temperament of the soul is well-suited to Socrates' desire to see the just city at war (19B). The scale of Timaeus is thus a sort of cosmic "background music" for Critias' promised story about the war between Athens and Atlantis. But even apart from the designs of Critias, the world of Timaeus is one in which the war against chaos is constantly being waged. The war mode of the cosmic soul reflects the central role played by *thymos* or spiritedness throughout the dialogue. It is that power of the soul that reason uses to subdue the irrational desires (70A).

As in all technical accomplishments, the very ingenuity of the Pythagorean solution tends to obscure the original problem: the incompatibility of perfections, the impossibility of making a perfect whole out of perfect parts. The refusal of the pure, small-number ratios to form a perfect scale recalls the reluctance of Other to mix with Same. The Pythagorean solution, for all its beauty, cannot prevent the thirds from being "off" or the **256:243** leftover from being ugly. It is haunted by what one might call a tragic necessity in the realm of tones. The scale is not a complete victory but a beautiful compromise.[10]

The tuning of the scale functions as a technical paradigm for what it means to exercise good judgement or prudence in the establishment of a beautifully ordered whole. As such, it is a sort of parable for statesmen, who, in their noble attempt to harmonize human nature in the context of political life, must constantly deal with that nature's recalcitrance to perfect order—the refusal of human nature to *stay in tune* with the *nomos* that is both law and song.

APPENDIX B—ASTRONOMY

The purpose of this appendix is not to present Timaeus' astronomical system in detail but to give a sense of its overall scheme.[11] The scheme is essentially the geocentric system of Ptolemy's *Almagest*. The all is a perfect sphere with the Earth at its center. Around it move the Sun, Moon, Mercury, Venus, Mars, Jupiter and Saturn—seven "wanderers" or *planêtai*, whose radial distances from the earth are somehow governed (Timaeus does not explain how) by the terms of the previous two geometric proportions (**1, 2, 3, 4, 8, 9, 27**). The so-called **fixed stars** are fixed in the sense that they maintain their positions relative to one another.

---

[10] Modernity makes an even greater musical compromise in equal temperament, the tuning in which the octave is violently but effectively broken down into twelve equal semitones. The result is that, with the exception of the octave, all the beautiful small-number ratios are gone: all intervals but the octave are *impure*. The whole tone's **9:8** ratio, for example, becomes the $\sqrt[12]{2}$.

[11] For a fuller account of Timaeus' astronomy and the various problems attending it, see Cornford, pp. 72-137. There is a very helpful "Table of Celestial Motions" on pp. 136-137. See also D. R. Dicks, *Early Greek Astronomy to Aristotle*, Ithaca, NY: Cornell University Press, 1970, pp. 92-150.

Over the centuries, the astronomical part of the *Timaeus* has given rise to heated debates and disagreements. The most notorious problem has to do with the sentence about the Earth at 40A-B. Does the Earth move, for Timaeus, or not? And if it moves, how does it move? In the translation of the disputed sentence, I have opted for a motionless Earth (see note to 40A-B). Nevertheless, the problem remains obscure, and there are plausible arguments for alternative solutions.[12] Perhaps the most interesting fact is that Timaeus, for whatever reason, has chosen to cloak the condition of the Earth in mystery. Indeed, although the astronomical picture I am about to convey is extremely straightforward, there is nothing straightforward about the way Timaeus actually presents all this. A picture must be teased from his sometimes-obscure pronouncements and, furthermore, makes his account seem more finished and settled than it really is.

In the previous section, we saw how the god used his expertise to transform the indefinite soul-stuff (Being, Same and Other) into a sophisticated musical order. Now the god takes his diatonic strip, splits it down its length, lays one strip over the other to make a cross (the X-like shape of the Greek letter *chi*, χ) and then brings the ends of both strips together to make two intersecting circles (36A-B). In this way, there arise the intertwined **circles of Same and Other**. And while the circle of the Same is not further divided, that of the Other is cut along its circumference in six places to make the seven orbits of the planets or wandering stars (36D). As we noted earlier, all these circles taken together are mythically understood by Timaeus to be not only the outer circuits of the planets but also the inner revolutions of the soul's "unceasing and thoughtful life" (36E).

The circle of the Same can be imagined as the **celestial equator**. Thanks to its motion, the all rotates on its axis from east to west. If you observe the North Star (or pole star) in the course of a night, you will see the so-called fixed stars move around it in a counterclockwise direction. This is the motion of the Same, which produces the appearance of alternating day and night. The circle of the Other is a great circle tilted with respect to the circle of the Same like the brim of a cocked hat. This circle is the **ecliptic**, and the band that goes around its circumference is the **zodiac** with its twelve "signs." The zodiacal band is bisected by the ecliptic, as shown here.

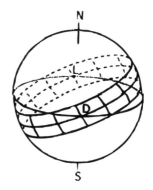

---

[12] R. Catesby Taliaferro has argued that the astronomical system of the *Timaeus* is in fact heliocentric. See his Appendix C to Ptolemy's *Almagest*, *Great Books of the Western World*, Chicago: Encyclopaedia Britannica, Inc., 1975, pp. 477-8.

The circle of the Other moves (slowly) from west to east. It carries the Sun around in its annual orbit. It also carries around the Moon and planets, which move within the band of the zodiac at different inclinations with respect to the ecliptic and at different speeds. Below is a much-simplified diagram of Timaeus' world-system.[13]

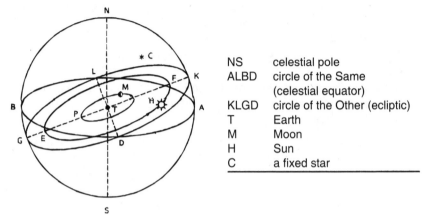

NS	celestial pole
ALBD	circle of the Same (celestial equator)
KLGD	circle of the Other (ecliptic)
T	Earth
M	Moon
H	Sun
C	a fixed star

As the Sun goes around its own yearly path in accordance with the motion of Other, it also gets swept around daily in the opposite direction by the motion of Same. The path that results from both motions put together is a *spiral* (see 39B). The top of the spiral is the **summer solstice**; the bottom is the **winter solstice**. The changes from upward to downward motion on the spiral, and from downward to upward, are the "turnings" or *tropai* to which Timaeus refers at 39D.[14] The **equinoxes** (when day and night are of equal length) occur when the Sun intersects the plane of the celestial equator. The *tropai* or "turns" of the planets are more complicated. In addition to moving up and down their spirals, the planets also appear to move ahead of, and then fall behind the Sun (which serves as a measure of their position in the heavens). The "outer planets" (Mars, Jupiter and Saturn) even appear to move backwards in their orbit with respect to the fixed stars and then to move forward again. This merely apparent moving in reverse is called **retrograde motion**.

The Sun, Moon and planets were made such that their speeds, although different from one another, were perfectly constant: the speeds were to each other in a ratio of whole numbers (36D). But this is far from how the motion actually appears. As with the scale, so too with the Sun, Moon and planets: there are apparent irregularities or so-called **anomalies** (literally, rough spots) that have to be accounted for. The Sun, for example, appears to speed up and slow down in its yearly course. Even worse, as we have noted, the outer planets appear to back up momentarily in their journey through the zodiac and then to resume their former direction. Can such irregularity

---

13   The diagrams are from the Ptolemy, Copernicus and Kepler manual used at St. John's College in Annapolis (1996).

14   See Taylor's note on this passage (p. 220).

really belong to the gods? The appearance of all these anomalies calls for the noble cunning of the astronomer. This cunning consists in inventing mathematical models called **hypotheses** that "save the appearances." They do so by showing how apparent irregularity is the result of regular, circular motion.

We find such models in Ptolemy's *Almagest*, which owes much of its spirit and its vision of the whole to the *Timaeus*.[15] And although Ptolemy belongs to a much later period (second century AD), his mathematical astronomy is the most systematic response to the astronomical problem laid down by Plato according to Simplicius: "What circular motions, uniform and perfectly regular, are to be admitted as hypotheses so that it might be possible to save the appearances presented by the planets?"[16]

The Ptolemaic astronomer's construction of mathematical models, his use of eccentric and epicyclic hypotheses, is perhaps the clearest technical embodiment of what Timaeus means by a likely story. The models are not the truth but the likeness of truth. They embody the astronomer's resourcefulness tempered by moderation and piety. The mathematical astronomer is healthy-minded. He loves the divine but also knows his limits—knows the image-nature of his mathematical models. In a direct reference to the *Timaeus*, Ptolemy tells us that the perfect freedom of motion that is the prerogative of the divine is not found "in the *likenesses* [*eikosin*] furnished by us."[17]

Ptolemaic astronomy helps us to formulate the problem involved in Timaeus' appeal to mathematical likely stories. Like the tuned scale, the "tuned" sky or heaven, for Timaeus, is a beautiful ordering in response to an inescapable fact: the all is in tension with itself, simultaneously moved in contrary directions, and is consequently suffused with a wide range of apparent irregularities. This tension is the kinematic version of the difficulty of mixing Other with Same. Otherness here takes the form of the seemingly infinite complexity that we find in celestial motions. With every anomaly comes the need for another refinement of the basic hypotheses, or even an *ad hoc* hypothesis.[18] The more inventive, ingenious the astronomer is compelled to become by the complexity of the appearances, the more removed he is from the noble

---

[15] Ptolemy's two main devices for deriving apparent irregularity from regular circular motion are the eccentric hypothesis and the epicyclic hypothesis (an epicycle is a circle *on* a circle). He introduces them in *Almagest* 3.3 (ibid. p. 86 ff.).

[16] The quotation from Simplicius' commentary on Aristotle's *On the Heavens* is taken from Pierre Duhem, *To Save the Phenomena: An Essay on the Idea of Physical Theory from Plato to Galileo*, tr. E. Dolan and C. Maschler, Chicago: University of Chicago Press, 1969, p. 5. Theon of Smyrna (second century AD) attributes the basic idea of looking for regularity within apparent irregularity to Pythagoras (ibid., p. 98).

[17] Ibid. 13.2, p. 429. I have slightly emended Taliaferro's translation of the phrase.

[18] Ptolemy's infamous *ad hoc* hypothesis was the so-called *equant*, which allowed for a circular motion to be irregular. The extreme inelegance of the equant played a key role in the Copernican revolution.

simplicity of his divine objects. The original or paradigmatic objects run the risk of being displaced by their beguiling, and understandable, mathematical models.

APPENDIX C—GEOMETRY

Stereometry is the study of solid figures (from *stereon*, solid). It is what we call solid geometry. In Euclid's *Elements*, the crowning moment of this study is the construction of the five regular Platonic solids: the **tetrahedron** or **pyramid, octahedron, cube, icosahedron** and **dodecahedron** (13, 13-17). Solid geometry was quite new in Plato's day. In Book 7 of the *Republic*, where we get the mathematical studies leading up to dialectic, Socrates tells Glaucon that the study of geometric solids "doesn't seem to have been discovered yet" (528B). He goes on to say, however, that although cities at present do not hold it in honor, the charm of this kind of geometry no doubt guarantees its future development. Glaucon, ever the lover of beautiful things, agrees that it is "exceptionally charming."

Although inquiry into the construction of the regular solids was already under way with the Pythagoreans, the full study of these figures was first achieved by Theaetetus, the young geometer we meet in the dialogue named after him.[19] The study of solids is intimately bound up with the study of ratio and proportion, most especially with the ancient theory of irrational lines. Theaetetus was able to give the regular solids a rigorous treatment because he had also advanced and systematized this theory of the irrational. We see him in Plato's dialogue practicing for his future claim to fame by defining the *dynamis* or square root.

The first appearance of something geometrical in the likely story is at 31C, where Timaeus introduces the mean proportion (*analogia*). The passage sets the stage for the two geometric proportions used in the construction of soul: **1:2::2:4::4:8** and **1:3::3:9::9:27**. In these examples, **4** and **9** are square number with respective "sides" **2** and **3**. **8** and **27** are cubic numbers also with respective "sides" **2** and **3**. The use of geometric language as applied to numbers is typical of Greek mathematics. Numbers for them were assemblages of units or monads ("one," therefore, was not a number) and were thought of as having shape.[20]

In our present passage, Timaeus alludes to three mathematical problems: the finding of numbers in continued proportion, doubling the square, and doubling the cube. The purely arithmetic problem is solved in Euclid's *Elements* (8. 2). The doubling of the square is the geometric example of recollection in the *Meno* (82A ff.). Meno's slave-boy discovers that the double square is produced by constructing it not on the side but on the diagonal of the given square. Now the side and diagonal

---

[19]   See Sir Thomas Heath, *Greek Mathematics*, New York: Dover, 1963, pp. 133-134.

[20]   For a thorough discussion of the Greek understanding of number, and the assumptions of Greek mathematical thought in general, see Jacob Klein, *Greek Mathematical Thought and the Origin of Algebra*, pp. 46-69.

of any square are **incommensurable**; that is, there is no unit of length that can measure them both. If we translate the geometrical magnitudes into numbers, then the length of the diagonal of the first square becomes the mean proportional between the area of that square and the area of the second, double square. (If the area of the first square is taken as **1** and that of the second as **2**, then this mean proportional is equivalent to our modern irrational number, $\sqrt{2}$.) The problem of doubling the *cube* is in turn reducible to the problem of finding *two* mean proportionals.[21]

It is easy for us moderns to fail to appreciate the crisis that the discovery of incommensurability produced for the Pythagoreans, for whom, as it is sometimes put, "everything is number," and for whom there was no such thing as an irrational *number*. The impossibility of there being a common measure of length for the side and diagonal of a square was, in effect, a crisis of intelligibility: it meant that there was a ratio or *logos* in the world that was unspeakable or *alogos*, for the being and determinateness of things resided, for the Pythagoreans, in our ability to count them. What does one call a line to which no whole number can be assigned?

The construction of the solids in the *Timaeus* is very different from the rigorous one we find in Euclid's *Elements*. Almost comically unsophisticated, Timaeus' method is that of cut and paste. He builds two elementary right triangles—one scalene, the other isosceles. Then he sticks together scalene triangles with one another, and isosceles triangles with one another, to form the faces of his three-dimensional figures. The fifth solid, the dodecahedron (a figure with twelve pentagonal faces), is not constructed at all but simply used for the god's interior decorating (55C).[22] At the end of his *Elements*, Euclid proves that there can be only five regular solids (13. 18). In other words, these solids are not only individual models of perfection: they also constitute a complete or perfect *set*.

On the following page is a picture of the two elementary right triangles. The one on the left is **scalene**, the one on the right **isosceles**. In the scalene triangle, the two sides are incommensurable; in the isosceles triangle, the side and diagonal (or hypotenuse) are incommensurable. In the scalene triangle, the square constructed on the greater side is three times the square on the lesser side (54E). In the isosceles triangle, the square on the hypotenuse is twice the square constructed on the side.

---

[21] See Heath, ibid. p. 154 ff. Albert Rivaud has an excellent presentation of how the doubling of geometric figures involves mean proportions. See his *Platon, Oeuvres Complètes, Timée-Critias*, Tome 10, Paris: Budé, 1970, pp. 72-74.

[22] On the mystic significance of the dodecahedron, Walter Burkert writes: "In the background of the mathematical problem there stands the dodecahedron as a cult object. Numerous dodecahedra made of bronze have been found in Gaul and thereabouts; and one made of stone has been found in northern Italy, dating back to pre-historic times. Their significance and use is unclear; the best conjecture seems to be that they were a kind of dice, used for oracular or mantic purposes" (*Lore and Science in Ancient Pythagoreanism*, [Cambridge: Harvard University Press, 1972], p. 460).

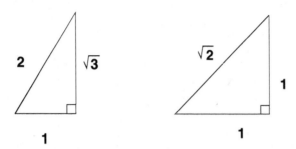

These facts are here expressed with the aid of our modern irrational numbers.[23] The numbers that correspond to the sides and diagonal in each triangle follow from the Pythagorean Theorem. According to this famous theorem, in any right triangle the square constructed on the diagonal is equal to the sum of the squares constructed on the sides. Euclid proves the Pythagorean Theorem in *Elements* 1, Proposition 47.

Timaeus proceeds to build an **equilateral triangle** (which will become the face of his pyramid, octahedron and icosahedron) from *six* of the scalene elementary triangles, and the square (the face of the cube) out of *four* of the isosceles elementary triangles. Here's what they look like:

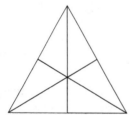
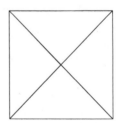

It is easy to see how Timaeus could have used fewer elementary triangles to get the faces he needs: two of the scalene triangles are sufficient for an equilateral triangle, and two isosceles triangles are sufficient for a square. Cornford explains that the god uses more triangles than seem necessary in order to insure the existence of varying sizes or grades of the elements—kinds within the kinds.[24]

Having built the faces of four of the solids, Timaeus proceeds to construct the solids themselves. The most important thing about them in the likely story is their sheer beauty. They, more than any other solids, possess that charm for which Socrates praised this branch of mathematics. Each is a model of structural perfection, a marvelous complexity of parts made to cohere in a simple whole. Their charm derives

---

[23] I wish to thank Jennifer Coard for all the illustrations in this section of the Appendix.

[24] Cornford, pp. 230-239.

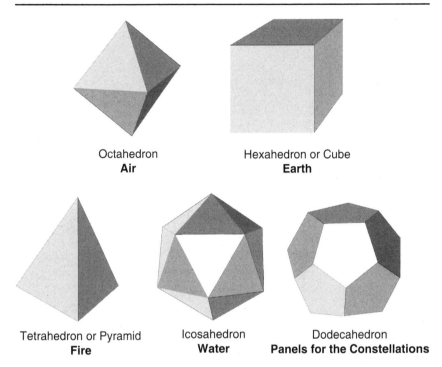

Octahedron	Hexahedron or Cube
Air	**Earth**

Tetrahedron or Pyramid	Icosahedron	Dodecahedron
Fire	**Water**	**Panels for the Constellations**

largely from the fact that they are all planar approximations of a sphere, a fact to which Timaeus refers at 55A. The regular solids are thus *mikrokosmoi*, microcosms, of the whole. Above are all five of these "most beautiful bodies" (53E) presented as illusions in the plane.

Music had to contend with the Pythagorean comma and the incompatibility of perfections, astronomy with the disjunction between being and appearance. The central problem of solid geometry is nothing less than the *irrational*. As we have seen in the case of the elementary triangles, the side and diagonal are incommensurable. There is no common measure of length for both magnitudes, which is equivalent to saying that they do not have to one another the ratio of a number to a number (Euclid, *Elements* 10. 5). But they *are* "commensurable in square." That is, the squares constructed on them do have a common measure and are to one another in the ratio of a number to a number. Now, in Greek geometry, there are lines that are commensurable with a given line in neither length nor square. They are called "irrational," *alogoi* (*Elements* 10, Def. 3). These are precisely the sort of lines that are incorporated, as Euclid shows, into the structure of the regular solids. In the context of the *Timaeus*, the presence of such lines within the structure of the regular solids suggests that beauty, even in "pure" mathematics, is inseparable from some element of irrationality—an irrationality beautifully suited to the waywardness of becoming.

SELECTED BIBLIOGRAPHY

EDITIONS, TRANSLATIONS AND COMMENTARIES CONSULTED

Apelt, Otto, *Platons Dialoge: Timaios und Kritias*, Leipzig: Der Philosophische Bibliothek, 1922.

Archer-Hind, R. D. *The Timaeus of Plato*, New York: Arno Press, 1973.

Burnet, John. *Plato's Timaeus*, Oxford: Oxford University Press, 1968.

Bury, Rev. R. G. Plato's *Timaeus* in the Loeb series, Cambridge: Harvard University Press, 1975.

Cherniss, Harold. Articles on the *Timaeus* in *Selected Papers*, Leiden: E. J. Brill, 1977.

Cornford, Francis MacDonald. *Plato's Cosmology*, New York: Library of Liberal Arts, 1957.

Jowett, Benjamin. *Plato's Timaeus*, *The Collected Dialogues of Plato*, ed. E. Hamilton and H. Cairns, Princeton: Princeton University Press, 1971.

Rivaud, Albert. *Platon, Oeuvres Complètes, Tome 10, Timée-Critias*, Paris: the Budé series, 1970.

Taylor, A. E. A *Commentary on Plato's Timaeus*, Oxford: Oxford University Press, 1928.

Zeyl, Donald. J. Plato's *Timaeus*, Indianapolis: Hackett Publishing Co., 2000.

SOME INTERESTING INTERPRETATIONS OF THE DIALOGUE

Benardete, Seth. "On Plato's *Timaeus* and Timaeus' Science Fiction," *Interpretation*, Summer, 1971. Difficult but very rewarding. The ideas are brilliant if at times incomprehensibly presented.

Brague, Rémi. "The Body of the Speech: A New Hypothesis of the Compositional Structure of Timaeus' Monologue" in *Platonic Investigations*, Washington, D. C.: The Catholic University of America Press, 1985. A fascinating attempt to show how the likely story is crafted in the image of the human body.

Brann, Eva. *What, Then, Is Time?*, Lanham, Maryland: Rowman and Littlefield, 1999. Contains an extremely interesting discussion of the *Timaeus* in an early section entitled, "Plato and Einstein: Time as a Clock" (pp. 4-12).

Cropsey, Joseph. "The Whole as Setting for Man: Plato's *Timaeus*," *Interpetation*, Winter, 1989-90. A clear summary of the drama and its central themes.

Derrida, Jacques. *Khora*, Paris: Galilée, 1993. This essay on the *Timaeus* can be found in *On the Name*, tr. Ian McLeod, ed. Thomas Dutoit, Stanford: Stanford University Press, 1995 (pp. 89-127). A fascinating and difficult essay on the problematic nature of the name usually translated "space" or "place."

Friedländer, Paul. "Plato as Physicist" in *Plato: An Introduction*, Princeton: Bollingen Series, 1973. A brief overview of Timaeus' physics in relation to modern scientists.

Gadamer, Hans-Georg. "Idea and Reality in Plato's *Timaeus*" in *Dialogue and Dialectic*, New Haven: Yale University Press, 1980. A provocative account of Timaeus' second beginning and the "persuasion" of necessity.

Klein, Jacob. *A Commentary on Plato's Meno*, Chicago: University of Chicago Press, 1989. This book contains one of the best and most helpful discussions of the *Timaeus* in a section entitled "The Problem of Solidity in the *Timaeus*" (pp. 193-199), as well as an excellent discussion of imagination and the divided line in the *Republic* (pp. 112-125).

Lampert, Laurence and Planeaux, Christopher. "Who's Who in Plato's *Timaeus-Critias* and Why," *The Review of Metaphysics*, September, 1998. A good introduction to the historical-political dimension of the projected trilogy. The authors argue that the missing fourth is Alcibiades.

Plutarch. *On the Generation of the Soul in the Timaeus*, tr. Harold Cherniss, Plutarch's *Moralia* (Vol. 13, Part 1), Loeb Classical Library, Cambridge: Harvard University Press, 1976. A detailed account of the construction of the cosmic soul, especially helpful on the musical part of the construction. The reader must beware, however, of the neo-Platonic tendency to make systematic connections among the dialogues without sufficiently attending to differences.

Sallis, John. *Chorology: On Beginning in Plato's Timaeus*, Bloomington: Indiana University Press, 1999. A highly perceptive account of the dialogue that centers on Timaeus' second beginning and the mysterious *chôra* (usually translated "space" or "place").

Welliver, Warman. Character, *Plot and Thought in Plato's Timaeus-Critias*, Leiden: E. J. Brill, 1977. A spirited examination of the prologues of both dialogues that reveals the antagonism among the characters and the political implications of this antagonism.

WORKS OF RELATED INTEREST

Aristotle. *Aristotle's Physics: A Guided Study*, tr. Joe Sachs, New Brunswick, NJ: Rutgers University Press, 1995. A literal translation with an extremely helpful glossary. Readers of the *Timaeus* would do well to examine Aristotle's non-mythical, non-mathematical treatment of nature, cause, motion, time and place in the *Physics*.

Brann, Eva. "The Music of the *Republic*," AGON: Journal of Classical Studies 1, pp. 1-117. [Reprinted in *The St. John's Review* (1989-90) 39, pp. 1-104.] A provocative introduction to the *Republic* with insightful comments on the *Timaeus*.

Brann, Eva. *The World of the Imagination: Sum and Substance*, Lanham, Maryland: Rowman and Littlefield, 1991. A vast treasury of philosophic reflections on image and imagination. Extremely helpful for thinking about the bond between human nature and likely stories.

Descartes, René. *The World*, tr. M. S. Mahoney, New York: Abaris Books, Descartes puts forth his laws of motion in the context of a modern likely story (Chapter 6). He invites us to re-create the world in thought, a project he continues in his *Treatise of Man* (tr. T. S. Hall, Cambridge: Harvard University Press, 1972).

Guthrie, Kenneth Sylvan. *The Pythagorean Sourcebook and Library*, Grand Rapids: Phanes Press, 1987. Contains many interesting items helpful to the understanding of the *Timaeus* and its Pythagorean spirit. Especially helpful is Iamblichus' *Life of Pythagoras*, which stresses the fact that for Pythagoras and his followers, philosophy was above all a way of life.

Husserl, Edmund. *The Crisis of European Sciences*, Evanston: Northwestern University Press, 1970. In the early parts of the book, Husserl gives an incisive account of the philosophic presuppositions of modern mathematical physics. He argues that this physics is in fact a kind of likely story or, as he puts it, a "garb of ideas" (p. 51).

Jonas, Hans. *The Phenomenon of Life: Toward A Philosophical Biology*, Chicago: University of Chicago Press, 1966. Contains an essay of great importance for the *Timaeus* entitled "Is God a Mathematician?"

Kirk, G. S., Raven, J. E. and Schofield, M. *The Pre-Socratic Philosophers: A Critical History with a Selection of Texts*, 2nd edition, Cambridge: Cambridge University Press, 1983. Contains the fragments (in Greek with English translations) attributed to Pythagoras and Empedocles, the two most important pre-Socratics for the *Timaeus*.

Klein, Jacob. *Greek Mathematical Thought and the Origin of Algebra*, tr. Eva Brann, New York: Dover Publications, Inc., 1992. An absolute must for a proper understanding of Greek mathematics in relation to Greek philosophy.

Leibniz, G. W. Leibniz is in many ways the modern Timaeus. His attempt to ground the world in divine wisdom and final causes appears throughout his writings. The best introduction to his thought is the *Discourse on Metaphysics*.

McClain, Ernest G., *The Pythagorean Plato: Prelude to the Song Itself*, York Beach, Maine: Nicolas-Hays, Inc., 1978. A detailed and thorough treatment of music and mathematics in the *Republic, Timaeus, Critias*, and *Laws*.

Straus, Erwin. "The Upright Posture" in *Phenomenological Psychology*, New York: Basic Books, 1966. An amazing study of how our human nature is revealed in our upright posture. The essay goes beautifully with Timaeus' effort to give human meaning to the details of our body.

Strauss, Leo. *The City and Man*, Chicago: Rand McNally, 1964. The book is composed of three essays on the political thought of Aristotle's *Politics*, Plato's *Republic* and Thucydides' *History*. It is the best introduction to the political themes that the *Timaeus* presupposes but does not directly address.